Making Research Work

MAKING RESEARCH WORK

Promoting Child Care Policy
and Practice

Edited by

Dorota Iwaniec and John Pinkerton

JOHN WILEY & SONS

Chichester · New York · Weinheim · Brisbane · Singapore · Toronto

HQ
778.7
.G7
M35
1998

Other Wiley Editorial Offices

John Wiley & Sons, Inc., 605 Third Avenue,
New York, NY 10158-0012, USA

WILEY-VCH Verlag GmbH, Pappelallee 3,
D-69469 Weinheim, Germany

Jacaranda Wiley Ltd, 33 Park Road, Milton,
Queensland 4064, Australia

John Wiley & Sons (Asia) Pte Ltd, 2 Clementi Loop #02-01,
Jin Xing Distripark, Singapore 129809

John Wiley & Sons (Canada) Ltd, 22 Worcester Road,
Rexdale, Ontario M9W 1L1, Canada

Library of Congress Cataloging-in-Publication Data

Making research work: promoting child care policy and practice /
   edited by Dorota Iwaniec and John Pinkerton.
         p.   cm.
   Includes bibliographical references and index.
   ISBN 0-471-97952-X (alk. paper)
   1. Child care—Research—Great Britain.   I. Iwaniec, Dorota.
II. Pinkerton, John, 1953– .
   HQ778.7.G7M35   1998
   362.71'2'07'20941—dc21   98-5759
                                                           CIP

British Library Cataloguing in Publication Data

A catalogue record for this book is available from the British Library

ISBN 0-471-97952-X

Typeset in 10/12 pt Palatino by Best-set Typesetter Ltd., Hong Kong
Printed and bound in Great Britain by Redwood Books, Trowbridge, Wilts
This book is printed on acid-free paper responsibly manufactured from sustainable
forestry, in which at least two trees are planted for each one used for paper
production.

CONTENTS

ABOUT THE EDITORS

PROFESSOR DOROTA IWANIEC is Professor of Social Work at The Queen's University of Belfast. She is also Director of the Centre for Child Care Research at Queen's and Head of the Department of Social Work. She was previously based in Leicester where she engaged in child care research and practice, particularly in the areas of 'failure-to-thrive children', children's behaviour management and parenting. She has published widely and is particularly well known for her work on the emotionally abused and neglected child.

Dr JOHN PINKERTON is Senior Research Fellow in the Centre for Child Care Research, The Queen's University of Belfast where he is engaged in work on family support. He also has responsibility for the day to day work of the Centre. He previously worked as Lecturer in Social Work at Queen's. His research and publication interest is in rights based social work practice with children, young people and their families, young people leaving care and family support. He has undertaken government funded research on both 'home in care' placements and young people leaving care.

ABOUT THE CONTRIBUTORS

Dr *KAROLA DILLENBURGER* is a Lecturer in Social Work at The Queen's University of Belfast. She is a chartered psychologist and social worker and is a Member of the Association for Behaviour Analysis. She has worked, both in Germany and Great Britain, as a social worker, therapist, trainer and lecturer and has published widely in social work and family therapy journals.

KATHRYN HIGGINS is Research Officer in the Centre for Child Care Research, The Queen's University of Belfast, where she is engaged in work on family support. She previously worked as Research Co-ordinator for the Tayside Behavioural and HIV Prevalence study which focused on drug injectors and she continues her research and publication interest in the drugs field.

GREG KELLY is a Senior Lecturer in Social Work and programme director for the Master/Diploma in social work course at The Queen's University of Belfast. His research and publication interest is in social work in child care generally, but with a particular focus on foster care and adoption. He has undertaken government-funded research on both decision making in child care and long-term foster placements.

Dr *COLETTE McAULEY* is a Lecturer in Social Work at the Queen's University of Belfast where she is responsible for teaching on child care and on law. Her research and publication interests are in children's perspectives on the care experience, foster care and family support. She has undertaken research on the emotional and social development of children in long-term foster placements and is currently funded to research the effectiveness of Home Start in the Northern Health and Social Services Board, Northern Ireland. This includes children's perspectives on this form of family support intervention.

PATRICK McCRYSTAL is Research Fellow in the Centre for Child Care Research, The Queen's University of Belfast, where he is engaged in work on children in need. He also has responsibility for developing training and consultation for child care agency staff on undertaking research. He previously worked as Research Officer at the School of Education, University of Ulster, and at the Health and Health Care Research Unit, The Queen's University of Belfast. His research and publication interests are in child care and vocational education.

MARINA MONTEITH is Research Fellow in the Centre for Child Care Research, The Queen's University of Belfast, where she is engaged in work on developing services to children with a disability. She also has responsibility for setting up and maintaining a system for accessing regional, UK and international child care statistics and research findings. She previously worked as Senior Research Officer in the Northern Ireland Housing Executive and in Human Resource Planning and Policy in the NHS in London. Her research and publication interests are in services for children with disabilities and their families, the expressed needs of young disabled people and the impact of homelessness on family life.

VALLERI SWITZER is researcher with the Health Research Board, Dublin, working on a study examining the extent of the use of folic acid by pregnant women. Previously she worked as Statistician in the Centre for Child Care Research, The Queen's University of Belfast, and in the private sector on drug trials in Germany. Her research and publications interest is in the application of statistics to research design and to the interpretation of data.

INTRODUCTION

These are difficult times for children, and for adults who care for and about children. Perhaps it was ever so, but it is now recognised just how complex a challenge it is to ensure that all children receive the recognition and praise, the love and security, and the opportunities for new experiences and responsibilities they need if they are to thrive. Developing an adequate and useful understanding of that complexity requires research. This book seeks to promote the relationship between child care and research. It demonstrates that this requires not only the informed and skilled application of research methods but also attention to how research can be fostered and used more effectively as part of the mainstream of child care policy and practice.

The book has been written primarily by the staff from the Centre for Child Care Research, The Queen's University of Belfast, a partnership bridging the worlds of academic research, policy making and service provision. It also includes material by three academics in the Department of Social Work, which is mainly concerned with professional training. Reflecting their backgrounds, all the authors believe that child care research must be made to work. In this there is a resonance with the strongly emerging philosophy, as postulated by the United Kingdom government Research and Development strategy, that policy and practice have to be based on evidence deriving from research rather than personal attitudes and beliefs. As part of that strategic vision, there is also strong emphasis that practice has to be evaluated in order to make progress in service provision and methods used to help children and their families.

The child care research issues discussed here are based on individual and collective research experiences and reviews of the literature and official government documents. The hope is that anyone interested in child care, whether primarily from a research, a policy or a practical perspective, will find at least some of the topics discussed both useful and informative. The purpose of the book is to draw together in one volume discussion of key issues associated with researching child care. It aims to help with the recognition of, and response to, both the fundamental and the specialist issues which arise as problems at the various stages of the research process. These problems, due to their novelty or through being regarded as too mundane, are either not covered in basic research methods texts or only dealt with comprehensively outside of any subject context and certainly without reference to child care. Accordingly, this book should be seen as a complementary text to existing general or specialist research literature.

The book is organised in three parts. Part I, entitled *The Relationship of Research to Policy and Practice*, deals with current issues relating to the strategic use of research generally and in relation to child care policy and practice specifically. Chapter 1 gives a historical background of research and development strategies in the National Health Service and Personal Social Services in the United Kingdom. It points to the growing recognition of the importance of research and the strongly evolving agenda that has developed in recent years to provide a secure and challenging Research and Development Strategy. Chapter 2 discusses the impact of research on policy and practice in child care and argues that understanding both the bridges and the blocks to this relationship is greatly enhanced by taking a systemic perspective. Chapter 3 discusses the extraordinarily influential role a single piece of research played in the development of the child care permanence movement in the United Kingdom and suggests that this was more to do with professional and political agendas than with the quality of the research.

The second part of the book is entitled *Child Care Research: Some Challenging Contemporary Developments*. It deals with six areas which make it clear that, in building the relationship between research and child care policy and practice, there are important issues to be addressed that are as much about the business of doing research as its application to child care. The first chapter in this part, Chapter 4, presents a detailed, illustrated account of how to undertake single-case design research. It is argued that what is already a well-established methodology in other fields has much to offer in measuring the effectiveness of child care interventions. Chapter 5 discusses literature reviewing as an integral part of the research process and sets out six steps to follow to ensure a more methodical approach, which is less open to unrecognised biases and is more explicit about limitations. The need to recognise limitations is also a theme in Chapter 6, which presents an illustrated critique of official child care statistics while still arguing for their importance as a central source of accessible data. Chapter 7 is concerned with the hidden populations that inevitably form an important part of what interests policy makers and practitioners and, therefore, child care researchers. It demonstrates that there is much that can be learnt about how to reveal these populations from research techniques in other fields, such as that of illicit drug use. Paradoxically children themselves, at least as active participants, have been something of a hidden population until recently in child care research, but, as Chapter 8 argues, this is no longer ethically acceptable and important advances are being made in understanding how to conduct child participatory research. Finally in this section, attention is given in Chapter 9 to developing a planned, strategic approach to dissemination. This requires innovation, which builds on traditional approaches but takes advantage of theories of interpersonal communication and the ever-growing advances in information technology.

Quality research requires a secure financial and administrative infrastructure and so Part III, *Promoting and Securing a Basis for Research*, addresses issues that have a direct bearing on achieving the necessary resources for child care research. The chapters in this third part should be of interest to both individual researchers and to institutions attempting to secure a base for a particular project or trying to set up a research centre or unit. Chapter 10 deals with the practical matters involved in preparing a research proposal to submit to a funding body. The other side of that coin is commissioning research, and how to go about doing that in a clear and managed fashion is set out in Chapter 11. There are well-established systems of funding within the social sciences and the further development of child care research will require that they are fully used. Chapter 12 draws attention to the boundaries within which proposals for funding have to be made and introduces a number of the major funding bodies likely to be relevant to child care research. Increasingly it is recognised that research centres, with their sustained cultures and administrative structures, have a great deal to offer to child care, and the final chapter in the book, Chapter 13, draws on the experience of the Centre for Child Care Research (The Queen's University Belfast) to demonstrate one successful approach to establishing such a centre.

ACKNOWLEDGEMENTS

We would like to express our appreciation to Margaret Coyle for her work on the preparation of the manuscript and Maura Dunn for a range of essential administrative support.

I

THE RELATIONSHIP OF RESEARCH TO POLICY AND PRACTICE

1

RESEARCH AND DEVELOPMENT STRATEGIES IN THE NATIONAL HEALTH SERVICE AND PERSONAL SOCIAL SERVICES IN THE UNITED KINGDOM

Dorota Iwaniec

Chapter Outline

INTRODUCTION

RESEARCH AND DEVELOPMENT STRATEGY IN THE NATIONAL HEALTH SERVICE

LAUNCH OF THE NATIONAL RESEARCH AND DEVELOPMENT STRATEGY IN WALES, ENGLAND, SCOTLAND AND NORTHERN IRELAND

THE CULYER REPORT

A WIDER STRATEGY FOR RESEARCH AND DEVELOPMENT RELATING TO PERSONAL SOCIAL SERVICES
- The Research Record
- Proposals for Future Improvements in Research and Development Strategies
- Future Developments

Making Research Work: Promoting Child Care Policy and Practice
Edited by D. Iwaniec and J. Pinkerton
© 1998 John Wiley & Sons Ltd

INTRODUCTION

Major changes have occurred in the United Kingdom in the area of research and development in the last decade. These changes came about as a result of growing concerns, especially among medical scientists, that research was starved of resources, was declining, and that the newly re-organised National Health Service (NHS) was run with little awareness of the needs of research or what it had to offer. The same concerns were raised in relation to services provided by Personal Social Services (PSS) notably in the child care and child protection fields. Numerous public inquiries into the deaths and maltreatment of children raised many concerns and begged many questions. There was a strongly emerging realisation that formation and implementation of policies were reactive, not research led, and the effectiveness of practice was not evaluated.

It was generally felt that there was the absence of a research culture and appreciation of the importance of research in service delivery among the managers and practitioners. Available research findings were not used to inform policies and practice, and dissemination of research was not properly addressed. Increasing demands on service provision within the scarce resources have also contributed to the reduction of research funding and support. Corrective measures were necessary and urgent. As a result the Government has set up mechanisms to review the situation and evolve strategies to implement change. A political will emerged that established research within the NHS as a vital part of its activities, and encouraged further expansion of research. This new climate was made possible through pressures from well-established and powerful professional institutions and other bodies that argued effectively for the necessity of research as an essential part of NHS function. Many positive strategies have been implemented as a result of this change within the last few years, and substantial progress has been made in research and development (R&D) across the United Kingdom.

However, a grave shortage of financial resources within the NHS has contributed to a severe reduction of funding for research purposes, as service provision was given priority. While this was understandable in the context of an impoverished NHS allocation of money, it caused a crisis in research capacity and productivity that, in turn, weakened practice, cost-effectiveness, and the evolution of knowledge—perhaps, in some cases, even causing social damage.

For the purpose of the chapter, R&D will be defined as follows:

- *Research:* the search for new knowledge using scientific methodologies and approaches.
- *Development:* the evaluation of new methods of care and techniques and their experimental introduction into service using scientific methodologies and approaches.

This chapter will outline how R&D strategy in the NHS evolved in the United Kingdom. Promoted at central government level, it was first launched in England in 1991 and was soon followed by Wales, Scotland and Northern Ireland. Further improvements in R&D in the NHS were recommended as a result of the publication of the Culyer Report (DoH, 1994a). A *Wider Strategy for Research and Development Relating to Personal Social Services* (DoH, 1994b) will also be described. Some examples regarding the working of the R&D strategy in the formation of child care policy and practice will be provided.

RESEARCH AND DEVELOPMENT STRATEGY IN THE NATIONAL HEALTH SERVICE

The House of Lords Select Committee on Science and Technology Report (HMSO, 1988) expressed concerns about the deterioriation of medical research. The Committee found UK medical research in a condition of despondence and low morale. Lack of coherent and adequate funding left many good proposals unsupported; career prospects for clinical researchers were poor; clinical research was under pressure from the demands of clinical services; and, most importantly, the NHS was run with little awareness of the needs of research or what it had to offer (HMSO, 1995).

Several recommendations were put to the Department of Health for consideration such as: appointment of the Director of Research and Development in the Department of Health; a marked increase in funding for public health and 'operational research' such as research into the organisation and management of health services; the creation of the National Health Research Authority (NHRA) and equivalent bodies for

Scotland, Wales and Northern Ireland. The Committee also recommended the creation of a National Forum, comprising various research councils, charities, industry and the NHRA, to determine research priorities.

The Government response to the Select Committee recommendations was very positive and was published in the form of a White Paper entitled *Priorities in Medical Research* (HMSO, 1988). The Government agreed to appoint a Director of Research and Development for the Department of Health and the NHS, whose terms of reference would be setting up a coherent, adequately funded, well-managed and organised national research strategy. However, the Government rejected the proposal to create a National Forum and National Health Research Authority.

LAUNCH OF THE NATIONAL RESEARCH AND DEVELOPMENT STRATEGY IN WALES, ENGLAND, SCOTLAND AND NORTHERN IRELAND

The NHS Research and Development strategy was launched in England in 1991 with the appointment of Professor (now Sir) Michael Peckham as Director of Research and Development. He was to be responsible for advising the Secretary of State for Health and Social Services on research issues and matters. This included not only the NHS R&D strategy but wider R&D, which covered the Department's centrally supported research programmes for Health and Personal Social Services (PSS), and was named the Department of Health Policy Research Programme. The establishment of Regional R&D Directorates in each of the Regional Health Authorities (RHAs) followed soon after.

Following the launch of R&D strategy in England (1991), the three other home countries—Wales, Scotland and Northern Ireland—published their own R&D strategies, addressing their specific needs and priorities within their own organisational structures. As in England, the documents of R&D strategy in Scotland, Wales and Northern Ireland recognised the gulf between research workers and the health care market. Lack of translation of research finding to policy and practice, as well as deficiencies in testing effectiveness of practice policies through systematic and vigorous evaluation, the short-comings in funding of R&D in the NHS and a need for collaboration with various research councils and institutions, was apparent and required urgent improvement across the UK.

In December 1992, the Welsh Office NHS Directorate issued *Sharpening the Focus: Research and Development Framework for NHS Wales* (Welsh Office, 1992). The Director of Research and Development (DRD) was appointed in 1996 and the Welsh Office of R&D for Health and Social Care was created. Unlike England, but like Northern Ireland, the Welsh Office of R&D embraces both health and social care, which includes research into policy and practice.

In 1993, the Chief Scientist Office of the Scottish Office Home and Health Department issued *Research and Development Strategy for the National Health Service in Scotland* (HMSO, 1993). The R&D strategy in Scotland is managed by the Chief Scientist Office (CSO), which was established in 1973, and the first Chief Scientist was appointed in 1974. The CSO is part of the Scottish Office Home and Health Department, and manages a R&D programme in which the Health Department is the customer, and the research workers—Scottish Higher Education Institutions, Health Boards and other institutions—are the contractors. The CSO advises the Department on how research can contribute best to policy development and health service efficiency.

Following announcement of R&D strategies in England, Scotland and Wales, the Department of Health and Personal Social Services in Northern Ireland (DHSS, 1993) published the consultative paper entitled A *Strategy for Research and Development in the Health and Personal Social Services in Northern Ireland.* This put forward a proposal to improve the scope, significance and quality of R&D in both health and social care in the Province. Since organisational and management structures in the HPSS in Northern Ireland are different from those in the other home countries as health and personal social services structures are amalgamated, the proposed R&D combined health and social care into one strategy. A Director of R&D was appointed in April 1997 and the new Research and Development Office (RDO) was established with that appointment. The RDO will commission R&D on behalf of the HPSS, including the HSS Boards and the Department.

THE CULYER REPORT

In response to clinicians' concerns about the internal market, the Department of Health set up in 1993 the NHS Research Task Force of wide-ranging composition, chaired by Professor Culyer, to consider whether to recommend changes in NHS R&D, and to advise on alternative funding and support mechanisms, including transitional measures within available resources (DoH, 1994a). The Task Force team, after wide consultation, found that, in spite of much progress achieved by the NHS R&D, strategy funding for research and related costs continued to be haphazardly allocated. They found that there was inappropriate duplication of research, that priorities were not always properly addressed, and that the selection and approval of research was not always diligent enough, allowing poor-quality research projects to continue at the expense of high-standard ones. Additionally, they found that the market for NHS services sometimes conflicted with research priorities, and that the views of the purchasers of services and of the provider-managers were not well represented to set up national research priorities. Funding for research and for service support was unco-ordinated and in need of clearly specified rules. There was a need for better co-ordination of service provision between the NHS and external research funders such as the Medical Research Council (MRC), the Higher Education Funding Council (HEFC), major charities, industry and local voluntary funders.

As a result of these exercises, the Task Force produced a set of recommendations proposing changes in the consultative mechanisms, in order to establish (a) the R&D that should be supported within the NHS; (b) the alterations that should be made in funding, commissioning, costing and accounting; and (c) the time-span that should be allotted to implement those changes.

Professor Culyer, in a letter to the Minister of Health, emphasised three main areas for consideration:

1. The necessity of separating funds for R&D and for service support for R&D from funds for other activities, because, only by separating them can health R&D be properly identified, managed, and accounted for, and only by such clear separation can investment in R&D be assured, and not cut as providers attempt to keep prices of services as low as possible.
2. Those involved in R&D must justify claims on resources, in competition with others, and should be accountable for their R&D.
3. Primary and community care sectors should be put on equal footing with the acute sector in terms of access to funding both for R&D and its associated service cost.

On the basis of this emphasis the report developed a comprehensive set of recommendations. To start with, it urged that in order to make R&D funding clearer and easier to manage, all spending on R&D (and its servicing) should be brought within a single explicit funding stream to avoid cross-subsidisation between patients' care and R&D. Thus single transparent R&D funds would be created (and determined annually) through a levy on all health authorities' allocations. This explicit budget should cover three categories of R&D:

- cost of research supported by the NHS;
- excess service cost of non-commercial research conducted in NHS settings, whether supported by the NHS or by another funder; and
- costs of maintaining research facilities, providing they are not attributable to a particular piece of research.

Funds for research in the first two categories should be awarded in response to bids from researchers, research institutions, or host NHS providers, from any discipline or NHS settings. Research facility funding should be available only to institutions (such as research centres) with substantial and continuous R&D programmes, and it should be awarded on the basis of formalised assessment by research rating, similar to the Research Assessment Exercises (RAEs) used at the universities by HEFC. Such programmes should be reviewed every three to five years.

- NHS executives should develop and publish statements of the scope of research facilities' funding and work out systems for business planning, monitoring, and accountability required to secure it.
- Most high-quality research should continue to be concentrated in the relatively few institutions capable of providing:
  (i)   the appropriate scale of resources;
  (ii)   critical mass of expertise, momentum, and continuity;
  (iii) academic links necessary to sustain long-term research programmes; and
  (iv)   satisfactory career structures for researchers.

Short-term research contracts for staff were felt to be a poor basis for building and maintaining top-rate research teams, as they tend to impede any long-term strategic development of research and can lead to opportunistic accumulation of unrelated research projects in order to protect positions of researchers and keep them in posts. Staff loyalty can be undermined as a result, making it difficult to keep research teams together. Senior research staff often are forced to spend an inordinate amount of time seeking funds. Core funding would help to retain scarce and expert research skills and allow more time for research.

- Purchasers of health care should allow providers freedom to support curiosity-driven pre-protocol research, both administratively and financially, in cases where it cannot be funded by external sponsors.

- Purchasers and providers of health care should be able to supplement levies to meet national and regional priorities more quickly.
- A single funding system would be achieved through a complex developmental process of Trusts declaring their R&D activity, costs and related income. Between 1996 and 1998 a new system of R&D funding was intended to have a neutral effect on total NHS income in Trusts for patient care and R&D. However, from 1998/99 the *status quo* will be replaced by contracts for costed R&D activity that has met minimum quality standards.
- To improve co-ordination and decision making regarding internally and externally commissioned research, the Task Force proposed the creation of a National Forum, chaired by the Director of R&D, to exchange information about research strategies of the various national funding bodies, that sponsor and support R&D in the NHS.
- The Director of R&D and the Regional Directors should remain the principle decision makers, assisted by an expanded CRDC, and new regional consultative bodies, and R&D commissioning units.
- The Task Force felt that the membership of CRDC was not wide enough to represent the views of service purchasers and provider managers. It recommended the recasting of CRDC membership to ensure that the perspectives of NHS purchasers and providers and of major commissioners of R&D (such as higher education institutions, research councils, charities, and industry) were represented.
- Greater emphasis should be put on recognising and supporting local research needs and on developing further regional structures and research programmes. The Task Force recommended that Regional Directors of R&D should be the focal points for R&D within each region, leading consultative bodies (to include local research interests and NHS service purchasers and providers), identifying research priorities for the region, acting as promoters of R&D, and playing key roles in commissioning and managing R&D.
- Primary and community services in the NHS have fared less well in developing research capacities and getting support for them. It was recommended that primary and community care establishments should be put on equal bases with the acute sector, and that funds for service support as well as for the direct costs of R&D should be made accessible to professionals working in primary and community health care settings and to those professions allied to medicine.

- Access to research findings by providing a national database was considered as urgent, and each region was asked to declare its research activities.
- The Task Force recognised that there was a need to develop research skills in order to make its recommendations effective, although it was not within its remit. The obvious deficit of primary care and the professions allied to medicine was seen as in need of urgent consideration. In addition, skills required to implement research findings and to promote an evaluative culture required development across all sections of the NHS. The shortage of trained researchers, a lack of career-paths and incentives for researchers, and a predominance of short-term contracts for research staff should be given attention. Four main areas of training and skills development were identified:
  - (i)   the articulation of health and health care problems and issues so as to identify the need for R&D;
  - (ii)   the commissioning and managing of R&D projects and programmes;
  - (iii) the formulation of R&D proposals; and
  - (iv)   the implementation of research findings.
- The development of a human resource strategy for R&D, embracing training and more general personnel issues, was recommended.

The first stage in the implementation of the Culyer Report (DoH, 1994a) recommendations in England involved the identification of the amount of research being carried out in the NHS and the cost to the NHS of undertaking that research. This exercise, termed 'the declaration process', required declarations of R&D activity and associated cost and income to be submitted by all NHS Trusts, hospitals and community health service providers, Special Hospital Service Authorities and London Postgraduate Health Authority. The information acquired from this exercise formed the 'Provider Declarations', outlining the main blocks of research going on with the organisation and the associated costs of that research. A validation exercise was undertaken to ensure that declaration of R&D activity and associated costs were completed in accordance with NHS guidelines.

The changes recommended by the Culyer Report are being broadly implemented across the UK, but reflecting each home country's individual organisational differences. For example, the new funding arrangements in Northern Ireland embrace the entire Health and Personal Social Services. This includes commissioning and both health and social care providers.

A WIDER STRATEGY FOR RESEARCH
AND DEVELOPMENT RELATING TO
PERSONAL SOCIAL SERVICES

Following the establishment of the Task Force to take stock of R&D in the NHS, the Department of Health appointed an independent review group to examine current provisions of R&D in Personal Social Services and to make recommendations for the improvement of future development within the same financial resources. This review group consulted extensively with the senior officials of DoH, PSS directors and senior managers, research units, academics, research councils supporting social care research, charities, voluntary organisations, social work journals, social work and health practitioners, and users. Research was commissioned by the review group to assist them with this task. As a result a report entitled *A Wider Strategy for Research and Development Relating to Personal Social Services* (DoH, 1994b) was produced. The first part of this report described the state of R&D in PSS as it existed then, while the second contained a set of recommendations for future improvement.

It was found that there was a substantial amount of high-quality research available related to the policy in the field of child care, but less in relation to practice. Strategic and applied PSS research, largely commissioned by the DoH, has had a more effective impact on many aspects of the Department's policy than was generally perceived. Research has played a major role in informing the Children Act (1989) in England and Wales, the first major child care legislation, and was influential in service delivery and practice through regulations and guidance accompanying the legislation. The Department commitment to examine effectiveness of the changes introduced by the Children Act were shown by the number of centrally commissioned research projects to learn how research-led policy can impact upon practice. There was consistent development of research initiatives into child protection, residential care, and fostering and adoption. Policy has been built on regular evaluation as to which research has made a major contribution to effective practice. The Review Group found that the management of research into child care was a model to follow in other areas of social care.

On the other hand, R&D in community care was more patchy, uncoordinated and difficult to absorb. The reasons might lie in the barriers between various services. The users need a mix of health and social care, and for that reason PSS research should be brought closer to health care research and other relevant services, and better understanding was needed of the interdependence of the professions to develop well-co-ordinated community care. In spite of greater resources provided for research in this area, it did not acquire the same high level of reputation as that achieved in child care research. While much enthusiasm and interest in research existed among practitioners, they were generally ill-prepared to understand research processes and methodologies, were unfamiliar with the information technology relating to the accessing of research, and were uncertain of how to translate research findings into everyday practice. Indeed, the review group found serious inadequacies in the whole spectrum of research dissemination and implementation.

Many of the dissemination initiatives were *ad hoc* and did not fit into any overall policies or strategies. Few organisations had formal policies covering the dissemination of research, its objectives, the audience intended, the methods used, and the resources to achieve an efficient dissemination. There was little systematic evaluation of the success of different strategies. Practitioners, in particular, found little time to read, or to find relevant material: they were unfamiliar with literature searches, and found it difficult to understand some research papers (which were all too often full of jargon and complicated statistical analysis). There were concerns that research literature was not 'user-friendly', and that social work journals were few and far between. There was also a lack of an easily accessible database. Additionally, many practitioners felt excluded from research, and felt that their views and needs were not taken into the agenda-setting process. The group felt that the approach to setting up research questions and priorities should be less top-down and more bottom-up.

As far as research literacy was concerned it was felt that professional and managerial training did not cover the research curriculum adequately, and that professional training (both at qualifying and post-qualifying level) required the inclusion of research-awareness in teaching. The organisation of the PSS to inform policy at governmental level was effective, particularly in child care, but links with health research were rather weak. Interdisciplinary and inter-agency research was almost non-existent in spite of the legal requirements relating to the provision of a mixture of services by the various departments (education, health, housing, and social services) involved.

The Research Record

Resources for R&D for PSS were small (less than 1% of the cost of service delivery). The *Survey of Resources* (Statham, 1992), conducted by the Thomas Coram Research Unit, found that in 1989 £9.6 million was spent on PSS research, 54% of which was provided by the DoH, 18% by universities, 15% by trusts and charities, 8% by the Economic Social Research Council (ESRC), 2% by local authorities and 3% by other commissioning agencies. During that year 58% was devoted to community care, 26% to child care, 14% to AIDS and 2% to the workforce. The DoH commissioned more than half of all PSS research. A significant proportion of PSS resources of £2.7 million was devoted to five core-funded units dedicated to PSS research. These were:

- the Dartington Social Research Unit (DSRU);
- the National Institute of Social Work (NISW);
- the Personal Social Services Research Unit (PSSRU);
- the Social Policy Research Unit (SPRU); and
- the Thomas Coram Research Unit (TCRU).

Departmental support varied from between 36% for SPRU and 100% for NISW; four units were attached to the universities, but NISW stood alone; 28 members of staff in these units were core funded.

The universities ranked next in the productivity of research in areas related to PSS, usually carried out by social policy and social work departments. Projects were funded either by HEFC, research councils, charities, or the DoH. Research in social services departments (SSDs) was undertaken only by some larger local authorities that had research divisions mostly addressing areas of intelligence.

The academic and conceptual framework of social services, and therefore of PSS research, was found to be still underdeveloped. There were no powerful long-established institutions providing leadership (such as that which the Royal Colleges give to the health services). The NISW had a long way to go to fulfil its tasks. Social work departments at universities received low grading in RAEs, and in 1992 only two obtained Grade 5. *The British Journal of Social Work* was seldom read by social care workers, and *Community Care*, although widely circulated, gave little space to research findings. However, they found that there was eagerness for sound knowledge to improve practice and to use new validated ideas: practitioners were aware of their inexperience and lack of skills in evaluating research and ability to distinguish between good and bad.

Proposals for Future Improvements in Research and Development Strategies

The review group made several recommendations as a way ahead. Knowing that extra money was not going to be available, priorities had to be established for R&D and PSS within the existing budget. Several aspects were considered as essential to improve research in PSS. Development and dissemination were seen as primary objectives for an R&D strategy. In order to encourage a broader conceptual framework regarding research needs and priorities, the involvement of purchasers, providers, policy makers and users was seen as necessary. Interdisciplinary decision-making regarding research questions and agendas was considered essential to organise and evolve comprehensive research programmes. Housing authorities, social security departments, and the police should be involved (both locally and centrally) in discussions underlying the formulation of policies. It was recommended that the DoH should take the lead in encouraging a broadly based occasional research forum which could take a long-term view on needs and draw together the many interests involved including the voluntary sector. Occasional two- or three-day conferences featuring well-prepared papers on chosen themes, as well as half-day seminars, were proposed. Academics and practitioners should work in partnership—academics on such occasions should be involved in the presentation of theories and research, while practitioners should share their actual professional experiences. It was also proposed to involve practitioners in the research process from the beginning to the end: to achieve this end, informal *ad hoc* partnerships should be established to encourage locally initiated research. Involving practitioners from the beginnings of the project, and keeping them informed throughout, would not only create a new sense of partnership and relevance, but also create an appreciation of understanding research, therefore facilitating a new climate of intellectual endeavour.

Generally agreed mechanisms were needed to ensure the reliability and validity of information before any wide dissemination took place. There was a clear need for facilities to carry out the review and digest functions, filtering and testing completed research against accepted standards, and drawing out lessons for policy and practice. It was recommended that more of the DoH's resources should be made available to establish a specialised development unit on a trial basis, perhaps in one region, where applying research to practice in one particular field could be tested.

It was recognised that there was a wealth of research knowledge already available, including Social Services Departments and that contained within unpublished theses. The review of dissemination initiatives was found to be unco-ordinated, largely autonomous and often carried out by different agencies on a competitive basis. It was felt that in order to facilitate access to research the DoH should commission:

- a collation of existing research;
- the establishment of a recognised national clearing-house available to practitioners and service users; and
- the preparation and publication of research and development reviews which would be stylistically accessible, have an easily recognisable format, and carry authority and credibility.

It was acknowledged that while such a proposal would be expensive, it was felt to be essential to have one authoritative source providing consistency in presentation, which all would understand and use when needed.

In order to abstract the messages from research projects and make informed use of them, reports should be clearly and simply written and presented. Dissemination should be provided in various ways: interim and final reports; executive summaries; publications in professional journals; seminars; and conferences.

Budgets should be allocated to those researchers who have writing skills and the capacity or willingness to undertake dissemination. It was proposed that the Joseph Rowntree methods of reporting research and findings by journalists experienced in writing on scientific subjects should be used. Comprehensive dissemination is not cost-free, and therefore it was recommended that the DoH and others commissioning research should adopt the practice in the USA of ensuring dissemination from the start of any research project by including a funding element in the budget, usually set at 5%.

Professional social work journals play an important role in dissemination, so it was suggested that editors should encourage practitioners and researchers to write joint papers (in particular, interdisciplinary ones) which could help lessen the divisions between health and PSS research. By involving practitioners in joint publications, interest and understanding of research would increase along with a much needed new sense of participation and personal involvement. To make research findings known to all ranks, each of the SSDs should have a known plan to keep staff informed by adopting various methods of dissemination. The Social Services Inspectorate (SSI) played a major positive role in the dissemination of research and its implementation into child care policy and practice. It was recommended that the SSI should continue promoting research-informed practice, but in relation to adult services this should be hand-in-hand with health care research dissemination. The SSI should also ensure that inspection was properly informed by research.

In relation to training in qualifying courses, the aim should be to make social workers research-literate, if not research-competent. This could be achieved through findings presented as part of course work, assessment demanding evidence of research knowledge, and by an insistence that professional journals should be read. Postgraduate research programmes run by some universities should be supported by SSDs, and more opportunities created to enable people to enrol for higher degrees. Research councils and charities provide some funding for these purposes, but on a very small scale. SSDs training sections should take responsibility for research-awareness training, helping all staff to recognise the value of research in practice and the need for quality assurance of research findings.

Future Developments

Although the review group was not asked to set an agenda for future research in the PSS, as a result of consultations it drew some conclusions of its own, and proposed possible organisational changes to promote developments for an R&D strategy in the PSS. It considered various organisational options to improve research culture, commissioning research and its dissemination, as well as strengthening the involvement of practitioners and bringing PSS research and health services research closer together. After considerable deliberation it concluded that present arrangements for R&D worked well and were effective in particular child care fields and that there was no need for breaking links between research and policy making. However, the position of PSS research would be strengthened if there was a clear location of responsibility for it within the management structure of R&D.

It was recommended that a senior manager should chair a small, separate committee, to include external advisers from service providers, users and academic researchers, to oversee the development of PSS research strategies. The committee would be accountable to the Department for R&D. Impressed by the strength of the link between research and policy making in child care and the role played by the Research Liaison Group (RLG), it was proposed that that group should become a subgroup of the committee proposed, in order to give strategic direction and provide quality control to the centrally commissioned programme for child care. In order to encourage integration of health and PSS research, a much stronger PSS presence was seen to be required on the CRDC of the NHS. At least two members should be included.

In line with NHS devolution from the centre to the regions, the development of PSS R&D consortia in three or four regions and the appointment of a Director for each of the regions (the Regional Directors to be accountable to the Director of R&D centrally) was proposed. Regional Directors of PSS R&D should enjoy the same status as those in the NHS. The remit of the Regional Directors of R&D in PSS would be to chair a regional commissioning group consisting of the Directors of Social Services, service users, carers, practitioners and researchers. The group would commission research and development based on research findings, and it was suggested that the research questions should be worked out collectively.

In order to focus research into practice issues, and to enhance collaboration between health and PSS research related to practice, the regionally commissioned projects should meet the following criteria:

• Research should be where the boundaries of social care, health and other related services, such as housing, meet.
• Research should involve collaboration between research and practice agencies at all stages from design to evaluation.
• The commissioning and dissemination of research should involve representatives of service users and their carers.

Each region would need a research budget: an estimated need per year was between £3.5 and £4 million; funding should be built up over four to five years; and a third of the Department research budget should be allocated to the regions. It was envisaged that centrally funded research would continue as before and would not impinge on the proposed arrangements. Bidding processes would be competitive and open to university departments, specialist research units, and private and voluntary sector agencies.

Advantages were seen in establishing a small number of long-term focused core-funded research centres. R&D should play the key role in negotiating agreements for each research centre, but thereafter keep clear of detail unless there was a clear breach of agreement or quality control was not met; and the existing programme of research funding should continue, but focus on the build-up of a number of teams to achieve critical mass.

EFFECTIVENESS OF THE RESEARCH AND DEVELOPMENT STRATEGIES IN THE NATIONAL HEALTH SERVICE AND PERSONAL SOCIAL SERVICES

Substantial progress was made within a relatively short time, as stated by the House of Lords Select Committee (HMSO, 1995). A Central

Research and Development Committee (CRDC) was set up to advise the Director of R&D on priorities for centrally and regionally funded R&D. The members of CRDC included NHS managers and academic researchers. Liaison links were established in order to co-ordinate and accommodate various needs, to establish priorities and to set up unified research mechanisms throughout the UK. The Committee liaised with the regions and Special Health Authorities (SHAs), the Department of Health and the Scottish, Welsh and Northern Ireland Offices, the Higher Education Funding Council (HEFC), the universities, the research councils, the charities, industry, and various professional bodies. The CRDC established six perspectives from which to assess priorities for R&D: diseases; management and organisation; client groups; consumers; health technologies; and research methodology. In contrast to the science-driven approach to research as promoted by the research councils, the CRDC adopted a 'problem-led' approach. It put strong emphasis on applied research and evaluation. In order to identify and prioritise particular problems suitable for commissioned research, the Committee appointed a time-limited multidisciplinary advisory group to help them with the selection of appropriate projects. Once a decision was made as to which projects required attention, a region was identified in order to oversee the commissioning of centrally funded research, whether from within that region or elsewhere.

Further developments followed. *Research for Health* (DoH, 1993) provided an update of papers since the initial 1991 R&D strategy document. It strengthened the role for R&D in the Regional Health Authorities. Regions were asked to appoint Directors and Managers of R&D. Regional Directors for Research and Development (RDRD) had an overall responsibility to develop regional research programmes, using their own resources, in collaboration with local universities, and to contract with the Central Research and Development Division (CRDD) to manage centrally funded programmes chosen by the CRDC. A programme of Health Technology Assessment was set up in 1994 to describe and evaluate methods used by health professionals to promote health, prevent and treat disease and improve rehabilitation and long-term care. Information systems have been established which provided the means to disseminate and promote the effective use and exchange of research information. The objective was to transfer up-to-date research findings to practitioners and policy makers and to the research community.

As part of the Information System Strategy (ISS), two major centres—the UK Cochrane Centre and the NHS Centre for Reviews and Dissemination—have been established to support the production of systematic reviews of evidence about the effects of health care. The

National Research Register (NRR) was also established to provide information about research projects being funded to avoid duplication. The NRR will provide information about R&D projects funded by the Department, NHS Executing, the NHS and other bodies. The UK Cochrane Centre has given rise to the Cochrane Collaboration, comprising review groups of Cochrane Centres in several countries. Cochrane Collaboration are preparing and maintaining systematic reviews of Research Control Trials in areas of health care, drawing upon national and international expertise, and designing systems for assembling and maintaining a database of systematic reviews. The Cochrane Library contains four databases which are regularly updated. These are: the Cochrane Database of Systematic Reviews; the Database of Abstracts of Reviews of Effectiveness; the Cochrane Controlled Trials Register; and the Cochrane Review Methodology Database.

The NHS Centre for Reviews and Dissemination (CRD) in York University commissions and supports reviewers to undertake reviews in areas of importance to health policy or NHS services. It disseminates research-based information to decision makers. Two databases of abstracts of systematic reviews of effectiveness and of economic evaluations of health care have been established. The Centre also produces Effective Health Care Bulletins.

A research capacity strategy in the NHS is being introduced to assist career researchers, research managers and supervisors, and to encourage the development of critical appraisal skills for practitioners and managers. The emphasis of the research capacity strategy is on general medical practice, nursing, health visiting and professions allied to medicine, including social work. R&D Offices in England, Scotland, Wales and Northern Ireland have devoted some resources to education and training in both the conduct of research and the assessment of research findings (critical appraisal) in the forms of post-doctoral fellowships, research-training studentships and bursaries. This is a most welcome initiative, and is fundamental to the success of the R&D strategy. Without skilled researchers from all disciplines, and well-informed managers with knowledge of what research can offer, progress is not going to be made. Research capacity is not going to be achieved quickly, but the wheels are on the right track:

- personal bursaries providing support for individuals to undertake courses in research or part-time programmes of research training (such as MSc or PhD);

- studentships providing support for individuals to undertake fully developed programmes of research as part of a higher degree; and
- fellowships providing support for individuals at a post-doctoral level to incorporate research into evolving professional functions as a means of developing a research career.

Studentships and fellowships have been provided over the years by research councils, such as the Medical Research Council, Higher Education Funding Council, Economic and Social Research Council, and some charities (such as the Rowntree Foundation), but they have been insufficient to meet demand, so the new injection of money is most welcome.

The new R&D spirit also reflected on the criteria of the HEFC Research Assessment Exercises, 1996. Emphasis was put on quality (rather than quantity), applied research was included (giving it an equal value to basic and strategic research) and evidence of research culture and support mechanisms to maintain input and output of all research activities was required (see Chapter 10 for full discussion on RAEs).

As far as child care research is concerned, it has not only expanded at governmental, university and PSS levels but also has been enhanced by the voluntary sector organisations such as the National Children's Bureau, Barnardo's and NSPCC. All of these agencies have well-developed research sections and are carrying out extensive research programmes. They play a significant role in the development of knowledge in a wide range of child care and child protection issues. Social work academics from various parts of the UK have played an important role in executing and enhancing research in child care. Two recent developments have taken place in Social Work Departments at Exeter University and The Queen's University of Belfast. At Exeter, for example, the DoH, eleven Departments of Social Services in the South-West of England, and the University established, in 1997, a Regional Centre for Dissemination and Implementation of Research Findings. In Belfast, a Regional Centre for Child Care Research (CCCR) was established in 1995, in partnership with the DHSS, the four Health and Social Services Boards, and The Queen's University in order to undertake original research, provide a wide range of dissemination activities, set up a database on child care research in Northern Ireland and elsewhere, and provide research training for practitioners and students (see Chapter 13 for further information on the Centre for Child Care Research).

THE IMPACT OF RESEARCH AND DEVELOPMENT STRATEGY ON CHILD CARE POLICY AND PRACTICE

Most studies embracing child care policy and practice are initiated and funded by the DoH Policy Research Programme. The current research projects centre around four major programme areas which have been commissioned as integrated groups of studies in response to major developments in services and policy. These include; an evaluation of early implementation of the Children Act (1989), studies in residential child care, and studies in adoption. In addition, there are numbers of smaller groups of studies relating to key policy topics or issues. Eleven studies were commissioned in 1992/93 to examine the impact of early implementation of the Children Act (1989) on children and families. Two projects focused on new provision for child protection, reviewing statutory intervention in the courts and the application of new criteria of risk by social workers. Four studies examined provisions of family support. Two studies investigated provisions for planning and review of children 'looked after', and registration and inspection of day care and pre-school services to children under eight respectively. Two studies examined new provisions for leaving care and the Guardian Ad Litem Reporting Officers' services. Five inter-linked studies on residential care were commissioned in 1993 in response to a series of incidents in children's homes. The focus is on describing what happens in children's homes, what promotes good practice, what inhibits it and how this can be recognised and prevented. Six studies on adoption aim to assist preparation of the proposed Adoption Act and accompanying guidance. Research on 'Supporting Parents' has recently been commissioned. The central aim of this initiative is to investigate the ways in which parents can be better supported to look after their children effectively. Eleven studies have been designed and are grouped under four headings: Children in the Community with Behaviour Problems; Families with Disability; Children at Risk; and Parenting and Support in Poor Environments. The studies commenced in 1996 and will run until 2001.

In addition to the four programmes of studies described above, there are several smaller groups of studies, in the areas of child abuse and protection, family support and services to under eight and juvenile justice. Two important studies in the area of juvenile justice are taking place: one aims to produce an updated version of *Juvenile Delinquence: Trends and Perspectives* by Rutter and Giller, while the second, *Protective Factors in Juvenile Offending*, is a longitudinal follow-up by the

Dartington Research Group of subsequent offending behaviour among a cohort of earlier juvenile offenders.

SUMMARY

This chapter discussed the state of research in the NHS as the House of Lords Select Committee found it in the 1980s. It went on to give an account of how, as a result of concern expressed and of recommendations made to the Government, a coherent R&D strategy has been developed. This was launched for the NHS in England with the appointment of a Director of R&D and various committees to revitalise, organise, set priorities, give direction, and deal with thorny funding issues. Scotland, Wales and Northern Ireland then published their R&D strategies based on the specific needs and organisational structures of each country. The Directors of R&D were appointed and R&D offices were created to oversee and manage R&D programmes and policies. In order to protect the necessary quantum of high-quality research from threats posed by the internal market of the NHS, DoH established a Task Force, chaired by Professor Culyer on *Supporting R&D in the NHS*. The Culyer Report, published in 1994, identified a number of problems and proposed a range of radical solutions. The changes being implemented in Wales, Scotland, England and Northern Ireland aim to improve consultative mechanisms, including consultation with purchasers and providers, and to improve arrangements for identifying, prioritising, supporting, commissioning, costing and accounting for NHS, R&D and for support of externally funded R&D. The goals are (1) to provide all parts of the NHS, including the primary and community care sectors, with access to R&D funding and (2) to ensure that those who carry out and support research not only justify their claim for funding, in competition with others but are also made accountable for their work. To achieve these aims and to support R&D properly, a single explicit stream of funding was proposed to avoid cross-subsidisation between patient care and R&D.

In 1994, the report commissioned by DoH, *A Wider Strategy for Research and Development Relating to Personal Social Services*, was also published, giving an account of the research in PSS then and making proposals for improvements. Special attention was given to the enhancement of research culture among social workers and their managers in order to understand the value of research and to use it to inform policy and practice.

The latter part of this chapter described the impact of R&D strategy on child care policy and practice. The DoH policy research programme on child care has proved to be highly successful, especially on policy formation, and has embraced and instigated new areas for research which require urgent attention. There is now ample evidence that major decisions made in relation to child care policy and practice are being based on lessons learned from research. The key to this was the development of a coherent government strategy for R&D in Health and Personal Social Services.

REFERENCES

DHSS (1993). *A Strategy for Research and Development in the Health and Personal Social Services in Northern Ireland*. Consultative Paper. Belfast: DHSS.

DoH (1993). *Research for Health*. London: HMSO.

DoH (1994a). *Supporting Research and Development in the NHS*. NHS Research and Development Task Force. London: HMSO. [The Culyer Report.]

DoH (1994b). *A Wider Strategy for Research and Development Relating to Personal Social Services*. An Independent Review Group Report. London: HMSO.

HMSO (1988). *Priorities in Medical Research*. Report of the House of Lords Select Committee on Science and Technology. London: HMSO.

HMSO (1993). *Research and Development Strategy for the National Health Service in Scotland*. Scottish Office, Chief Scientist Office, Home and Health Department. HMSO: Edinburgh.

HMSO (1995). *Medical Research and the NHS Reforms*. House of Lords Select Committee on Science and Technology. London: HMSO.

Statham, J. (1992). *Survey of Resources for Research Relevant to Personal Social Services*. London: Thomas Coram Research Unit.

Welsh Office (1992). *Sharpening the Focus: Research and Development Framework for NHS Wales*. Welsh Office, NHS Directorate. Cardiff: Welsh Office.

2

THE IMPACT OF RESEARCH ON POLICY AND PRACTICE: A SYSTEMIC PERSPECTIVE

John Pinkerton

Chapter Outline

INTRODUCTION

THE CHILD CARE SYSTEM AS RESEARCH CONTEXT

SOCIETAL CONTEXT

KEY ACTORS: PROCESSES AND OUTCOMES

DEVELOPING AN IMPACT STRATEGY

SUMMARY

INTRODUCTION

In 1991 a European seminar brought together representatives from twenty countries to discuss applied research and social policies for children (Casas, 1995, p. 10). What emerged was a mixed but overall fairly bleak view.

> In most European countries, maybe with the exception of Scandinavia, the study of the social problems of childhood seems to have a dual

---

Making Research Work: Promoting Child Care Policy and Practice
Edited by D. Iwaniec and J. Pinkerton
© 1998 John Wiley & Sons Ltd

common denominator: a low budget and a low status for the researcher
engaged in the field. Low status and limited resources are naturally
associated with the low popular impact of scientific achievements in the
childhood field, even though these achievements are obviously of the
greatest importance. (Casas, 1995, p. 6)

In addition to Sweden, with its experience of a long-lasting and wide-
ranging relationship between research, policy and practice, a number
of other countries were able to report positively for at least some
areas. One of these countries was the United Kingdom. The 1989
Children Act in England and Wales and the closely associated Children
(Scotland) Act 1995 and Children (Northern Ireland) Order 1995 are
generally recognised as marking a watershed for child care in the UK. It
is also generally accepted that one of the major influences on the new
legislation was research (Hill & Aldgate, 1996). Throughout the 1980s a
steady stream of research was both commissioned and published with a
leading role being played by the then Department of Health and Social
Security (DHSS), now the Department of Health (DoH). Particular attention was given to dissemination of findings, with the publication and
active promotion of a review of nine major pieces of research under the
title *Social Work Decisions in Child Care* (DHSS, 1985)—the 'Pink Book' as
it came to be known from its distinctive cover. This was followed in the
1990s by *Patterns and Outcomes in Child Placement* (DoH, 1991), which
reviewed findings from a wide range of research projects, and by *Child
Protection: Messages from Research* (DoH, 1995), known as the 'Blue
Book', which drew together a set of twenty studies that made up a
programme of research into child protection commissioned by the DoH.
     This growth in the importance of research to policy and practice
within child care was noted by an independent Review Group appointed by the DoH to take a strategic look at the place of research
within Personal Social Services (PSS) (DoH, 1994). However, in looking
at the impact of research on policy and practice the Review Group also
drew attention to a range of general difficulties from which child care
is not exempt—the complexity of PSS as a subject area; the difficulty of
researching social care outcomes as clinical probabilities; the diffuse
nature of research undertaken in the area; the place of research as only
one of a variety of competing influences on the direction of policy and
practice; the restrictions of limited resources and market mechanisms;
the blocks caused by organisational issues and professional demarcation lines. Thus even though the situation in the UK may be better than
in other countries it still demonstrates that there is clearly a complex
and difficult relationship between research, policy and practice.
     As Bullock and Little (1995) have pointed out for child care in the
field of PSS:

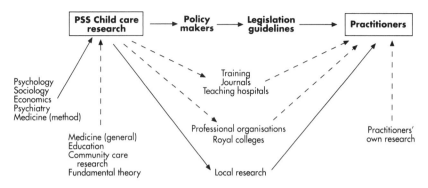

Figure 1: Links between research, policy and practice

> some links, such as those between research and central government policy, are relatively strong, but in other areas, for instance, social work training and practitioners' own work, we have made little headway. (Bullock and Little, 1995, p. 30)

They usefully illustrate their assessment of the existing relationships in Figure 1, which is useful because it not only reinforces a sense of the complexity of the means by which research impacts on policy and practice but also suggests that it depends on a process involving relationships between a range of interests. The aim of this chapter is to take that idea further by arguing for a systemic perspective on the relationship of research to policy and practice. Such a perspective suggests that child care researchers concerned with ensuring that their work helps to develop policy and practice need to understand the system of which they become a part through researching it and, based on that understanding, need to develop an 'impact strategy' as part of their research design.

This chapter sets out a systems model of how outcomes of various types are achieved in child care, as a way of understanding the position and potential impact of research. This is then discussed with illustrations from a study commissioned by government and undertaken by academic researchers, in which practitioners and service users were surveyed and interviewed about the needs and service experiences of young people leaving state care (Pinkerton & McCrea, 1996). The model draws attention to the general societal context of research, as registered in the characteristics of the scientific community, the state and civil society. It highlights four key groups—child care researchers, policy makers, practitioners and service users—and notes areas of similarity and of difference relevant to their coherence as an interacting system. Attention is then given to the way each group achieves its outcomes through a process more or less particular to itself and the potential for synchronising these is discussed. The overlaps between the various outcomes resulting from the activity of the four groups is discussed and attention drawn not only to their variety but also to the degree of interdependence. On the basis of that discussion, suggestions are made on how to develop an impact strategy as part of designing and undertaking child care research. The chapter finishes with a summary which stresses that child care researchers need to believe that their work can make a difference to policy and practice and should put effort into developing and implementing an impact strategy.

THE CHILD CARE SYSTEM AS RESEARCH CONTEXT

The DoH Review Group which examined the place of research within Personal Social Services identified as a weakness the tradition of a diffuse process of knowledge dissemination. This is not peculiar to child care but is an expression of a wider experience which has been called the 'limestone model' as it accepts that the influence of research on policy and practice will be long term and indirect—like water entering and gradually percolating through limestone without it being clear where or when it will emerge as a trickle (McWhirter, 1993). While there may be some descriptive accuracy in that view, it is increasingly unacceptable not only to funders (whether state or charitable foundations) but also to researchers themselves who increasingly have professional and clinical backgrounds and want their work to play a role in the development of policy and practice.

Until now a major alternative to the 'limestone model' has been the 'engineering model' (Hammersley, 1995), which in the current climate could perhaps more accurately be termed a 'commissioner-provider model'. This model assumes a linear sequence running from the recognition of a policy or practice problem about which research is required, to the commissioning of a researcher who undertakes the research and the development of a policy or practice solution to the original problem based on that research. In this model the development of a policy or practice solution is seen as a direct output of research—a dependent variable. Yet as one commentator who has experience of being both a university researcher and a government commissioner has bluntly put it:

> It is a myth that social research, if properly conducted, will always find its results incorporated into social policy. The expectation of direct and

immediate policy effects from research is in fact unrealistic. (McWhirter, 1993, p. 4)

Even advocates of the 'engineering model' would accept that there are likely to be other influential social, technical, economic and political inputs that contribute to the final policy or practice output. Instead of having to choose between these two unsatisfactory models, child care researchers need an approach that draws from both in such a way as to encourage researchers to aspire to and maximise the impact of their work while recognising that their contribution is only one part of a complex interplay between all components in the child care system which, together, generate changes in policy and practice. The competing influences to which the DoH Review Group drew attention are an inevitable and necessary part of the system. Understood in that way, in what can be called the 'social system model', the problem of how to ensure research has an impact on policy, and practice becomes a strategic matter of how researchers can best influence other key players through the particular contribution they have to offer child care. The researchers then need to understand where they and their work fit into the system and its dynamic.

A social system can be usefully defined as a set of component parts in which both the system as a whole and each of the components derive their characteristics from their interaction. Accordingly, to understand the individual components it is necessary to understand the system and to understand the system it is necessary to understand the components. Thanks to the work of family therapists and of social systems analysts, particularly in the field of juvenile justice, the importance of a systemic perspective to child care is securely established within research, and among policy makers and practitioners. The argument here is that it should also be applied to the place of research within the child care system.

In order to locate child care research in such a systemic manner it is helpful to map out the societal context, key child care actors, processes and outcomes in the form of a model, as in Figure 2.

Looking at Figure 2, it is apparent that the researchers as key child care actors are linked within the process section of the model by lines of communication with three other types of actor—policy makers, practitioners and service users. In the case of the Leaving Care Study being used here for illustration, the key actors were the academic researchers, the policy makers were civil servants and social services inspectors, practitioners were field work and residential care staff, and young people leaving care were the service users. There are other important actors, a point that will be returned to later, but for the argument here

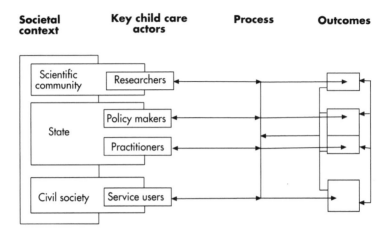

Figure 2:   Research in the context of the child care system

the four noted are sufficient. The model also indicates that what follows from process is a variety of outcomes which are specific to the different types of actor but reinforce each other to a greater or lesser degree. It is with that question of degree that *impact* is concerned. Impact in this sense can be defined as the extent of mutual reinforcement between the outcomes achieved by the different actors. This raises the following questions: Did the work of the researchers in gathering, describing and making informed comment on data about a cohort of care leavers reinforce the policy makers' stated commitment to promoting services that were more proactive and flexible (SSI, 1994)? Did it reinforce the concern of practitioners to ensure that individual young people on their case loads moved on successfully from the care system? Did it contribute to the capacity of young people to make their personal transitions to adulthood?

A research project offers the opportunity to bring the four identified groups of key actors together to form an alliance of interests in pursuit of their own outcomes but reinforced by each other. Such an alliance is not just a matter for the end of the research process when findings are available; it should be pursued throughout a project's development from the initial idea, through the design of the project, to data collection, analysis, write up and dissemination. As each of the four groups advances its own concerns through a process particular to itself, any alliance must take account of these differences and attempt to synchronise the process. Within the process section of the model in Figure 2 these links are denoted by the vertical line cutting across the 'process' arrows. There is the potential for the processes to touch and feed off each other. Each process arrow connects one of the key actors groups to its own separate outcome. The arrows within the outcomes section suggest the possible reinforcement. The arrow returning from the outcomes section to the process section represents the feedback loop that must exist in any functioning system. Each of the key groups takes what it requires as feedback but does it in a manner that is affected by and affects the others. Thus the impact of research on the activities and concerns of each group is not just a matter of time and chance, as in the 'limestone' model, nor is it the result of direct, managed inputs, as in the 'engineering' model. Rather the model demonstrates impact as depending on the forging and sustaining of social alliances within the context of a dynamic system.

In addition to highlighting the interplay of the four groups of key players the model also draws attention to the context in which these relationships are played out. It is society in the broadest sense that sets the overall context of the child care system in which researchers and the other key actors have to operate. It is important to recognise that ideological, economic and political structures determine the space within which any child welfare system has to function and it can be a very narrow space squeezed between other, more dominant forces within the state and civil society. For researchers there is also the wider scientific community of which they are a part and which is also dependent on the broader forces of ideology, economics and politics. This reminds researchers that they are part of a wider society in which they have responsibilities and are connected to the other key players as citizens as well as researchers. It is also important to recognise the global dimension to this societal context.

> As nations become globally aware and increasingly interlinked, it becomes more necessary to relate any social action concerning children to an international framework, encompassing both policies specific to children and social policies in general. (Casas, 1995, pp. 2–3)

Any actor in the child care field is now part of a global agenda set by the United Nations Convention on the Rights of the Child (CRDU, 1994).

Attention to societal structures also asserts as central to any consideration of impact, the recurring social science theme of the relationship between 'structure' and 'action' (Giddens, 1979, 1997). The process and outcomes sections of the model can be seen as representing a focus on social action while the context section draws attention to social structure. The core strategic question for researchers, as for any other social actors, is what are the structural boundaries to the possibilities of their social action. This raises the question of power and the politics of research (Harvey, 1990; Hammersley, 1995).

SOCIETAL CONTEXT

For researchers to make useful strategic calculations about the social space and the balance of power within which they are operating, it is helpful to focus on how structural limitations and the possibilities for action are expressed in the particular nature of the scientific community, the state and the civil society in which they are working. This requires researchers to give thought to their own power and status within a broader and far from homogeneous scientific community. It also requires researchers to consider how their social positioning relates to that of the other key actors—policy makers and practitioners as part of the state, and service users as part of civil society.

In the UK, hierarchies still exist within the scientific community that would privilege the natural sciences over the social sciences and pure research over applied research. However, there is also a growing recognition that a sterile pure versus applied distinction needs to be replaced with a more graded and interlocking view of different types of research. Three types of research are generally, though by no means universally (Hammersley, 1995), recognised as applying in both the natural and social sciences. First, 'basic research', sometimes called 'blue skies' research, is experimental or theoretical work on understanding the underlying foundation of phenomena with no particular use in view. Secondly, 'strategic research' has the goal of an eventual application but is at a stage where it is premature to specify what that application might be. Thirdly, 'applied research' is undertaken with a particular practical aim or objective in mind. It is applied research that is the focus of discussion here. The distinction between the three types is not made to elevate one over the others but rather to recognise their different contributions and interdependence.

Within the UK there is also a long tradition of applied social research which can be traced back at least a hundred years (Alcock, 1998). This is an important asset which should not be taken for granted. It has been pointed out by others that even 'when faced with pressing social problems, in many countries, such as France, there is no tradition of seeking remedies by reviewing empirical evidence' (Bullock and Little, 1995). Applied social research in the UK has also, in the main, avoided being fragmented by endless abstract debates between rival schools of thought and theoretical paradigms, as complained about in other countries (Casas, 1995). If anything, the tendency has been to underplay the importance of developing basic theory, though the growing disenchantment with the capacity of the welfare state to resolve major social problems which grew from the late 1960s did prompt more basic theoretical citiques from both the left and right (Taylor-Gooby, 1991). An unfortunate result of the general lack of theory within child care research is that the loose interdisciplinary allegiances based on pragmatism and empiricism have made the research community an equally loose-knit, disparate group lacking the authority of a clear professional identity.

This lack of a strong independent research identity has allowed other professional, occupational or organisational identities to dominate and set the research agenda—especially where the group has been either traditionally powerful, as with medicine, or in the ascendancy, as with groups associated with the 'new managerialism' of the public sector (Clarke, 1998). This has the disadvantage of generating professional rivalry, demarcation disputes and organisational blocks. The lack of a strong independent identity may also be one of the reasons why, to a large extent, the development of social research in the UK has depended on the sponsorship of the state. This had clear benefits during the post-war development of the welfare state. It has been argued that the 1969 Children and Young Persons Act, an important landmark in British child care because of its promotion of prevention, resulted from a Labour Government whose respect for social science rigour and its application to policy and practice 'led it to a dependency on Fabian academics and social work professionals' (Bolger et al., 1981, p. 90). The collapse in the consensus about the nature of the state and the ascendancy from the late 1970s of a politics driven by an ideology which held as axiomatic that 'there's no such thing as society' (Thatcher quoted in Taylor-Gooby, 1991, p. 85) inevitably undermined the position of the social sciences.

However, as with many other aspects of the Thatcher years, the undermining of the relationship between the state and social research may have been more apparent than real. In order to pursue its distributive and regulatory functions in an increasingly complex domestic and international environment the state continued to require the knowledge and information that research can provide. Accordingly, public policy continued to be characterised by an incrementalism based on rational problem solving which required the data, key ideas and explanatory conceptual frameworks that research can provide. As noted earlier, it was during the 1980s that significant strides were made in both the volume and influence of child care research. Leaving care is a good example of a growing research base becoming influential. In 1986 the first major study was published (Stein and Carey, 1986) and ten year later there were at least six major pieces of empirical work in the area and a burgeoning literature. Much more significant during the 1980s and 1990s has been the political promotion of the market as the means of economic management. This forced research along with every other resource-hungry activity to become more focused on purpose and competitive in costs.

While the basic function of the state may not have changed, there has been a growing awareness of the complex of institutions through which the state may operate, including those which might more readily be regarded as private rather than public. In part this reflects political choices during the last decade and a half about rolling back the state through the creation of various forms of quasi-autonomous non-government organisations, promotion of the private sector and reasserting expectations of the family as the basic unit of social reproduction. But it also represents recognition, signified by the increasingly commonplace use of the term 'governance', of the importance of developments within theoretical work which highlight that the contemporary state depends on much more than its formal administrative and security appartatus to sustain and extend its influence (Althusser, 1971; Parton, 1994; Hill, 1997).

It may be true that, ultimately, public policy is whatever those in control of the state decide to do but the notion of governance directs researchers concerned about impact on policy and practice to give attention to more than just the corridors of power. There is a need to take into account that 'a decision network, often of considerable complexity, may be involved in producing action, and a web of decisions taking place over a long period of time and extending far beyond the initial policy-making process may form part of the network' (Hill, 1997, p. 7). The impact of research has to be considered within the more fluid and amorphous networks of civil society. Within the UK the pace of change within civil society has raised fundamental questions about the environment, social institutions, social relationships, value systems, rights and obligations. Nowhere is this more apparent than in relation to children, as evidenced in debates about family life, child protection, school and youth crime (Scraton, 1997). Young people leaving care epitomise many of these themes—family failure, children as victims, young people as dangerous, teenage mothers, youth homelessness (West, 1995). The popular social perceptions of childhood and youth, rooted in personal experience and moulded by the media, tends to be imprecise, often contradictory and yet immensely potent (Morrison, 1997). The result is a deep-seated ambivalence to acknowledging and understanding these changes which is reflected in attitudes to research in this area.

However, there continues to be considerable respect for science, particularly the biological and physical sciences, as providing objective understanding on the basis of which technological advances can be made—not least in the area of information technology where such rapid developments have occurred. Effective social policy is also seen to require debate and judgement based on facts and explanatory frameworks. This is attested to by the importance given to research by so many pressure groups. It is also important to note, as a significant feature of contemporary civil society, its capacity to generate single issue campaigns and organisations. So much so that some commentators have argued that the UK is a 'post-parliamentary democracy' in which public policy is the result of negotiations between government agencies and pressure groups (Richardson and Jordan cited Hill, 1997, p. 31). Thus civil society as much as the state is both highly significant for, and receptive to, the impact of research—though in a more random and unpredictable fashion.

KEY ACTORS: PROCESSES AND OUTCOMES

In recognising the diversity within the broad societal context, a wide range of groups potentially become important to ensuring the impact of the research. Casas has drawn attention to five key groups who need to be drawn together in order to promote the convergence of research and practice in child care: professionals in the field, researchers, the media, the general public and politicians. He suggests that a major block to drawing these groups together is that each approaches the issue of childhood from a different perspective.

Professionals in the field focus on solving the practical problems presented by individuals, communities and other specific groups. They tend to be wary of politicians, defensive about research and suspicious of the media. The researcher's focus is on truth, approached cautiously and slowly through accurate and meticulous measurement, careful observation and continuous verification. Information professionals need novelty: dramatic and spectacular events and issues which will capture the public attention. The public themselves need information of a human, immediate kind which will be relevant to them in their daily lives. In addition, they need to feel that they are participating, that they are being listened to, that their opinions, needs and wants are receiving attention. The politician's task is to formulate a coherent, legal framework of service, establishing priorities, standards and procedures which embrace, as far as possible, the different and often conflicting needs of all the other players. (Casas, 1995, p. 15)

What is important here is that Casas draws attention to how different social groups have their own particular and legitimate perspectives. These reflect different concerns and are pursued in their own ways. They cannot be reduced to a single 'correct' or 'accurate' view but they do impinge on each other and need to be bonded together in some form of coherent unity. This reinforces the systemic approach being advanced here, but suggests a degree of possible consensus which is not implied in the social systems model set out in Figure 2. On the contrary, the four groups identified in the model—the child care researchers, policy makers, practitioners and service users—are those whose interests and interactions seem particularly crucial to the impact of research but their relative autonomy, as regards both process and outcomes, is clearly registered in the model. The problem of how to ensure that research has impact on policy and practice is the strategic question of how researchers can best use the process and outcomes distinctive to their work to influence other key actors. This involves giving attention to synchronising processes and achieving mutually reinforcing outcomes within the context of a dynamic system. Thus, it is not a matter of pulling the other actors into line behind the 'truth' uncovered by research; nor is it a matter of making research the servant of policy makers, practitioners or service users. The integrity of research requires its relative autonomy from the imperatives of other key actors (Hammersley, 1995).

In the case of the leaving care study, the outcome that was aimed for was to provide, on a once only basis, after two-and-a-half years' work, a baseline of empirical data and informed comment on young people leaving state care (Pinkerton & McCrea, 1996). This outcome was seen as overlapping with the needs of policy makers and practitioners to review, plan, monitor and evaluate services for this group of service users. For policy makers the concern to do this was determined by impending legislation which had been taking shape for over a decade and commitments expressed in strategic plans spanning over five-year periods. For practitioners it was the more pressing concern to help individual young people cope with their transition from care in the immediacy of their day-to-day living. While it is clear that there is an overlap between the outcomes pursued by these three sets of actors, it is equally clear that they are different outcomes working to different time-scales.

The planned research outcome took as given the overall strategic direction for leaving care services, as set out by the impending legisla-

tion and existing regional and agency strategic planning. It also accepted as best practice what was being advocated by practitioners. In
doing so it was also taking account of findings and recommendations
of relevant English research (Stein, 1991) and the wider child care
literature. The impact issue was therefore not how to change the emerging direction of policy and practice, but how to reinforce it by providing an informed and critical view of it in the light of an empirical
account and commentary on existing types and levels of need and
service delivery. The other important point to make about the early
stage of the research was the absence of young people as active participants. The research made assumptions about the outcomes appropriate
for these young people. Thus at the point of engagement with
which the research process commenced there was a clear hierarchy in
the attention given by the researchers to their relationships with
the other actors: the policy makers first, not least because they were
also the funders; the practitioners next; and the service users only as
potential beneficiaries. It was a case of 'eyes on the down
people . . . palm out to the up people' (Nicolaus quoted Hammersley,
1995, p. 104).

   This hierarchy was also apparent in the synchronising of the processes. Considerable time and effort went into discussions between the
researchers and the policy makers as funders to convince them that the
idea and the research design were worthy investments—in particular,
that the research would overlap with an outcome which they were
committed to by the Regional Plan. By contrast, although in the research design assumptions were made about the participation of practitioners and the young people leaving care, no consultations took
place about those assumptions. The young people were very much
'objects of concern', to borrow both Justice Butler-Sloss's term from the
Cleveland Inquiry and her concern for the inappropriateness of this
attitude (HMSO, 1988). The young people leaving care were passive
subjects to be researched. It is important to recognise that, despite these
limitations, even at this early stage of the research its impact had begun
to emerge.

   In the research review *Patterns and Outcomes in Child Placement*
(DoH, 1991) it is noted that there are similarities between the skills and
attitudes required of researchers and those required of social workers
in child care, but it is also noted that there is a marked difference in
emphasis on the various aspects of these skills and attitudes.

   Researchers are constantly challenging themselves and each other to get
   accurate complete data, to avoid bias, assumptions and the drawing of
   unwarranted conclusions. A social worker's role as service provider
   and/or therapist has inevitably meant more emphasis has been given to

empathy, negotiation and building relationships and less to objectivity
and a rigorous search for reliable evidence. (DoH, 1991, p. 78)

There is indeed this difference, and as the review suggested 'perhaps
the most important message from recent research is for practitioners
to pay greater attention to objectivity and the reliability of evidence'
(DoH, 1991, p. 78). Similarly, successful engagement of practitioners
and service users requires that researchers attend to 'empathy, negotiation and building relationships' (DoH, 1991, p. 78).

Once the process of the Leaving Care research got underway and in
particular during data collection, it was necessary to directly engage
both practitioners and service users. The researchers were able to benefit from establishing a small support group made up of practitioners
and a foster parent directly involved in leaving care provision and
discussions from time to time with an existing Aftercare Practitioners
Group. This at least sensitised the researchers to the differences between the practitioners' concerns, working practices and timetables
and their own—including, at one point, the knock-on effect of indus-
trial action on questionnaire returns. Attempts were made to do something similar for the young people leaving care through a focus group
and including young people in the support group. But these were
gestures that would have required more commitment of time and
resources than were available as the importance of this work had not
been recognised at the design stage. Again, it is important to note that,
whatever the limitations, in the process of negotiating contacts, in
completing questionnaires and taking part in interviews, the research
was impacting. This was happening through raising the profile of
leaving care and prompting people to think about different ways of
care careers, outcomes and coping mechanisms in relation to particular
young people and for leaving care in general. This was further encouraged by the production of interim reports and dissemination events at
the end of each of the four stages within the research design.

The least impact which was noticeable during the process of research was on service users because fewer of them were involved.
Conscious of this dilemma, the final report (Pinkerton & McCrea, 1996)
included not only recommendations about policy and service provision
but also two recommendations which were intended to boost the relationship between the research, young people and practitioners:

• The development of peer support groups among young people
  leaving care should be promoted as a possible intermediary network linking formal services to the informal support networks of
  family friends and community.

- Consideration should be given to an Aftercare Consortium which could draw into partnership users, service commissioners and providers, researchers and trainers to share information, encourage co-ordination of services, monitor policies and practice and promote staff training and support.

In response to the above recommendations two initiatives emerged from the research project's dissemination strategy, which included the publication of both an easy-to-read six-page summary booklet and a full 160-page final report, briefings with civil servants, a conference plus action seminar for practitioners and operational managers. The first initiative was a project involving the Voice of Young People in Care and one of the researchers in producing an 'A to Z of Leaving Care' for young people, in order to incorporate the research findings and recommendations with advice, information and accounts of personal experience from care leavers. The other initiative was that First Key—a voluntary organisation with a brief focusing solely on promoting the interests of care leavers through providing information, training and consultancy—undertook a feasibility study to explore the possibility of a role for themselves in promoting the Consortium. This was led by the second researcher and led to a mandate for First Key to set up in the region which won government funding for the initiative. These two initiatives are tangible indicators of the impact of research, as it is highly probable that neither would have occurred without the research.

DEVELOPING AN IMPACT STRATEGY

If child care researchers are committed to maximising the impact of their work they need to recognise that their contributions are only a part of a complex interplay between components in the child care system which, together, generate changes in policy and practice. To make the most of their contributions researchers need to be developing an impact strategy from the start of any project. As with any strategic thinking, this requires attention to six key principles:

- have vision
- accept that the only answers are those forged in practice
- assess the possibilities and constraints of the present position
- work collectively
- accept, understand and work the unexpected
- stay unfinished.

Child care researchers have to be clear what their vision is. While this may well include values relating to the substantive issues of child care such as those codified in the UN Convention on the Rights of the Child, it more importantly expresses the value of research. It has been argued that both functionalist and critical variations of the Enlightenment paradigm, with its belief that 'through the exercise of human reason, it was possible to produce knowledge whose validity is absolutely certain . . . valid for all human beings in all places at all times' (Hammersley, 1995, p. 121), have encouraged excessive expectations about the contribution to policy and practice of research. To abandon belief in the practical value of research is to open the way to 'celebrate irrationality, unthinking reliance on tradition, or spontaneous playfulness . . . leaving practice as a realm of mystery, and one where policy makers and practitioners can always appeal to their authority and wisdom' (Hammersley, 1995, p. 143). Child care researchers need to be clear on what they believe to be the possibilities and the limitations of a worthwhile and distinctive role for research.

As a second principle of strategic thinking, researchers need to accept that it is only through active participation that they will achieve the possibilities and explore the limitations of their vision for research. Research is essentially a social practice like any other in which outcomes are pursued by social actors who are constrained and empowered by their involvement in a social process. The answers to whether outcomes can be achieved are forged in practice. However, provisional assessments of the likelihood of achieving identified outcomes and, where necessary, appropriate modifications is an important part of strategic thinking. For researchers, this includes not only an assessment of the general context in which they work but, very importantly, the knowledge, methodologies and skills available and the resources for realising them. A part of that assessment will include looking for allies, discovering the other key actors, and finding out what they bring in the way of help or hindrance. Either way they cannot be ignored. As the fourth strategic principle highlights, the researcher has to work collectively and, as already noted, will need the skills of 'empathy, negotiation and building relationships' (DoH, 1991, p. 78).

As part of engaging in the social process of research it is important to accept that the unexpected will occur—sometimes involving gains, sometimes losses. This can be anything from the discovery of a similar study, complete with methodology, late in the design stage, to having to deal with time delays in data collection caused by having to do house calls to set up interviews because a large proportion of service users may not have telephones. Accepting the inevitability of this allows researchers to better understand these things when they occur so as to take advantage of any gains and manage the impact of losses. Expecting the unexpected also reinforces the sixth strategic principle of staying unfinished—which is a way of saying that research is creative. The best-planned project, with the most detailed design, the most meticulous approach to data collection and analysis, the clearest writing plan for the report and a coherent dissemination strategy will still need to be brought alive by the creative endeavours of individuals.

To help pursue these principles in the light of the systems model set out in Figure 2, it is important to make explicit the impact strategy to be pursued in any particular project. This raises key questions that must be answered for the project and requires certain features to be included in the research design. The most important question is: What impact do the researchers want to achieve? This means both the extent and type of impact. The answer can be minimal or ambitious but needs to be clear and be reflected in the planned outcomes as expressed in the formal aim and objectives of the research. The latter are unlikely to be purely at the discretion of the researchers, but require negotiation with other key actors. In that negotiation it is important to clarify the outcomes and processes that make up their daily concerns and how they anticipate the research process and outcomes meshing and reinforcing their concerns. It is not unknown for research to be commissioned as a means of shelving an uncomfortable issue or buying time (McWhirter, 1993). Alternatively, other actors may not know what they want, because they either cannot see the connection between the research and their concerns or just assume there is one. Framing these negotiations in terms of problem solving and timeliness can help gain the necessary focus.

The model also emphasises that all of the actors need to take account of the wider societal context. Within the particular contexts of the research community, the state and civil society it is necessary to consider what are the constraints and the encouragement. These are likely to be relevant, not only to determining what outcomes the actors are pursuing but also to the processes in which they are involved. There is a need to address such questions as:

- Are new research methodologies being developed?
- Are government departments being reorganised?
- Are additional funds being made available to particular areas of practice?
- Are shifts underway in the division of labour within households?

It is also through attention to the societal context that the broader forces of ideology, economics and politics can be identified. These will set the balance of power between the key actors and will determine the likely points of contact between them. These things, however, are not immutable and attempts can be made in the research design to re-order the hierarchies of power and build in mechanisms for contact during the process that promote different outcomes. A Save the Children Fund Project on leaving care was explicitly designed with young people to empower them to take on the role of researchers about their own experiences and those of their peers (West, 1995).

The research design is also crucial to the development and implementation of an impact strategy. The design can ensure the opportunities and resources for connecting the key actors in a meaningful way from the earliest point, with the opportunities to review not just the progress of the research but also its impact. Steering Groups and Support Groups can provide forums in which the researchers can prompt other key actors to give thought to how they are using the research process to promote impact. They can also be used to advise the researchers of emerging impact opportunities which may reinforce the importance of maintaining existing work schedules or may require some re-ordering of priorities in order to take advantage of an opportunity. The relevance of this becomes increasingly apparent as a project draws to a close and information and recommendations become available. But at that time of maximum capacity for engaging the other actors and aligning the research outcome with their outcomes, attention also needs to be given to disengagement. Having a prepared exit strategy as part of the original design can help to ensure that maximun use can be made of the research outcome. Audiences can be targeted in advance and discussion can take place to decide which key actors are likely to be able and willing to take forward particular areas of the findings and recommendations. Such discussion may also suggest a variety of formats for presenting material in order to facilitate the needs of specific groups.

SUMMARY

There are two basic assumptions underlying this chapter. The first is that child care researchers are concerned to ensure that their work has an impact on policy and practice. On the basis of the experience of research within the child welfare system in the UK, this is not easy to achieve. The challenges it poses are not peculiar to this particular area of child care research, nor just to child care research, but they are variations on themes to be found in any area of applied social research.

The second assumption is that 'research is itself a form of practice, in the sense that it is an activity pursued by human beings which takes place in the world, is directed towards a particular set of goals and uses social resources' (Hammersley, 1995, p. 141). Accordingly it makes sense to take a social systems perspective in considering how best to manage the relationship of researchers with other key actors within the child care system, and thereby promote the impact of research on policy and practice.

In order to advance a systemic perspective on research, policy and practice a model was presented of how outcomes of various types are achieved in child care. The model drew attention to the general societal context of research, as registered in the characteristics of the scientific community, the state and civil society. It also highlighted four key groups within the system—child care researchers, policy makers, practitioners and service users—and indicated that they are engaged in their own particular processes in order to advance their own outcomes. The discussion that followed was illustrated by reference to a study, commissioned by government and undertaken by academic researchers, in which practitioners and service users were surveyed and interviewed about the needs and service experiences of young people leaving state care (Pinkerton & McCrea, 1996).

Attention was first given to the implications of the societal context for constraining or encouraging the impact of research on policy and practice. This was followed by considering in more detail the relationship between the processes engaged in by key players in pursuit of their particular outcomes. It was noted that these relationships reflected their areas of similarity and of difference. Attention was given to the way each group achieves its outcomes through a process, more or less particular to itself, but also to the potential for synchronising these processes. The potential for overlaps between the various outcomes resulting from the activity of the four groups was discussed, and attention was drawn not only to their variety but also to their degree of interdependence.

On the basis of the model and discussion, the importance of developing an explicit impact strategy was presented. Six strategic principles were put forward along with more detailed suggestions of how to develop an impact strategy as part of the design and implementation of child care research. Here again the two basic assumptions were critical. Researchers actually have to believe that, at least to some degree, their work can make a difference to policy and practice and improve the lives of children. They need to apply all their knowledge and skills relevant to understanding and managing social phenomena to their own situation in order to work the system and make that difference.

REFERENCES

Alcock, P. (1998). The discipline of social policy. In P. Alcock, A. Erskine & M. May (eds) *The Student's Companion to Social Policy*. Oxford: Blackwell.

Althusser, L. (1971). Ideology and ideological state apparatuses. In *Lenin and Philosophy and Other Essays*. London: NLB.

Bolger, S., Corrigan, P., Docking, J. & Frost, N. (1981). *Towards Socialist Welfare Work*. London: Macmillan.

Bullock, R. & Little, M. (1995). Linking research and development: return home as experienced by separated children. In M. Colton, H. Ghesquiere & M. Williams (eds) *The Art and Science of Child Care*. Aldershot: Arena.

Casas, F. (1995). Social research and policy making. In M. Colton, H. Ghesquiere & M. Williams (eds) *The Art and Science of Child Care*. Aldershot: Arena.

Cheetham, J. (1991). *Research and Practice: Bridging the Gap*. Stirling: Social Work Research Centre, University of Stirling.

Clarke, J. (1998). Managing and delivering welfare. In P. Alcock, A. Erskine & M. May (eds) *The Student's Companion to Social Policy*. Oxford: Blackwell.

CRDU (1994). *UK Agenda for Children*. London: CRDU.

DHSS (1985). *Social Work Decisions in Child Care: Recent Research Findings and their Implications*. London: HMSO.

DoH (1991). *Patterns and Outcomes in Child Placement*. London: HMSO.

DoH (1994). *A Wider Strategy for Research and Development Relating to Personal Social Services*. London: HMSO.

DoH (1995). *Child Protection: Messages from Research*. London: HMSO.

Everitt, A. & Hardiker, P. (1996). *Evaluating for Good Practice*. London: Macmillan.

Finch, J. (1986). *Research and Policy*. London: Falmer Press.

Giddens, A. (1979). *Central Problems in Social Theory: Action, Structure and Contradiction in Social Analysis*. London: Macmillan.

Giddens, A. (1997). *Sociology* (3rd edition). Oxford: Blackwell.

Hammersley, M. (1995). *The Politics of Social Research*. London: Sage.

Hardiker, P. (1993). Research in Social Work: Process, Promises and Payoffs Conference Paper. Belfast: Department of Social Work, The Queen's University of Belfast.

Harvey, L. (1990). *Critical Social Research*. London: Unwin Hyman.

HMSO (1988). *Report of Inquiry into Child Abuse in Cleveland* (Cm 412). London: HMSO.

Hill, M. (1997). *The Policy Process in the Modern State*. Cornwall: Prentice Hall/Harvester Wheatsheaf.

Hill, M. & Aldgate, J. (1996). The Children Act 1989 and recent developments in research in England and Wales. In M. Hill & J. Aldgate (eds) *Child Welfare Services*. London: Jessica Kingsley.

Morrison, B. (1997). *As If*. London: Granta Books.

McWhirter, L. (1993). Social Science Research and Policy Processes: Relationships, Tensions and Skills. Conference Paper. Belfast: Department of Social Work, The Queen's University of Belfast.

Parker, R. A. (1987). *A Forward Look at Research on the Child in Care*. Bristol: School of Applied Social Studies, University of Bristol.

Parton, N. (1994). Problematics of government, (post) modernity and social work. *British Journal of Social Work*, **24**, 1, 9–32.

Pinkerton, J. & McCrea, R. (1996). *Meeting the Challenge? Young People Leaving the Care of Social Services and Training Schools in Northern Ireland.* Belfast: Centre for Child Care Research, The Queen's University of Belfast.

SSI (1994). *Promoting Social Welfare.* Annual Report of the Chief Inspector. Belfast: DHSS.

Stein, M. (1991). *Leaving Care and the 1989 Children Act—The Agenda.* Leeds: First Key.

Stein, M. & Carey, K. (1986). *Leaving Care.* Oxford: Blackwell.

Scraton, P. (ed.) (1997). *Childhood in Crisis.* London: UCL Press.

Taylor-Gooby, P. (1991). *Social Change, Social Welfare and Social Science.* London: Harvester Wheatsheaf.

West, A. (1995). *You're on Your Own—Young People's Research on Leaving Care.* London: Save the Children Fund.

3

THE INFLUENCE OF RESEARCH ON CHILD CARE POLICY AND PRACTICE

The Case of *Children Who Wait* and the Development of the Permanence Movement in the United Kingdom

Greg Kelly

Chapter Outline

INTRODUCTION

THE BACKGROUND

THE STUDY
- Basic Assumptions
- Methodology
- The Findings and their Presentation

THE IMPACT
- The Permanence Movement
- Reasons for the Impact

Making Research Work: Promoting Child Care Policy and Practice
Edited by D. Iwaniec and J. Pinkerton
© 1998 John Wiley & Sons Ltd

- The Rise of Child Abuse
- Political and Organisational Change
SUMMARY

INTRODUCTION

The impact of research on policy and practice in social work generally, and in child care in particular, is unpredictable. Some research findings, although confirmed by different studies over decades, appear to have little impact on policy or practice. Other studies are credited with major influence on legislation as well as changing policy and practice. An example of the former is the findings on foster placement breakdown. Despite many years of research having shown associations between placement breakdown and the presence of foster parents' own children near in age to the foster children, this pattern continues to recur in practice unfettered by clear policy or legislative change (Parker, 1966; Berridge & Cleaver, 1987). On the other hand, the positive influence of research is exemplified by the United Kingdom's recent children's legislation where an extensive programme of research 'played a fundamental part in bringing about the changes contained in the Act' (DoH, 1991, p. vi).

In the hope of shedding light on at least one side of this enigma, this chapter considers one study which, although modest in scale and with serious weaknesses, is widely held to have had a profound impact on British child care (Parton, 1985). The study was *Children Who Wait* by Jane Rowe and Lydia Lambert, published by the Association of British Adoption Agencies in 1973. Bean (1984), ten years after the publication of *Children Who Wait*, dedicated his book (*Adoption*) 'for those who wait'. Its influence is still felt today as a touchstone and starting point for discussion about this area of child care (Thoburn, 1996).

This chapter will consider the background to *Children Who Wait*, its methodology, findings and their presentation. The importance of the study's background in the adoption agencies of the early 1970s will be explored. It will examine the impact of the study and consider the professional and organisational context. It will explore the coincidence of the report's publication with the rising concern about child abuse generated by the death of Maria Colwell in 1973. It will conclude that the impact of the research owed much to external factors. However, the origins of the study, the emphasis within it and how it was reported were very important in determining the precise nature of its influence.

THE BACKGROUND

The commissioning of *Children Who Wait* was a response to the crisis in the adoption service in the late 1960s. As Hall (1984) has shown, until then adoption was still widely regarded as a service for childless couples. It was generally seen as a way of providing 'healthy white babies' for such families. Children who were thought to be handicapped by illness, intellect, age or colour were considered 'unadoptable'. Prospective adopters had 'to be young and usually middle class, with a secure and healthy income, a house and garden' (Hall, 1984, p. xiv). The adoption service was provided by a network of mostly church-affiliated voluntary organisations and centralised units within local authority Children's Departments. The crisis was caused by the sudden drop in the numbers of 'illegitimate' children being placed for adoption with strangers. Numbers fell from a peak of 14,500 in 1968 to 3,300 in 1982 (Hall, 1984, p. xiv). This was the result of more widespread use of contraception, the availability of abortion under the Abortion Act 1968 and a more tolerant view of single parenthood. The immediate impact on the work of adoption agencies was summarised at the beginning of *Children Who Wait*:

> ... the number of babies needing adoptive families declined rather dramatically and in the next three years (1968–1971) placements by adoption agencies dropped by approximately 40%. (Rowe & Lambert, 1973, p. 13)

With the collapse of its traditional market the adoption service was faced with a stark choice: find a new role, through broadening the scope of adoption, or close. Many agencies did close or rationalise their remit. The leaders of the Association of British Adoption Agencies (ABAA), the leading national adoption organisation, saw the potential for expanding adoption to include 'categories of children other than easy to place ordinary white babies' (Child Adoption, 1970). The most obvious place to look for such children was among those who were spending their lives in local authority care; often in residential care. ABAA set out to answer the question of whether or not there were children in care who needed permanent substitute parents. The implication of organisational self-interest was avoided by arguing that: 'members of the public have become confused by long lists of people on adoption waiting lists on the one hand and adverts for foster homes on the other' (Child Adoption, 1973, p. 59).

Research in the form of *Children Who Wait* was the means by which ABBA set out to answer these questions. The initial impetus came from a member of its council (Rowe & Lambert, 1973, p. 5). Jane Rowe, the agency's director at the time, was to become the study's principal researcher. The agency published and publicised the findings, producing not just the main report in paperback form but also an attractive 30 page summary (Rowe & Lambert, 1975); setting an early precedent for the popular dissemination of child care research findings.

Drawing attention to the political and organisational background to the research illustrates an often ignored motivation for research—that of professional self-interest. It does not fit easily with the image of the objective, scientific researcher, nor with the child care profession's claim to be selflessly promoting the 'best interests of the child'. Rowe and Lambert (1973) were somewhat coy about the move by adoption agencies to extend their services to children with special needs. They attributed it to a decrease in numbers of children coming forward for adoption (Rowe & Lambert, 1973). Others were clearer about the organisational imperatives around at the time.

> We expect the adoption figures to continue to go down, unless the policy of adoption agencies as a whole takes in categories of children other than the easy to place ordinary white babies and legislation supports efforts to place for adoption children whose natural parents show no interest in them. (Child Adoption, 1970, p. 3)

Subsequent commentaries have stressed that practice emanating from *Children Who Wait*, which has become known as the 'permanence movement', has been the result of an expanding professional knowledge base regarding the understanding and meeting of the needs of children. This shift was helped by the results of studies showing how well older children placed for adoption were doing (Triseliotis, Shireman & Hundleby, 1997). However, its origins in the adoption agencies' struggle for survival has been largely forgotten.

Since the early work of Barnardo's and the NSPCC in the last century, campaigning sectional interests and pressure groups have played an important role in the development of child care policy in the UK. Their success is dependent on having their agenda accepted by influential sections of the public and then adopted by public policy makers. They are more likely to achieve this if they can convince that they are driven by the common good rather than their sectional interest. The argument of this chapter is that the influence of *Children Who Wait* has been due to the extent to which it succeeded in achieving this transition. A discussion of the reasons for that success follow a summary of the study.

THE STUDY

Basic Assumptions

The *Children Who Wait* study made two basic assumptions: firstly, that 'every child has a right to a family of his own' and, secondly, that 'foster care and adoption cannot be looked on as completely separate categories' (Rowe & Lambert, 1973, p. 15). The first was an uncontroversial ideal, but one which, as the study showed, was not being achieved often enough in practice. Bowlby's work on attachment theory was standard fare on social work courses at the time and the effects of institutional care on young children was well documented. Substitute family care was, even then, widely accepted as preferable to residential care (Robertson & Robertson, 1971; Adamson, 1972). The second assumption was radical and central to the study's purpose of seeking to explore the use of adoption for children in care. Adoption and fostering were, and were seen as, very separate and even opposing entities. There was a fear that many prospective foster parents might really want to adopt and were using fostering as a 'back door' route, so any association between the two was heavily discouraged. The services within local authorities were usually organised separately. Parker's description of adoption as 'frighteningly final', in his foreword to *Children Who Wait*, summed up the feelings of most social workers in the mainstream of child care at the time. As will be seen in later discussion of the research's findings, fewer social workers were seeking adoptive placements for the children waiting in residential care than those seeking foster placements.

Methodology

The study was conducted in eight local authorities in Scotland, twenty in England (12% of the total number of such authorities), and five voluntary child care societies. This generated a sample of 2,812 children, who were over 6 months and under 11 years of age and had been in care for a minimum of six months. The sample size and national coverage showed a great determination to ensure the study's national relevance and clearly justifies the claim that the children studied were adequately representative of children in care. It was in stark contrast to most studies of child care practice at the time which had small local samples and a more qualitative methodology.

The information on the children and their families was collected from one source only—the social workers, either directly or from their case records as read by the research team. The central findings were based on the social worker's judgement as to whether the children needed a substitute family placement.

As they stated:

> The team did not consider it their responsibility to develop objective criteria for placement, to decide which children ought to be placed, ... The aims were the more limited ones of counting, describing, considering and commenting on the children thought by their social workers to need placement. (Rowe & Lambert, 1973, p. 16)

The weakness of this uni-dimensional approach in such a highly con-tested area as the long-term placement of children in care was evident at the time and has become more evident since the study. Social work judgements had previously been shown to be very variable in these matters (Packman, 1968) and were found to be so in this study. Despite extensive efforts the research could offer no explanation for the wide range in the proportions of the children across the different local au-thorities judged to be needing placement. As the authors pointed out:

> there appeared to be no obvious, meaningful and consistent link between unusually high or unusually low need for placement and the character-istics of the authorities or of the children in their care (Rowe & Lambert, 1973, p. 81).

There were two additional and related problems. Firstly, the case records, which were either directly or indirectly the source of the study's data, were poor; 'recording more often tended to be superficial and lacking in assessments of situations, personalities or problems' (Rowe & Lambert, 1973, p. 93). Secondly, the competence of social workers to make the judgement as to the need for family placement is further questioned by the findings on the inconsistency of social work involvement with the children and their families. There was direct casework with only one child in three of those thought to need family placement and 39% of the children's parents had not been visited in the past 12 months.

Basing the research solely on the views of social workers and their records, therefore, had serious weaknesses. However, the reality was that, in those days, it was the social workers who were charged with the central, if not the sole responsibility, for making placement deci-sions. Their judgements—however constructed and, indeed, however 'wrong'—were the first and perhaps the most important step in the placement process. Their views were in a real sense a measure of 'felt need' within agencies. Basing the study exclusively on the social workers' views was also important in political terms. If the study had been based on the assessment of 'experts' (particularly experts from the Association of British Adoption Agencies) the findings would have been much more clearly open to questions of bias and sectional interest. As it was there was enough concern for the report to comment that some social workers thought that the purpose of the study was to find more children for adopters (Rowe & Lambert, 1973, p. 24). The study's design enabled it to report its findings as the views of the workers in the agencies who were responsible for children in care, rather than the views of outside researchers. This made it less likely that the research would be questioned and more likely that it would be accepted by those agencies. Acceptance of the need for the development of family placement was, as noted earlier, an aim of those who established the study.

Whether the sole reliance on social workers was a consciously developed strategy by the researchers is not clear. In sheer logistic terms, if a study with limited resources was to have a nationally representative sample it inevitably had to be economic in the depth of data it collected and the key source for the core data on child placement was the social worker's opinion and the social work file. It is, however, notable that in the presentation of the findings in the report the methodological weaknesses were not highlighted. The findings were reported by the researchers and, as we shall see below, by other commentators and policy makers, as reliable indicators of need. The competence of the social workers alone to make these judgements was not alluded to.

In summary, *Children Who Wait* had some serious methodological weaknesses. It had, however, real political strengths in terms of the constituency it was being aimed at. Principal among these were:

• national coverage making the 'not true for us' argument difficult to sustain; this has been a common reaction to research in a service provided by a patchwork of the local authorities and voluntary organisations;
• being able to report the findings as the views of the agencies in the form of their social workers' assessments.

These strengths in the study and the lack of a critical research tradition within child care at that time proved more significant in determining the study's influence than narrower questions of methodological weakness. *Children Who Wait* was the first of what has become a continuous and impressive series of national studies of child care policy and practice in the UK, and its principal researcher, Jane Rowe, was at the heart of much of what followed (DHSS, 1985; DoH, 1991).

The Findings and their Presentation

A major problem in any national service, particularly where responsibility for its delivery is devolved to local authorities, is knowing accurately how the system is working in practice. In child care the official statistics recorded the entry and exit of children from care but told little about what happened when they were actually in state care. In reporting a later study, Jane Rowe and her colleagues presented their findings by way of challenges to generally held beliefs about how the child care system was working (Rowe, Hundleby & Garnett, 1989). The picture that *Children Who Wait* presented could have been similarly framed. Following the reforming legislation of 1963 and 1969 much professional energy had been focused on preventive and rehabilitative services. The widely held belief that this was making long-term care a thing of the past was overturned by the *Children Who Wait* findings. Large numbers of children were still set to spend their childhood in care; 25% of the children were expected by their social workers to return home; 61% were expected to remain in care until they were 18 years old. This overall picture of the system moved the research's core question of how these children should be cared for to centre stage.

The answer to the study's key question of whether there were children in care who needed permanent substitute parents was a resounding 'yes'—in the opinion of social workers:

> There were 625 children (22% of the whole group) who were thought by their social workers to need a substitute family. When translated into national terms this means that there probably were about 7,000 children waiting to be placed in a foster or adoptive home. (Rowe & Lambert, 1975, p. 95)

However—and this is of great importance when we consider the study's origins and the influence of the report on the UK permanence movement in the years that followed—there were only 35 of the 625 children or 6% for whom a direct adoption was planned. The largest groups, 68% of the children, were thought to need permanent foster homes or foster homes for an indefinite period. The role of adoption was enhanced by the finding that 26% of the children were said to need a foster home with a view to adoption.

In the discussion of the results and their implications for practice, adoption is emphasised out of all proportion to its position in the findings. Suppose that the study had been conducted by independent researchers coming to the project from a neutral professional background in relation to how the services developed subsequently. In line with the findings it is reasonable to speculate that they would have advocated a radical expansion of foster care with a range of long-term provision: permanent foster homes, foster homes for an indefinite period, foster homes with a view to adoption, professional foster care. The final chapter of *Children Who Wait*, however, questions the suitability of foster care as the accepted solution for children needing long-term substitute family care and emphasises the advantages of adoption. This happens in subtle ways. The authorities and precedents that are used to encourage the development of family placements are predominantly from the field of adoption. For example, Rowe and Lambert pointed out that the North American experience indicated a high degree of success in the adoption of older children. They also drew attention to the expansion of the Adoption Resource Exchange and the contribution of groups such as the Parent-to-Parent Information Services. It also happens in more overt ways where the perceived deficiencies of foster care are set out and contrasted with the strengths of adoption in a number of areas: continuity for the child, a sense of possession for the substitute parents, legal security for both substitute parents and children. As they stated:

> Beneath the surface of many apparently successful foster homes also there is a pervasive anxiety about the permanence of the relationship. (Rowe & Lambert, 1973, p. 109)

These criticisms are asserted without supporting research evidence, as is their conclusion that adoption would better meet the needs of some of the children lacking permanent substitute care.

The authors clearly recognised that this view was not shared by the majority of social workers and stated that their emphasis on adoption would require a major re-think by many social workers. So we have the anomalous situation of research which relied on social work opinion to decide whether or not children need long-term substitute family placement, but did not rely on the same social workers' judgement as to what that placement should be.

It is not the purpose of this chapter to set out the adoption versus foster care arguments, but the British permanence movement's concentration on the 'exclusive adoption relationship as the cornerstone of permanency planning' (Fratter, 1996) was to run into serious difficulties (Thoburn, 1996). *Children Who Wait*, in its overall emphasis, provided considerable support for that view. It introduced social workers in the UK to the important developments in the USA, in the successful use of adoption for older and hard-to-place children (Kadushin, 1970). It also anticipated some of the difficulties and gave encouragement to consider the benefits of a limited form of open adoption where children would retain contact with siblings, other relatives or friends, but not parents. But, in pure research terms, how valid it was to do this on the back of a research study whose findings, at best, offered only limited support for the development of adoption as a resource for children in care is questionable. While being critical, it is important to recognise that child care is a value-laden subject, and most research and commentary will inevitably reflect this (Fox-Harding, 1997). *Children Who Wait* is no exception and its influence was greatly accentuated by the singularly favourable 'political' conditions that were to develop, coincidentally, in the wider child care world at the time of its publication. Child care was soon to be in a crisis dominated by the death of a child who had previously been discharged from long-term foster care.

THE IMPACT

The Permanence Movement

Children Who Wait is widely credited with beginning the permanence movement in the UK. In its early years the movement advocated adoption as the only satisfactory placement for children in long-term care. The permanence movement dominated thinking about children in long-term care for 15 years (Parton, 1985; Thoburn, Murdoch & O'Brien, 1986; Fox-Harding, 1997). Such a sea-change of policy tends to happen as a result of a number of factors that point in the same direction rather than a single event or influence. We shall see below that a range of circumstances and thinking provided fertile ground for the messages from Rowe and Lambert and facilitated their growth into the reality of widespread permanence policies.

There are other full expositions and explorations of the development of the permanence movement in Britain (McKay, 1980; Thoburn, 1990; Triseliotis, Shireman & Hundleby, 1997) and so this will not be detailed here. However, two elements of it that are directly related to the approach and thrust of *Children Who Wait* will be considered: firstly, the organisational change to bring fostering and adoption closer together and, secondly, the failure to develop innovatory and resourced return home programmes as preferred permanence placements.

One of the basic assumptions of *Children Who Wait* was that adoption and foster care should not be considered as separate categories, and yet a key finding was that adoption and foster home services were organised separately in all the agencies studied. The recommendation as to future practice was unambiguous:

> Foster care and adoption services also need a drastic overhaul. Both have out grown their traditional patterns and need a complete re-alignment to create a flexible range of provision for substitute family care. (Rowe & Lambert, 1975, p. 100)

A widespread reorganisation was further encouraged by the Houghton Report (1972) and the Children Act 1975 and did indeed occur. New policies, inspired by the pioneering work of Margaret McKay (1980) in Lothian, were developed in a range of local authorities, these brought adoption into the mainstream child care planning process. A well-publicised example was that in Lambeth (Hussell & Monaghan, 1982) where the policy was to review every child in care for six months in order to make a realistic plan for either a return home or for a permanent substitute family. Permanent placement was clearly seen as adoption. Adoption did not enter the process as an alternative of equal merit but was seen as the only true answer to the separated child's needs. The arguments against foster care were cruder but not dissimilar to those deployed in *Children Who Wait*. This can be illustrated by comparing the two quotes below:

> No placement in care whether in residential or foster home is ever sufficient for the needs of a child, even though it may provide consistency, continuity and parental contact, if it does not carry with it an expectation of a permanent parental relationship. (Hussell & Monaghan, 1982)

> If the benefits of permanence are to be achieved, the child and foster parents must be sure that they have a future together and that it is worth investing in the relationship. . . . Adoption might be a better alternative for some children needing permanent substitute care. (Rowe & Lambert, 1973, pp. 110–111)

The Association of British Adoption Agencies led the way in the incorporation of foster care into its title and remit in 1976 when it became the Association of British Adoption and Fostering Agencies (ABAFA) and eventually the British Agencies for Adoption and Fostering when it merged with the Adoption Resource Exchange in 1980. Here, too, fostering and, in particular, long-term fostering tended to receive a predominantly critical treatment. Permanent placement came to mean only adoption. 'It is a pity in some ways that long-term fostering still exists as an option because it is such a comfortable compromise for the decision makers' (Boswell, 1980). Adcock, assistant director ABAFA, co-authored *Effecting Permanent Placement*, which succeeded in not mentioning foster care at all and begins 'Adoption placements are now being sought for a range of children many of whom would never have been considered for placement' (Adcock & Levy, 1979). Thus, following *Children Who Wait*, the reorganisation it called for became, in the permanence movement, an attempted take-over of long-term foster care by adoption.

There were a number of problems with this approach. Firstly, there was a strong body of respected opinion that was implacably opposed to it on the ground that it was unfair to the poor in society from which the population of children in care was drawn (Fox-Harding, 1997). This thinking reinforced the doubts many social workers retained about the finality of adoption (Bean, 1984). Secondly, adoption against parental wishes was so difficult to achieve that its use in practice was a lot less dominant than its position on the conference platform and in the child care journals. Thirdly, attempts to develop practice to achieve permanence in ways other than 'closed' adoption were neglected. Now, in the wake of the Children Act 1989, new and more open ways of developing permanence for children are being explored (Fratter, 1996) and the supremacy of adoption generally is being questioned:

> There is insufficient evidence of the desirability of adoption, permanent fostering or residence orders, from the child's point of view. There appears to be ample evidence that the generally negative view of long-term or permanent fostering is not supported by recent research. (Sellick & Thoburn, 1997, p. 69)

The second way in which the dominance of adoption in *Children Who Wait* affected the development of the permanence movement in the UK was that it did not emphasise the 'return home' option which was an equal partner in the original US movement but made the term permanence synonymous with adoption. By contrast, as Thoburn (1985) has pointed out, in America permanence planning and research into permanence were always seen as including rehabilitation with the child's natural family as a major permanence option. Advocates of permanence may feel this to be unjust in that their policies always place return home as the first choice for all children, as does *Children Who Wait*, but it does reflect the overall tone of the policies where families were threatened with the loss of their children to adoption as a means of encouraging them to resume care of them (Parton, 1985). It was also evident in resourcing services where

> the biggest difference one sees . . . is that in America permanence placement units employ workers who are specialists at working with natural families whereas in this country, as far as I know, the units employ only specialists in adoption and fostering. (Thoburn, 1985, p. 29)

This was reflected in research in the two countries: in the USA research into permanence policies includes the study of the children returned home (Lahti, 1982); in the UK it concentrates on the children placed in substitute family placement (Thoburn, Murdoch & O'Brien, 1986).

Thoburn (1990) attributes this imbalance to UK social work having been preoccupied with prevention and rehabilitation since the Children and Young Persons Act 1963 and thus what was new and exciting about permanence was permanent substitute family placement and the use of adoption for children in care. While that may have been a factor, it is wrong to ignore the importance of *Children Who Wait*. It was the foundation of the permanence movement in the UK. It both highlighted the children who needed substitute family placements and showed how a reformed adoption service might contribute to providing such placements. As discussed in the next section, however, the climate of hostility to the parents of children in care that developed in the 1970s was also important in the shape that the permanence movement took in the UK and, in particular, its antipathy to natural parents.

Reasons for the Impact

It can be argued that there are other bodies of research which have been more influential than *Children Who Wait* in framing legislation, and so will ultimately have a greater impact on the service as a whole in the UK (DoH, 1991). However, *Children Who Wait*, in terms of its influence on the debate about policy in relation to children in care, could be seen as the single most influential piece of research in Britain since World War II. Almost all local authorities and voluntary agencies developed permanence policies, although they may have pursued them with varying degrees of success and enthusiasm. Rowe and Thoburn (in Fratter *et al.*, 1991) were able to review over 1,000 placements (mostly adoptive) of special needs children, made by voluntary agencies between 1980 and 1984. These placements would not have been contemplated prior to *Children Who Wait*.

Why had this research such an impact when it had serious methodological weaknesses and was the work of a relatively small sectional interest who, at the time of the research, would have been seen as out of step with mainstream policy and practice? The reasons, in large measure, lie beyond the research itself and can best be found in the fertile ground on which it fell—principally the child abuse crisis and the organisational changes that dominated the years that followed its publication. There was also a sympathetic professional climate primed by other supportive thinking and research.

Children Who Wait made much of the development of the use of adoption for disturbed and deprived older children in the USA. It quoted the high success rates for these placements, and also extensively from one English social worker's account of a visit to some American agencies where the message resounded with American confidence: 'If you believe it can and should be done it will be' (Sawbridge, 1973 quoted in *Children Who Wait*, p. 100). This was new and exciting practice for an adoption service facing retraction and for social workers weary of the problems in residential and foster care. The permanence movement in the UK developed with a different emphasis from the USA but it continued to use and draw strength from the high success rates of permanent substitute family placement in American practice (Thoburn, 1990). They were also much encouraged by what limited British research there was (Triseliotis, 1983; Fratter *et al.*, 1986).

The Houghton Committee (1972), of which Jane Rowe was also a member, was impressed by these developments and a number of its recommendations encouraged the use of adoption for children who might previously have remained in care. These were incorporated in the Children Act 1975 which gave far greater control to local authorities over the lives of children in their care and extended the grounds on which the consent of parents to adoption could be dispensed with (Parton, 1985).

Beyond the Best Interests of the Child was published in 1973 (Goldstein, Freud & Solnit, 1973). It was a polemical work by three distinguished academics and clinicians and it provided a major strand of the theoretical underpinning for the permanence movement. The message was stated clearly and authoritatively with an almost religious sense of conviction. They set out their guiding values as:

- 'the law must make the child's needs paramount';
- 'minimum state intervention' in family life.

They concentrated on the child's need for 'psychological parents':

> Only a child who has at least one person who he can love, and who also feels loved, valued, and wanted by that person, will develop a healthy self-esteem. (Goldstein, Freud & Solnit, 1973, p. 20)

If the biological parents could not provide this then we should seek new psychological parents who, with the child, should be left free from state or biological parent interference to form 'normal' parent–child relationships. They worried that some current adoption procedures did not facilitate this but they saw almost no chance of foster care promoting the psychological parent–child relationship. The child's need for one set of psychological parents and the lack of state interference were taken up by the framers of Britain's permanence policies. These stressed that the local authority should ensure the parenting for children in its care, but cannot itself provide it and so, if rehabilitation to birth parents has been ruled out, adoption should be seen as the most satisfactory alternative (Adcock, White & Rowlands, 1983, p. 13).

A major problem with this ideal of minimising the role of the state in the lives of children in care and their families, was that the means of achieving it, adoption, often involved extreme forms of state intervention such as denying to parents contact with their children in care. These measures provided both a focus for opposition to the movement, led by the Family Rights Group (1984), and criticism of aspects of its practice by the courts (Fratter et al., 1991).

Beyond the Best Interests of the Child was criticised for its lack of empirical support (Fox-Harding, 1997). It did not refer to a single empirical study. In terms of its influence this was less important than it might have been because, the advocates of the permanence movement maintained, the empirical evidence was in the studies of the care system, principally *Children Who Wait*. As Adcock, White and Rowlands (1983) stated:

> It was clear from the findings of the study that local authorities were not necessarily able to meet the needs of the child for both long-term security and in providing someone to meet parental responsibilities in relation to them.

The Rise of Child Abuse

The relentless rise of child abuse to dominate policy and practice agendas of welfare authorities across the UK has been extensively documented (Parton, 1985; Kelly & Pinkerton 1996). This began with the inquiry into the death of Maria Colwell in 1973 at the hands of her stepfather after she had been returned from foster care to live with her mother. The inquiry report (Secretary of State for Social Services, 1974) was published the year after *Children Who Wait*. The circumstances of Maria's death, the subsequent succession of child abuse deaths, the associated inquiries and the publicity they received changed child welfare services out of all recognition from those that preceded and, indeed, took part in the *Children Who Wait* survey.

The rise of child abuse and the associated 'moral panic' is important in understanding why a profession, seen to be so unenthusiastic about the widespread use of adoption for children in care in the Rowe and Lambert research, was within a very short time enthusiastically devising permanence policies that would seek to pave the way for its use. Adoption moved from the margins to the status of preferred place-ment, even where it was against parents' wishes. There was encourage-ment of this by BAAF and the other enthusiasts for permanence through direct reference to Maria Colwell's death (Adcock, White & Rowlands, 1983).

The important elements in the child protection agenda for the devel-opment of the permanence movement were:

- the parents of children in care became objects of suspicion rather than compassion;
- it was easier to argue that if parents did not meet their respon-sibilities then their children would be better of separated from them;
- the widespread use of court proceedings to take children into care (Parton, 1985; Kelly & Coulter, 1997) and then the growth in Ward-ship resulted in social services having the power to plan for chil-dren's future, although a lot of the evidence indicated that this was not wisely used (Vernon & Fruin, 1986; Sinclair, 1984);
- 'The subsequent procedures and practices developed to "manage" the problem of child abuse' (Parton, 1985) were available to those who would use them for children in care, and the apparent clarity of the permanence movement's position also fitted well with the new professional and management culture that surrounded child abuse.

Thus the importance of *Children Who Wait* and the strength of the subsequent permanence movement was greatly amplified by the rise of the concern over child abuse. Further evidence of this relationship is seen in the softening and revision of permanence thinking in tandem with the reforms of the Children Act 1989, which have been more sympathetic to parents and given them more rights (BAAF, 1997). These reforms followed a number of high-profile child sexual abuse cases where concern was expressed about the power of professionals and the need to curtail their interference in family life. Thus the perma-nence movement that was swept along by the tide of concern with child abuse, but was also prepared to harness that power to further its agenda, has been left in some disarray as that tide has receded some-what. Thoburn (1996) argues that the changed climate enables a better balance to be achieved that takes account not only of the children's need for permanence but also their need for continuity of relation-ships.

Political and Organisational Change

Change in child care policy and practice occurs within and is influenced by, if not determined by, changes in the society in which it is located. Two changes occurring through the 1970s and 1980s in Britain appear to have had a bearing on the growth of the permanence movement. The first has been alluded to above, the growth of a management culture within the social services; the second was the changing relationship between the state and the family and the changing role and perception of state services.

These changes and their effect on child care are dealt with extensively by Frost and Stein (1989) and Parton (1985). In summary they trace the shift from a politics dominated by social democracy to one dominated by the 'new right' and the consequent shift in welfare policies. This has seen the role of the state move from one governed by the ethos of help and support to families in need to one where the emphasis is on the responsibility of the family to look after its own and to conform to standards. In child care these standards have been enforced by the child protection procedures and ultimately by permanence policies that remove children from parents who are judged to have failed to care for, or have abused them. In terms of children separated from their parents, foster care with its continued state care and its concept of care shared between foster parents, birth parents and social services can be seen as embodying the values of social democracy. Permanence policies and adoption with their exit from state care, their firm standards and their lack of sympathy for the weak and the poor parents were much more in tune with the 'new right' that dominated British politics under Mrs Thatcher.

Thus Rowe and Lambert's relatively narrow agenda of trying to help the adoption service come to terms with radically changed times in the 1960s contributed to the formulation of policies that were, in many respects, tailor-made for the emergence of a society dominated by the conservative values of the 'new right' (Frost & Stein, 1989; Parton, 1985). The 'new right' was itself a political reaction to the liberalism of the 1960s and 1970s.

The elements of permanence policies that particularly fitted with the politics of the 'new right' were:

- the emphasis on the family and family values;
- the attempt to set standards and limits for families, including time limits, the breach of which would carry identified consequences;

- the critique of state services contained in the widespread dictum 'a local authority cannot be a parent' and the consequent quest to get children out of public care;
- adoption as a form of voluntary activity.

However, evidence developed of a contradiction at the heart of permanence policies, that in order to free children from state care, the state has to act in what many, including those from the 'new right', see as a draconian fashion; removing children under court orders, denying parents access to them and, ultimately, separating parents from their children totally. This, along with widespread criticism of professional power and state intervention in the family in the area of child abuse, created a momentum for change that has resulted in the Children Act 1989. It in many respects reversed the Act of 1975, giving parents increased rights in relation to their children in care and making it more difficult to take action without consulting them and without their consent.

SUMMARY

Children Who Wait has been, perhaps, the most influential single piece of research in child care in the United Kingdom. It was the early empirical base for the permanence movement which dominated thinking about the long-term placement of children for over 15 years. Adoption has, as a result, moved from becoming an increasingly marginalised area of practice to centre stage when the long-term placement of children separated from their parents is being considered. In this sense the research has been successful beyond the imaginings of those committee members of the Association of British Adoption Agencies who commissioned it in the early 1970s.

The research report reflected its background in the adoption societies of the 1970s. While it found that there were unexpectedly large numbers of children who needed family placement, it concentrated on the demand this represented for adoption. It largely ignored its finding that the social workers, who were the key informants, selected foster care as their choice of placement for the vast majority of the children. The reliance on the sole opinion of the social workers in such a disputed area was open to criticism but it did lend the research the political strength of reflecting the agencies' opinions back to them and not imposing the judgements of outsiders on their practice.

Given its national coverage and its uncovering of thousands of children destined to spend their childhood in residential care, it is likely that *Children Who Wait* would have had a considerable impact on child care practice in any circumstances. The reasons for its enormous and continued influence lay not, however, in its intrinsic merits but rather in the professional and political climate at the time of its publication and which developed in the years thereafter. The principal elements of this were:

- the early and selective promotion of the permanence movement from the USA, which Rowe and Lambert began;
- the emergence of child abuse as the dominant issue in child care with its associated hostile attitudes to parents and its reliance on procedures;
- the growing management culture that valued the clarity that permanence promised to bring to decision making;
- the hostile attitude to public services that the 'new right' brought to politics and its resonance with the hostility to local authority care of children inherent in the permanence movement.

The consequence of the success of the permanence movement as it developed in the UK after *Children Who Wait* was a lack of balance in policy, practice and research. Resources were concentrated on one aspect of permanence—adoption—at the expense of other alternatives. This led to thousands of successful family placements that would not have otherwise occurred and a huge development in the professional knowledge base. However, the failure to match this enthusiasm for adoption with an equal emphasis on the state's responsibility to creatively resource the support of parents as first choice permanent placements for their separated children has ultimately been divisive. The seeds of this division were sown in *Children Who Wait*'s concentration on children who needed substitute family placements and its emphasis on adoption. The growth of this division has been due to developments in child care and the role of the state in family life which *Children Who wait*'s commissioners and researchers could not have foreseen.

REFERENCES

Adamson, G. (1972). *The Caretakers*. London: Bookstall Publications.
Adcock, M. & Levy, A. (1979). Effecting permanent placement. *Adoption and Fostering*, **4**, 4, 29–33.
Adcock, M., White, R. & Rowlands, O. (1983). *The Administrative Parent*. London: BAAF.
BAAF (1997). Planning for Permanence. Practice Note 33. London: BAAF.

Bean, P. (ed.) (1984). *Adoption: Essays in Sociology, Law and Social Policy.* London: Tavistock.

Berridge, D. & Cleaver, H. (1987). *Foster Home Breakdown.* London: Blackwell.

Boswell, A. (1980). Alternatives to long-term foster care. *Adoption and Fostering,* **2**, 13–16.

Child Adoption (1970). No. 3 (Editorial).

Child Adoption (1973). No 4 (News Report).

DoH (1991). *Patterns and Outcomes in Child Placement.* London: HMSO.

DHSS (1985). *Social Work Decisions in Child Care.* London: HMSO.

Family Rights Group (1984). *Permanent Substitute Families; Security or Severence.* London: FRG.

Fox-Harding, L. (1997). *Perspectives in Child Care Policy.* London: Longman.

Fratter, J., Rowe, J., Sapsford, D. & Thoburn, J. (1991). *Permanent Family Placement a Decade of Experience.* London: BAAF.

Fratter, J. (1996). *Adoption with Contact.* London: BAAF.

Frost, N. & Stein, M. (1989). *The Politics of Child Welfare.* London: Harvester/Wheatsheaf.

Goldstein, J., Freud, A. & Solnit, A. S. (1973). *Beyond the Best Interests of the Child.* London: Burnett.

Hall, T. (1984). Introduction. In P. Bean (ed.) *Adoption: Essays in Sociology, Law and Social Policy.* London: Tavistock.

Houghton Committee Report (1972). Report of the Departmental Committee on the Adoption of Children. Cmnd 5107. London: Home Office.

Hussell, C. & Monaghan, B. (1982). Child care planning in Lambeth. *Adoption and Fostering,* **6**, 2, 21–24.

Kadushin, A. (1970). *Adopting Older Children.* New York: Columbia University Press.

Kelly, G. & Pinkerton, J. (1996) The Children (Northern Ireland) Order Prospects for Progress. In M. Hill & J. Aldgate (eds) *Child Welfare Services.* London: Jessica Kingsley Publishers.

Kelly, G. & Coulter, J. (1997). The Children (Northern Ireland) Order and Fostering and Adoption Services. *Adoption and Fostering,* **21**, 3, 5–13.

Lahti, J. (1982). *A Follow Up Study of Foster Children in Permanent Placements.* University of Chicago: Social Service Review, pp. 556–571.

McKay, M. (1980). The right to permanent placement. *Adoption and Fostering,* **1**, 19–21.

Packman, J. (1968). *Child Care Needs and Numbers.* London: Allen and Unwin.

Parker, R. A. (1966). *Decision in Child Care.* London: Allen and Unwin.

Parton, N. (1985). *Politics of Child Abuse.* London: Macmillan.

Robertson, J. & Robertson, J. (1971). Young children in brief separation. *Psychological and Analytical Study of the Child,* **26**, 19–29.

Rowe, J., Hundleby, M. & Garnett, A. (1989). *Child Care Now.* London: British Agencies for Adoption and Fostering.

Rowe, J. & Lambert, L. (1973). *Children Who Wait.* London: Association of British Adoption Agencies.

Rowe, J. & Lambert, L. (1975) *Extracts from Children Who Wait.* Association of British Adoption and Fostering Agencies.

Secretary of State for Social Services (1974). Report of the Committee of Inquiry into the Care and Supervision Provided in Relation to Maria Colwell. London: HMSO.

Sellick, G. & Thoburn, J. (1997) *What Works in Family Placement.* London: Barnardos.

Sinclair, R. (1984). *Decision Making in Statutory Reviews on Children in Care.* London: Gower.

Thoburn, J. (1985). What kind of permanence? *Adoption and Fostering*, **9**, 4, 29–33.

Thoburn, J., Murdoch, A. & O'Brien, A. (1986). *Permanence in Child Care.* Oxford: Blackwell.

Thoburn, J. (1990). *Success and Failure in Permanent Family Placement.* Aldershot: Avebury.

Thoburn, J. (1996). Psychological parenting and child placement. In D. Howe (ed.) *Attachment and Loss in Child and Family Social Work.* Aldershot: Avebury.

Triseliotis, J., Shireman. J. & Hundleby, M. (1997). *Adoption Theory, Policy and Practice.* London: Cassell.

Triseliotis, J. (1983). Identity and security in adoption and long-term fostering. *Adoption and Fostering*, **7**, 1, 22–31.

Vernon, J. & Fruin, D. (1986). *In Care: A Study of Social Work Decision-Making.* London: National Children's Bureau.

II

CHILD CARE RESEARCH: SOME CHALLENGING CONTEMPORARY DEVELOPMENTS

4

EVIDENCING EFFECTIVENESS: THE USE OF SINGLE-CASE DESIGNS IN CHILD CARE WORK

Karola Dillenburger

Chapter Outline

INTRODUCTION
- History of Single-Case Research in Child Care
- Empirically Based Practice
- Accountability

WHAT IS SINGLE-CASE DESIGN?
- Evaluating Practice
- Behavioural Measurement
- Taking a Baseline
- Intervention
- Generality and Maintenance

COMMONLY USED SINGLE-CASE RESEARCH DESIGNS IN CHILD CARE
- ABA Reversal Design
- Multiple Baseline Designs
- Changing-Criterion Design

Making Research Work: Promoting Child Care Policy and Practice
Edited by D. Iwaniec and J. Pinkerton
© 1998 John Wiley & Sons Ltd

INTRODUCTION

The majority of child care work is carried out on a case-to-case basis. A typical example is Mrs M., mother of John, who is 8 years old and Jamie, who is 6 years old. Mrs M. and her husband separated a year ago. Family M. came to the attention of child care workers after a teacher noticed bruising on John's arm. When interviewed Mrs M. admits to having bruised John in an attempt to restrain him from fighting with Jamie. She states that she is at her 'wits end' and asks for help. She says that she just cannot control the boys who seem to fight continually. She fears that she may seriously hurt John one day. Following a thorough assessment of the situation, an intervention is planned and implemented. A few weeks later the situation seems defused and Mrs M. seems to be able to cope. The boys seem to fight a lot less now.

Intervention in cases like this goes virtually unnoticed in a busy child care team. But what if this case was going to court? What if evidence was needed that the intervention was in fact effective? What if there was a complaint against the child care worker and the worker had to account for her choice of intervention? Usually the only evidence collected would be a general feeling that things had improved, and perhaps a statement from the mother to that effect. In order to collect evidence in retrospect the child care worker may hold an interview with Mrs M. to find out how she feels about the intervention now. On the other hand, the child care worker may remember her training in research methods at college and give the mother a questionnaire to complete. Perhaps she would look up some statistics about the prevalence of sibling quarrels after parental separation.

But all this information would do little to help the child care worker evidence that her intervention in this case was effective. It would also take a lot of time to gather all this information in retrospect. Wouldn't it be good to have evidence at her finger-tips? Wouldn't it be good if information was collected during the intervention to monitor how things were going? Wouldn't it be good if . . . ? It is too late to collect this information now. The child care worker swears that next time she will collect all this information during the intervention. But when the next case comes, she is too busy, she does not have the time to design a questionnaire or interview schedule. Wouldn't it be good if there was a methodology that would guide her and help to measure effectiveness, not in retrospect, but during the intervention—a methodology that would enable her to collect evidence of effectiveness of her intervention as a matter of routine, for every case.

Such a method would not only allow the child care worker to collect evidence of effectiveness, it would also allow her to find out which intervention method is effective, in which kind of cases and in what situations. It would allow her to communicate her findings to new, incoming colleagues, inexperienced, newly qualified workers, or senior managers. It would give her credibility in case conferences and confidence in multidisciplinary settings. She would quite simply know what to expect from different methods of intervention and would no longer have to rely on educated guesswork and a vague feel-good factor.

This chapter will discuss a research methodology which is designed specifically to look at the single case, the couple, the family with whom the child care worker is concerned. This methodology was pioneered by behavioural researchers (Sidman, 1960) and has since gained a well-established place on the table of research methodologies. This method is called single-subject or single-case or single-system evaluation.

History of Single-Case Research in Child Care

In 1981, Fisher wrote that the development of single-case design heralded a quiet revolution in social work and the same could be said for child care work in general. He envisaged that with this new research methodology practice would move away from '. . . vague, invalidated and haphazardly-derived knowledge traditionally used in social work toward more systematic, rational and empirically-oriented development and use of knowledge for practice' (Fisher, 1993).

Sadly, ten years later, Penka and Kirk (1991) found that 88% of social workers in the USA had not conducted single-case designs following their graduation. The picture was not much different in Britain until Kazi and Wilson (1996a, 1996b) implemented a major project training social workers in the use of single-case evaluations for their daily practice. Kazi and Wilson taught 21 social workers workers (69% of the service in a district in England) how to apply this methodology and found that a total of 83 cases were evaluated using single-case evaluations during the period of their study. Data for the prevalence of use of single-case designs in other child care professions do not exist.

Empirically Based Practice

While single-case methodology has not yet permeated through child care services as Fisher had predicted in 1981, there has been a clear shift in models of practice in the past decades. Today most child care workers subscribe to a model of practice that firmly integrates research into intervention planning and decision making. This model has variously been termed empirical practice, scientific practice, or research-led practice (cf. Fisher, 1993).

Most modern-day practitioners would argue that their practice is not founded on common beliefs or folk wisdom but on research findings and well-established theories (O'Hagan & Dillenburger, 1995). However, Macdonald and Macdonald (1995) argue that much of this research is descriptive, retrospective in nature, and concerned with '. . . process variables of social work, or the organisation of social services, rather than with the relative effectiveness of either in terms of bringing about desired change' (p. 51). They refer to Cabot, who already stated in 1931 that child care workers should 'measure, evaluate, estimate, appraise your results in some form, in any terms that rest on anything beyond faith, assertion, and the "illustrative case"' (p. 51).

What do we mean by empirically based practice? In the first instant, empiricism stems from the premise that knowledge is to be gained through experience. This earliest systematic philosophy of science emphasises that knowledge gained through observation or experimentation should be given priority over assumptions arrived at through purely scholastic deliberations. As Johnston and Pennypacker (1980) put it: 'The suggestion that a solution to the question of how many teeth a horse possesses might be more easily obtained by looking in a horse's mouth than by consulting panels of learned clergy expresses a central tenet of the empiricist attitude.' (p. 23) Logical as this may seem to today's empiricist, this attitude has still not permeated through all the echelons of social science. Child care workers who intend to take empiricism further need not be surprised if they experience opposition in their quest to establish an approach in their practice that is firmly based in science (Trinder, 1996).

In order to fully establish a new way of thinking in child care we have to break through similar barriers as those encountered by the discoveries of Galileo and Darwin in that 'the most fervent critics were those entrusted with preserving the intellectual traditions upon which the social order was founded' (Johnston & Pennypacker, 1980, p. 19). Yet we should not be disheartened, as Johnston and Pennypacker go on to say that 'the history of science consistently and clearly shows that ultimately the need to know exceeds the need to believe' (p. 19).

Accountability

The need to know rather than believe is at the heart of effective practice not only because knowledge allows us to base intervention on facts but also because intervention that is founded in a firm knowledge base leads to practice that is accountable to clients. The call for accountability in child care practice is not new. Preston-Shoot and Williams (1987–88) clearly outlined the advantages of an evaluative approach by stating that: it enables social workers to assess effectiveness of methods; it offers a structure for planning work and setting of achievable goals; it prevents vagueness, misunderstandings and loss of directions; and, most importantly, it provides consumers and workers with feedback on progress.

Feedback on progress and effectiveness means accountability to the service users. When workers are accountable for their practice, service users gain confidence in the worker's ability to have an impact on their lives and failures can be acknowledged as being a failure of intervention rather than a personal failure of the client. Single-case designs offer clear measures of effectiveness of a particular intervention on a particular client problem. As such, they offer a level of accountability to clients that few other methods can achieve. The vagueness and 'woolliness' (Howe, 1987) for which child care workers were criticised in the past is no longer acceptable. Not surprisingly, Fisher (1993) stated that 'Clients find (single-case design) procedures more acceptable than just the practitioner's opinion' (p. 35).

The main aims of this chapter are to encourage practitioners to apply single-case evaluation designs in their daily practice in order to evaluate the relevance and effectiveness of direct client services and to collect evidence which enables practitioners to be fully accountable to their clients, colleagues and agency. In the remainder of this chapter single-case methodology will be outlined and examples will be given of single-case designs applied to child care practice.

WHAT IS SINGLE-CASE DESIGN?

Evaluating Practice

What is single-case design and how is it done? In the first instance, this research methodology is concerned with evaluating intervention on a case-to-case basis. Traditionally many social science research methodologies rely on the comparison of one group of individuals with another. In many cases one group is exposed to a certain method of intervention while the other, the 'control group', remains untreated. Following intervention the two groups are compared and contrasted and the conclusion is that any difference between them was caused by the intervention. While this may well be the case in many situations, the comparison between two different groups of people remains somewhat vague since the researcher can never control for all independent variables that may affect one group of people and not another. Moreover, averages usually tell us little about the circumstances of the individual.

Single-case design does not rely on a comparison between one group of people and another but relates the behaviour of a certain person prior to intervention to the behaviour of the same person during and after intervention. In this way the comparison relates only to the person and not to others. This idea of intrapersonal comparison is one of the basic tenets of single-case design. Essentially four basic steps characterise these designs (Fisher, 1993):

- identification of a problem that requires change and ways to measure this;
- prior to the onset of intervention, collection of information on the problem on a repeated basis;
- identification of a specific intervention, implementation of it, and continuation of data collection on the problem during intervention; and
- analysis of the data by evaluating changes over the course of the entire process.

Behavioural Measurement

The first step in single-case designs is the need to identify the problem to be changed and to find ways to measure it. This requirement has already created much controversy within the social sciences. Many social scientists would argue that behaviour, while obviously the subject of study, is not quantifiable in the same way as other subjects of study, for example in physics or biology. However, as Johnston and Pennypacker (1980) point out: 'Measurement is the cornerstone of all scientific activity' (p. 55). If we subscribe to scientific methods of research we have to measure, evaluate and appraise our results in ways that go beyond faith or assertion. In order to gain a precise picture of the problem prior to intervention, as well as to enable the child care worker to monitor change during intervention and afterwards, we have to establish behavioural measurement.

Obviously our definition of what constitutes our subject matter has to be broad enough to incorporate the range of human problems that child care workers usually encounter. The behaviour of the individual is therefore best defined as anything people do—overt or publicly observable behaviours, as well as covert or privately observable behaviours, such as thoughts, feelings and emotions (O'Hagan & Dillenburger, 1995).

In order to be able to monitor changes during intervention we need to carefully assess and record the behaviour in question. This usually begins with a clear definition of the so-called 'target behaviour'. The target behaviour is the behaviour that is identified by the client and the worker as the desired outcome of the intervention. It is, of course, often the case in child care work that the desired outcome is not so clearly defined or that the client does not have much say in the matter. However, these are not satisfactory circumstances and one of the first advantages of single-case design is that it demands clarity from the outset as to the aim of the intervention.

The necessity for clarity forces the worker to be open and honest with the client. In the earlier example of Mrs M. and her sons, we need to establish with the mother what exactly she means when she says that the boys are always fighting. We need to establish which exact behaviours the boys engage in. Do they hit each other, bite each other, scratch, spit, shout, box, curse, or simply argue verbally? It is important to get a clear picture of what the boys can be observed doing, when the mother labels the behaviour as 'fighting'.

Once the target behaviour is identified, it needs to be measured along an agreed parameter. Measures most frequently used include those of frequency, duration, or intensity. In order to take a frequency measure, one simply counts the number of times a certain behaviour is performed during a specified time period. Duration measures involve collecting data about the length of time a behaviour occurs. Intensity measures involve some kind of measurement of the strength of the behaviour in question. Take, for example, the sibling fighting. The worker could count the number of fights, or she could measure the duration of fights, or measure their intensity. Better still, she could teach the mother to measure and record these behaviours along one of these parameters. If the behaviour has a certain product, such as bruises, this could become the focus of data collection—for example, the number of bruises after each fight could be counted.

The measure chosen depends obviously on the target of intervention. If we want to reduce the number of bruises, then we should chose the measure of 'number of bruises'. However, since we are most likely aiming to reduce the number of fights or length of fighting, the frequency or duration of fights should become the focus of our behavioural measurement.

Taking a Baseline

We now have a clear definition of the behaviour in question and have decided which measure is the most appropriate. It is time to collect information on the problem prior to the onset of intervention. In single-case design this is referred to as 'taking a baseline'.

Taking a baseline simply means observing the behaviour along the agreed measure prior to intervention. Baseline taking is one of the hallmarks of single-case design. Traditionally in most child care settings we would have taken a brief look, a quick assessment interview and immediately started with an intervention. Single-case design demands that we take a good clear measure prior to intervention. The importance of baseline taking cannot be underestimated. The baseline is the measure against which we decide whether or not the intervention is in fact effective. The baseline gives us an indication of what the behaviour or problem would be like if no intervention was implemented.

As mentioned earlier, social science researchers traditionally use control groups to establish effectiveness of intervention. This measure, however, does not give us the required information on a case-to-case basis. Taking average group data means that most people within the group fall either above or below the average. There are no Mrs or Mr Average. A good example of the mismatch between average statistics and the individual case is during pregnancy. The average pregnancy lasts 40 weeks. Commonly the expected date of confinement is, therefore, arrived at by adding 40 weeks to the date of conception. However, in reality only 5% of women give birth on the date calculated this way. That leaves 95% of women for whom the statistics are not correct. Another good example is the statistic that nowadays one in three marriages end in divorce. While this may dissuade some people from getting married in the first place, it tells us nothing about the circumstances that may or may not lead to marital breakdown in the family with whom a child care worker is presently working. In single-case design we take our control measure from the person whose behaviour is to be changed prior to intervention and our comparison from the same person during and after intervention. The measure taken prior to intervention is therefore of crucial importance. As Johnston and Pennypacker (1980, p. 225) point out:

At the heart of good . . . research is an intimate understanding of the typical characteristics of the behavior under study when no treatment is being administered. The obvious function of the information is to permit comparisons with the same behaviour when under the influence of an independent variable in order that any changes can be detected. The more detailed and accurate this information under both non-treatment and treatment conditions, the more exact will be the resulting knowledge of the relations between the independent and dependent variables.

Intervention

Once we have established the unit of measurement (the dependent variable), and taken a valid baseline, we can identify a specific intervention and implement it. In scientific terms, we identify independent variables of which the changes in the behaviour are a function (Dillenburger & Keenan, 1997). In order to achieve changes in the dependent variable we implement changes in the independent variables; put another way, we identify what needs to happen so that the behaviour (including feelings and thoughts) of a client changes to the benefit of the client. Change in the behaviour can then be directly related back to the intervention.

However, it is crucial to continue to collect information on the problem during the intervention. If the desired change does not occur the intervention should quickly and immediately be adjusted, until the desired change is achieved and measured. This continued measurement is one important advantage of using single-case designs.

It is important to note at this point that single-case designs have been used to evidence effectiveness of a range of methods of intervention (Kazi, 1995). As such this research method, while originating from behavioural research, is not ideologically linked to any specific form of intervention. It is only linked to the aspiration of scientific evaluation of effectiveness.

Generality and Maintenance

A final hallmark of single-case design is the emphasis on what happens after the intervention, or the analysis of the data by evaluating changes in the problem throughout the entire process (Fisher, 1993). The entire process includes follow-up data collection on at least two parameters. Firstly, it is important to see whether or not changes that were achieved during the intervention are maintained, Secondly, it is important to assess if changes generalise to other areas of concern.

Maintenance is the question of whether or not changes that have been achieved during intervention are, in fact, long term. Does the mother revert back to her old ways of dealing with the boys after intervention has finished, or does she continue to implement her new skills? Measures of maintenance must be taken in a follow-up of the intervention. As the child care worker you cannot presume that changes achieved during intervention will be maintained. If necessary, you may have to design a specific maintenance programme of intervention.

Generalisation refers to the question of whether or not changes that have been achieved in one situation occur in other situations. There is a need to monitor if this happens and a need for further intervention if it does not. Take, for example, Mrs M., mother of the fighting siblings. You may have been successful in teaching her how to handle one of the two boys, but does she actually apply these new skills to the other boy? Does she apply her new skills to other situations, say the supermarket? Does she apply these skills to other problems with the same boy? All these questions are concerned with generalisation. If the answer is 'No' to any of these questions, intervention is not finished. Intervention and measurement have to be designed to include generalisation.

COMMONLY USED SINGLE-CASE RESEARCH DESIGNS IN CHILD CARE

There are a range of commonly used single-case research designs. The following section will introduce some of the main designs; however, anyone wanting to go into more detail should refer to the literature (Alberto & Troutman, 1995; Cooper, Heron & Heward, 1987; Gabor, 1989; Gelfand & Hartmann, 1986; Miltenberger, 1997; Thyer, 1997).

ABA Reversal Design

The ABA reversal design is the most commonly used single-case design. Basically the idea is to take a baseline (A), monitor change during the intervention (B), and then return to baseline (A)—in other words, withdrawing the intervention for a short period of time in order to check if the changes that were measured were in fact caused by the intervention rather than by any other factor. Once this 'experimental question' is answered the intervention is usually reinstalled (B). So the design becomes *de facto* an ABAB design.

There is, of course, the obvious problem with this kind of research design. In most child care settings, once a change for the better has been achieved, it is not desirable to return to baseline. Therefore, most child care workers who use single-case design use an AB design rather than returning to baseline (Hudson & Macdonald, 1991). While this is clearly better than no monitoring during intervention, it does not answer the question of whether or not it was the intervention that caused the change. Other factors could have impacted on the behaviour and have been the cause for change.

The problem of answering the question of what exactly caused the change can be averted by measuring more than one behaviour. In child care setting we are often dealing with a range of different behaviours that require change, and by monitoring change on a number of levels we can introduce more rigour into the research design. Take, for example, the case mentioned earlier, of Mrs M. and her sons. The target behaviours were identified as increasing co-operative play and reducing sibling fighting. First, a clear definition has to be established; for example, Mrs M. stated that she considered co-operative play to be both boys playing either together or in parallel, doing their home work, helping each other with difficulties such as finding a toy. She defined sibling fighting as the boys verbally shouting at each other, physically hitting, kicking and scratching each other. Baseline observations were taken after school (Monday to Friday) from 4 to 7 o'clock. A frequency count during baseline of both of these behaviours established that co-operative behaviour happened two to three times per day while fighting happened about five to six times per day (see Figure 3).

Once a relatively steady baseline is established, the intervention is implemented and changes monitored. We can see in Figure 3 that the frequency of fighting reduced quite quickly while the frequency of co-operative play increased. Follow-up observations showed that this change was maintained over a three-month period. While it seems pretty obvious that changes that occurred in the M. family were due to the intervention, this question cannot be answered conclusively using a simple AB design. A more rigorous approach is offered by taking a multiple-baseline design.

Multiple-Baseline Designs

The basic idea of a multiple-baseline design is to measure a range of different behaviours during baseline and to introduce intervention in a staggered way for one behaviour at a time while continuing to take baseline measure of the other behaviours. This way, if the intervention

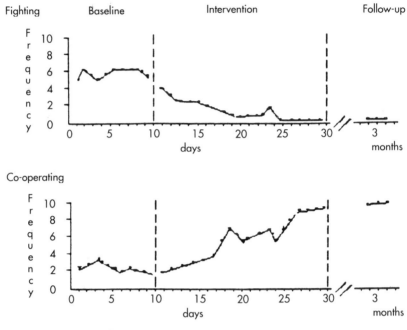

Figure 3: Frequency of sibling fighting and co-operative behaviour during baseline, intervention and follow-up (AB design)

only affects changes in the targeted behaviour the practitioner can be sure that it was in fact the intervention that caused the change rather than any other factors. Multiple-baseline designs can be used to monitor changes on a range of issues such as different kinds of behaviours of the same persons (so-called multiple-baseline-across-behaviours design), the same behaviour in the same person in different situations or settings (so-called multiple-baseline-across-settings designs), or the same behaviour across different individuals (so-called multiple-baseline-across-subjects designs). The basic design always takes the shape of Figure 4. In the example used in Figure 4 we are looking at a multiple-baseline-across-behaviours design. The figure is taken from a case of child abuse and neglect of a young baby. Before intervention started the child was voluntarily placed in care. The aim of the intervention was to re-unite mother and child. For this to happen the mother's child care skills, such as diapering, positive stimulation, bathing, etc., had to improve (for full report, see Greene *et al.*, 1995).

Baseline measures were taken for all target behaviours (Figure 4 shows three target behaviours). Intervention took place on target be-

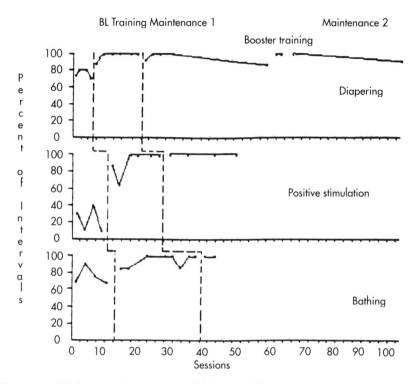

Figure 4:   Mother's performance of child care skills during baseline, training and maintenance conditions. (Multiple-baseline-across-behaviours design. Adapted from Greene *et al.*, 1995)

haviour one (diapering) first, while baseline measured were continued for the other behaviours. In the second step of the intervention target behaviour 2 (positive stimulation) was addressed and changes monitored. The same procedure was then applied to target behaviour 3 (bathing). The multiple-baseline-across-behaviours design applied in this case shows clearly that each behaviour changed following the training. Follow-up data show that changes were maintained over a 12-month period. This evidence was then used to argue for the safe return home of the baby.

Changing-Criterion Design

A useful design for cases where the target behaviour either does not exist, or exists on a very low level, is the changing-criterion design.

Following baseline taking, a range of criteria are agreed, ranging from very low demand to the full target criterion. A good example is dealing with homework trouble; for example, a child does not complete the full eight maths problems that constitute normal homework expectations. A low criterion, such as completing two maths problems in half an hour, may be set first. Once this is consistently achieved, the criterion can be raised to four maths problems in the same time period. Once this is achieved the criterion is raised to six problems solved in half an hour and, finally, once this is achieved, the full eight maths problems are required to achieve criterion.

A changing-criterion design was useful, for example, in the case of a 19-month-old baby boy (O'Hagan & Dillenburger, 1995). The boy and his mother were placed in a refuge for battered women. Although able-bodied the boy was unable to walk. The criteria ranged from pulling himself up on furniture (criterion 1), walking along furniture (criterion 2), walking between furniture and mother, two to three steps (criterion 3), walking for longer distances between furniture and mother, five steps (criterion 4), and finally free walking (criterion 5). Figure 5 shows how each of these criteria was met. Each time the criterion was raised only after the previous criterion had been met consistently (for further discussion of this case see Dillenburger & Keenan, 1997).

In this section we have concentrated on three of the most commonly used single-case designs and examples of their application to child care practice were given. There are, of course, other possible designs in

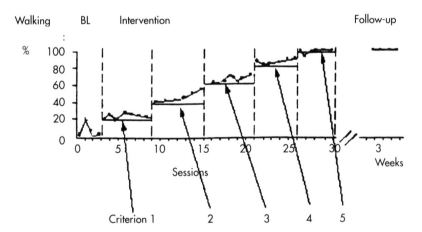

Figure 5: Percentage of infant's correct walking behaviour during baseline and training. (Changing-criterion design)

clinical practice; however, a full description of these is not possible in this chapter. For further exploration, interested readers are referred to Bloom (1993), Poling, Methot and LeSage (1995), Risley and Wolf (1973), Royce and Thyer (1996), or Sturmey (1996).

HOW TO CARRY OUT SINGLE-CASE RESEARCH

Having looked at three of the most commonly used single-case designs we will now consider some of their practical implications. Three main issues are apparent: the first relates to philosophical concerns such as differences in the concept of knowledge development; the second relates to practicalities such as workload and time constraints; and the third relates to the need for clearly identified outcome measures.

One of the first preconditions of using single-case designs is conceptual compatibility. As argued earlier, single-case design is based on a philosophy of science which states that knowledge gained through observation or experimentation should be given priority over assumptions arrived through purely scholastic deliberations. For example, knowledge about how best to teach a child to read is gained by using a variety of teaching methods and observing their effectiveness, rather than drawing conclusions about the effect of teaching methods solely from an academic debate without actually trying different methods.

Not every child care worker subscribes to this empirical philosophy of science. Some have even argued that 'empirical epistemology does not contribute to an understanding of practice (and) that interventions cannot be empirically validated' (Corcoran, 1993, p. 148). These arguments are, however, somewhat outdated and do nothing to promote the development of accountable practice. Those who are familiar with single-case designs realise the important implications of proper practice evaluation (Cheetham et al., 1992).

It is therefore important to ensure that all child care workers are at least familiar with the basic methodology of the actual single-case designs. This familiarity should be created during child care training. Students should be given the opportunity to practice the use of single-case designs during their practice training (Dillenburger, Godina & Burton, 1997; lwaniec, McAuley & Dillenburger, 1996; Jason, 1981). While this is stating the obvious it is surprising how few child care courses offer this opportunity. The infrequent use of single-case designs in practice (Kazi & Wilson, 1996a, 1996b) is probably first and foremost a reflection of inadequate training in this research method.

The second precondition of the use of single-case designs to evaluate practice is that their use does not substantially add to the workload of the child care worker. In general, child care workers have already a very full workload and may not even be able to meet statutory requirements. Anything that increases this workload will not be carried out. While single-case designs may be considered time-consuming, this is only the case in some situations and at certain times during the intervention.

Experience has shown that aspects of single-case designs, such as self-monitoring, can in fact save time. For example, a 15-year-old girl with chronic enuresis was asked to monitor her own baseline frequency of dry nights over a period of a few weeks. Without any further intervention the number of dry nights increased during this initial monitoring phase to a point that made further intervention unnecessary, thus saving the child care worker's time. Another example is the parent who complained about behaviour problems with her child, particularly during mealtimes. She complained that the child would never sit still at the dinner table. The parent was asked to take a baseline of the duration of the child's sitting at the table. She discovered that in fact the child was sitting 70% of the overall mealtime. In discussion with the child care worker the parent conceded that her expectations of the two-and-a-half year old may have been to high. When she looked at other problem areas she came to a similar conclusion and further intervention was not necessary, again saving the child care worker's time.

Obviously practice also increases efficiency of use of single-case designs. Child care workers who are very experienced in the use of this methodology will require much less time for its application than workers during training. It is therefore important that the use of single-case evaluation becomes a daily routine of child care workers, thus decreasing time requirements and increasing efficiency.

The third prerequisite of utilising single-case designs fully is that the outcome measure is clearly identified. A clear definition of the target of change should be the case in all child care work, preferably prior to, but certainly during, intervention. In other words, the direction of desired change must be identified and negotiated with the client or the client's representative. This requirement is all too often not met in child care practice when the identification of the desired outcome remains rather ambiguous and ill-defined, thus preventing the measurement of change on any kind of parameter (Cheetham et al., 1992). Thankfully recent legislation in the UK, such as the Children Act 1989, the Children (Scotland) Act 1995 and the Children (Northern Ireland) Order 1995 requires more clarity in this matter. One of its main principles—parental participation in decision-making processes—should encourage more clarity in regard to outcome targets and measures.

Nevertheless, there are some child care settings or methods of intervention such as once-only meetings, hospital settings, or crisis intervention that make it more difficult to adhere to single-case methodology. Furthermore, unexpected treatment termination by clients and unforeseen circumstances, such as clients moving house, can terminate the use of single-case designs even if initially started. In such cases child care workers can use aspects of single-case designs such as the notion of practice evaluation, observation and graphing of data (Corcoran, 1993).

A recent example from a probation setting illustrates this point. The juvenile probationer absconded frequently from his grandmother's house, where he resided. This behaviour was problematic because his grandmother did not know where he was and when to expect him home at night, thus increasing the probability of his re-offending. A baseline measure indicated a high frequency of this problem behaviour. Following baseline taking, but prior to any planned intervention, the young person decided to move back to his mother's house. While this move included a range of other, new problems, the absconding decreased to near zero levels. The importance of measuring this change became apparent when, later, the worker compiled the court report on this young person and was able to describe some positive changes that had occurred in his behaviour based on the data collected (Brady, 1997).

ETHICS OF SINGLE-CASE DESIGN RESEARCH IN CHILD CARE

All child care workers are bound by ethical guidelines and value statements (see, for example, APA, 1982; BASW, 1988; BMA, 1983). These do not change just because the worker uses a particular theoretical outlook or method of intervention. The same is true for the use of single-case designs. In fact, the proper use of single-case designs promotes values such as client self-determination, client choice and full participation. It is nearly impossible to carry out this kind of research without these ethical preconditions.

Child care workers who use single-case designs properly take the ethical issue one step further. The designs were developed from within a philosophy that states that the client has a right to the most effective treatment on offer and that the effectiveness of treatment has to be demonstrated (Kimmel, 1996; Van Houten et al., 1987). This means that workers have to evidence that the method of intervention they have chosen for a particular problem is in fact the most effective method on offer. When workers use single-case designs, data are collected during the intervention. Ineffective methods of intervention are therefore exposed early on and can consequently be terminated and replaced with more effective methods of intervention. Rather than being guided by an ideological stance, it is the effectiveness of the intervention that determines the choice of intervention. Macdonald and Macdonald (1995) point to the dangers if workers are married to a favourite method rather than being guided by effectiveness measures. 'This disinclination to be disturbed out of a lifetime's allegiance to a world view, often decided on at the outset of professional training, if not before, is both arrogant and dangerous' (p. 51).

Taken seriously, the right to the most effective form of intervention also means that the care worker is obligated to be accountable to the client, the agency and society as a whole. Workers who use single-case designs have the necessary data at their finger-tips.

> The best protections . . . do not come from ceaseless scrutiny of our own values, not just from empowering clients and seeking informed consent. They come—more prosaically but more effectively—from technically better research. (Macdonald & Macdonald, 1995, p. 61)

SUMMARY

Most child care work is carried out on a case-to-case basis. Child care workers usually visit families, one at a time, and investigate, intervene and evaluate intervention on each of these occasions. When child care workers work with groups they are typically small groups with a particular focus of intervention, such as groups to support single mothers, groups to teach assertiveness skills to battered women, groups designed to teach anger control skills, or small community groups.

However, when child care workers do research they typically use large group designs and statistical analysis either to assess need, such as family support needs, needs of disabled children, needs of teenage parents, or to evaluate provisions, such as respite care facilities, children's home or specialist care facilities (Cheetham et al., 1992). The results of this research is then used to determine policies on which the intervention in the single case of family X are to be based. While some of the information gained in statistical and group design research can be useful in guiding policy making or procedural developments, by and large, the results do not reflect reality for the individual family with whom the child care worker is involved.

In this chapter we looked at a methodology that is specifically tailored to the single case. Comparative data are collected, not by comparing averages of one group of individuals with those of another, but by comparing data collected of the same individual before intervention, during intervention and after intervention. By collecting these kinds of data this method of evaluations is ideally suited to evidence whether or not the intervention is in fact effective in achieving the desired outcome, with this particular client.

The increasing use of single-case evaluations in child care work clearly shows that, while we all learn from experience, just relying on our gut feeling is no longer good enough. People that turn to professionals for help expect professional intervention. In most cases these people have exhausted common knowledge and popular beliefs in their search for a solution of their problem. They expect and need more than this from a professional. As Fisher (1993) put it: 'If the trademark of the empirically-based practitioner is the use of single-system designs, then certainly the hallmark of this perspective is the attempt to identify intervention approaches that are clear, systematic, precise, and, above all, effective' (pp. 39–40).

Clarity and precision lead to interventions which, if successful, can be used in other similar cases. One of the expectations of good research is that it can be replicated. In child care work this is particularly important in the present climate of rapid staff turn-over. If evidence of effectiveness of intervention exists in child care cases, new incoming or inexperienced workers can utilise this knowledge. Valuable experience with certain cases or certain methods of intervention is no longer lost when a worker leaves. With the use of single-case methodology it can be communicated, efficiently and effectively, and consistency of intervention can be maintained.

When this approach is applied to child care services, people can expect effective intervention, accountable professionals, full participation, databased decision making, and a feeling of remaining in charge of their own lives. Clients, managers and child care workers who have learnt to expect such practice should demand that single-case designs are used routinely.

REFERENCES

Alberto, P. A. & Troutman, A. C. (1995). *Applied Behavior Analysis for Teachers* (4th Edition). Englewood, NJ: Simon & Schuster Company.

APA (1982). *Ethical Principles in the Conduct of Research with Human Participants.* American Psychological Association.

Bloom, M. (ed.) (1993). *Single-System Designs in the Social Services. Issues and Options for the 1990's*. London: The Haworth Press, Inc.

Brady, M. (1997). Single-Case Design: An Evaluation of the Use of a Behaviour Modification Approach in a Supervision of a Offender in a Probation Context. Master of Social Work Dissertation. Belfast: The Queen's University of Belfast. Unpublished.

BASW (1988). *A Code of Ethics for Social Work*. Birmingham: British Association of Social Workers.

BMA (1983). *Handbook of Medical Ethics*. London: British Medical Association.

Cheetham, J., Fuller, R., McIvor, G. & Petch, A. (1992). *Evaluating Social Work Effectiveness*. Buckingham: Open University Press.

Corcoran, K. J. (1993). Practice evaluation: problems and promises of single-system designs in clinical practice. In M. Bloom (ed.) *Single-System Designs in the Social Services. Issues and Options for the 1990's*. London: The Haworth Press, Inc.

Cooper, J. O., Heron, T. E. & Heward, W. L. (1987). *Applied Behavior Analysis*. Columbus: Merrill Publishing Company.

Dillenburger, K., Godina, L. & Burton, M. (1997). Behavioural social work training: A pilot study. *Research in Social Work Practice*, 1, 70–78.

Dillenburger, K. & Keenan, M. (1997). Human development: A question of structure and function. In K. Dillenburger, M. O'Reilly & M. Keenan (eds) *Advances in Behaviour Analysis*. Dublin: University College Dublin Press.

Fisher, J. (1981). The social work revolution. *Social Work*, 26, 199–207.

Fisher, J. (1993). Empirically-based practice: the end of ideology. In M. Bloom (ed.) *Single-System Designs in the Social Services. Issues and Options for the 1990's*. London: The Haworth Press, Inc.

Gabor, R. (1989). Increasing accountability in child care practice through the use of single-case evaluation. *Child and Youth Care Quarterly*, 2, 93–109.

Gelfand, D. M. & Hartmann, D. P. (1986). *Child Behavior Analysis and Therapy*. New York: Pergamon Press.

Greene, B. F., Norman, K. R., Searle, M. S., Daniels, M. & Lubeck, R. C. (1995). Child abuse and neglect by parents with disabilities: a tale of two families. *Journal of Applied Behavior Analysis*, 28, 417–434.

Howe, D. (1987). *An Introduction of Social Work Theory*. Aldershot: Wildwood House.

Hudson, B. L. & Macdonald, G. M. (1991). *Behavioural Social Work: An Introduction*. London: Macmillan Education Ltd.

Iwaniec, D., McAuley, R. & Dillenburger, K. (1996). Multi-disciplinary diploma in applied social learning theory in child care. *Child Care in Practice. Northern Ireland Journal of Multi-disciplinary Child Care Practice*, 1, 30–37.

Jason, L. A. (1981). Training undergraduates in behavior therapy and behavioral community psychology. *Behaviorists for Social Action Journal*, 3, 1–8.

Johnston, J. M. & Pennypacker, H. S. (1980). *Strategies and Tactics of Human Behavioral Research*. Hilisdale, NJ: Lawrence Erlbaum Associates.

Kazi, M. A. F. (1995). Experience in evaluation by practitioners: utility of single-case evaluation as part of a methodological-pluralist strategy. Paper presented at the International Conference Evaluation of Social Work Practice, Centre for Evaluation Studies, University of Huddersfield, England.

Kazi, M. A. F. & Wilson, J. T. (1996a). Applying single-case evaluation methodology in a British social work agency. *Research in Social Work Practice*, 1, 5–26.

Kazi, M. A. F. & Wilson, J. T. (1996b). Applying single-case evaluation in social work. *British Journal of Social Work*, **26**, 699–717.

Kimmel, A. (1996). *Ethical Issues in Behavioral Research*. Oxford: Blackwell.

Macdonald, G. & Macdonald, K. (1995). Ethical issues in social work research. In R. Hugman and D. Smith (eds) *Ethical Issues in Social Work*. Routledge.

Miltenberger, R. (1997). *Behavior Modification: Principles and Procedures*. Pacific Grove, CA: Brooks/Cole Publishing Company.

O'Hagan, K. & Dillenburger, K. (1995). *The Abuse of Women within Child Care Work*. Buckingham: Open University Press.

Penka, E. P. & Kirk, S. A. (1991). Practitioner involvement in clinical evaluation. *Social Work*, **29**, 332–337.

Poling, A., Methot, L. L. & LeSage, M. G. (1995). *Fundamentals of Behavior Analytic Research*. New York and London: Plenum Press.

Preston-Shoot, M. & Williams, J. (1987–88). Evaluating the effectiveness of practice. *Practice*, **4**, 393–405.

Risley, T. R. & Wolf, M. M. (1973). Strategies for analysing behavioral change over time. In J. R. Nesseiroade H. W. Reese: *Life-span Developmental Psychology. Methodological Issues*. New York and London: Academic Press.

Royse, D. & Thyer, B. A. (1996). *Program Evaluation. An Introduction* (2nd Edition). Chicago: Nelson-Hall Publishers.

Sidman, M. (1960). *Tactics of Scientific Research*. New York: Basic Books.

Sturmey, P. (1996). *Functional Analysis in Clinical Psychology*. Chichester: John Wiley & Sons.

Thyer, B. A. (1997). Single-system research designs. In R. M. Grinnell. *Social Work Research and Evaluation* (4th Edition). ltasca, Illinois: F. E. Peacock Publishers, Inc.

Trinder, L. (1996). Social work research: the state of the art (or science). *Child and Family Social Work*, **1**, 233–242.

Van Houten, R., Axelrod, S., Bailey, J. S., Favell, J. E., Foxx, R. M., lwata, B. A. & Lovaas, O. I. (1987). *The Right to Effective Behavioral Treatment*. Kalamazoo: Report of the Association for Behavior Analysis (ABA) Task Force on the Right to Effective Treatment.

5

LITERATURE REVIEWING: TOWARDS A MORE RIGOROUS APPROACH

Kathryn Higgins and John Pinkerton

Chapter Outline

INTRODUCTION

AN INTEGRAL PART OF THE RESEARCH PROCESS

SIX KEY STEPS
- Step One: Clarification of Purpose
- Step Two: Planning a Systematic Approach
- Step Three: Conducting a Search
- Step Four: Selecting and Reviewing Individual Items
- Step Five: Producing an Integrated Review
- Step Six: Making Use of the Review

FUTURE DEVELOPMENTS

SUMMARY

INTRODUCTION

In child care, as for any other topic, a thorough review of the literature is an essential component in planning and undertaking research. Ordering and evaluating the existing literature on a research topic can both improve the quality of new research and help ensure the most

---

Making Research Work: Promoting Child Care Policy and Practice
Edited by D. Iwaniec and J. Pinkerton
© 1998 John Wiley & Sons Ltd

effective use of time and resources while the research is being carried out. Given that there is general agreement on the importance of undertaking a literature review as a part of any research project, there is surprisingly little practical guidance on how to conduct it.

Although general advice is provided in research texts on how to search for items of literature and describe what is found, many do not go beyond that. If the object of the literature review was merely to describe research that has already been conducted, then the process would be fairly straightforward. But a review should go beyond that. Rather 'the goal is to synthesise, to draw the results together from disparate sources, to interpret their findings and to integrate them into broad conclusions' (Wood, 1995). That goal begs important questions how best to identify disparate sources, how to disaggregate different types of findings and how to integrate them in a valid and useful manner that will provide broad conclusions. These things are not easily done.

In this chapter we will attempt to provide guidelines for full and effective literature review within child care. Account is taken of both the general social science approach to review found in most contemporary child care studies and of the more challenging developments within the fields of medicine and psychology where attempts are being made to promote a 'science of systematic review' (CRD, 1996). Learning from those developments may not only improve the quality of literature reviewing within child care research but also encourage the development of a particular type of research. Following a discussion of why the literature review should be an integral part of any research design, a methodical step-by-step approach to carrying out a literature review is presented with examples for illustration. The approach and possibilities within the 'science of systematic review' is then introduced as a key future development. It is shown that this has implications not only for literature reviewing as a core activity within child care research, but also for current and future research methodology. Particular attention is given to 'meta-analysis' and the status of randomised control trials.

AN INTEGRAL PART OF THE RESEARCH PROCESS

As noted above, there is general agreement that any new research should take into account what has already been established in the area under study. This, in turn, is seen as endorsing the need for a literature review as something to be done early on in the life of any project. There are two problems with that view. The first is the assumption that the literature review only plays a role at the start of the research process. One of the confusions around reviewing is that it is often discussed as though it was a discrete stage at the start of the process. In fact the review can be crucial to any one of the five major stages of the research process: developing a research idea, working up a design, collecting data, undertaking analysis, and disseminating results. There is even a convincing argument that some reviews should be regarded as complete research projects in their own right. This is becoming increasingly important with the growing commitment to 'Evidence Based Practice' in the health and social care fields.

At the first stage of the research process it may be a review that has crystallised a research idea from the accounts of existing theories, concepts and data contained in the literature. In addition, for applied research a literature review may set a direction by allowing policy options and practice interventions to be considered in the light of existing accounts of different types of policy and practice and their effectiveness. At the second stage, methodologies employed by other researchers can be identified, assessed for strengths and weaknesses, and adapted as required for the research design of a new project. Findings from previous studies can be gathered up as part of data collection and used as a reference point to be taken as given, added to or challenged by fresh data. For some projects data from previous studies may be all the data collection that is required. At the analysis stage, it is highly likely that key concepts and theoretical frameworks derived from the literature will provide the means for ordering and making sense of the data. Even at the final stage of dissemination, the review is likely to shape the way in which material is presented and may have lessons to teach about techniques of presentation and target audiences.

The second issue is that even a cursory glance at the literature in any particular area is bound to reveal studies with contradictory and contrasting findings arrived at via various methodologies. In such circumstances how can researchers integrate results and draw conclusions? In all too many reviews the interpretation of the findings, the insights derived and the manner in which conclusions are drawn, are all dependent on the judgements of, at worst, a single reader or, at best, on a group of reviewers. In essence, they are highly subjective.

The strategy utilised by many traditional social science researchers is simply to side-step this issue and conduct what is perhaps most accurately described as a 'pseudo-synthesis' of the literature. This results in reviews being little more than annotated bibliographies strung together by the ingenuity of a narrative imposed by the author or authors. Because it has been accepted that social sciences research reviews take this narrative style, insufficient attention has been given to the detrimental effects of subjective assessments and comments, partial or selective coverage and other weaknesses (Hakim, 1987). While traditional reviews have the potential to be extensive and insightful, their validity has to be open to question when they are undertaken in a non-systematic fashion without adherence to explicit procedures.

From within their empiricist traditions, the medical and psychological disciplines have recognised this type of weakness within reviews and their detrimental impact on the effective use of research in practice. As a result there has been growing attention within those disciplines to what has been described as 'the science of systematic review'. The aim of the systematic review is to 'locate, appraise and synthesise evidence from scientific studies in order to provide informative empirical answers to scientific research questions' (CRD, 1996). Systematic reviews differ from other types of review in that they adhere to a strict scientific design as a means of making them more comprehensive, to minimise the chance of bias, and so ensure their reliability. They contain a comprehensive summary of the available evidence rather than reflect the subjective views of the reviewers or being based on only a (possibly biased) selection of the published literature.

This approach has much to recommend it, and will be reviewed later in this chapter, but within the child care field at present it is important to acknowledge the diversity of paradigms, theoretical frameworks and research approaches that are making important contributions. There is just as urgent a need for creative approaches to undertaking research and for seminal ideas for understanding a topic, as there is for 'hard' data representing the known facts. Accordingly, what is required is not necessarily the application of an empirical 'scientific' approach to literature reviewing, but certainly a rigour comparable to that which is required of any other aspect of the research process. At the very least that needs a methodical and systematic approach, which can be adopted whatever the particulars of the research in question. Such an approach will now be presented as a set of six steps.

SIX KEY STEPS

The question of how a researcher actually goes about effectively reviewing the literature requires exploration. It is being proposed here that there are six distinct but related steps involved in undertaking a review which generally should be followed in sequence. These are adapted from CRD Report No. 4, NHS Centre for Research and Dissemination at University of York. Each step has its own particular purpose and tangible output. Any step should only be regarded as successfully executed when its purpose is achieved and the output exists in tangible form. The six steps are:

- clarification of the purpose of the literature review in the form of a rationale statement;
- planning the literature review through drawing up of a blueprint document;
- conducting a comprehensive literature search, according to the blueprint, leading to an annotated list of items to be reviewed;
- selection and focused reviewing of individual items, according to the blueprint, creating a set of reviews;
- integrated or 'synthesis' reviewing, according to the blueprint, to produce the review document;
- use of the Review document in what ever forms are appropriate.

Step One: Clarification of Purpose

The first question to ask before embarking on any review of the literature is: What is its purpose? This requires clarity about its function and place in the process of the entire research project and the type of review being considered. The review should be directly linked to the overall aim and objectives of the study of which it is a part. It is important to recall, as noted earlier that, as with any component of a research design, the purpose and positioning of the literature review can vary considerably from project to project. For example, in projects where secondary analysis or theoretical critique are the core concerns, the literature review will be at the centre of the project whereas in others it may only provide background or a fairly limited 'kick start' to the research proper.

There are various types of review and it should be made clear which type, or combination of types, is appropriate to meet the requirements of the particular research project. One type of review provides the means of pulling together all existing empirical data in a specific area. A second type is that which focuses on theoretical developments within the area in order to identify the key concepts required to direct further research. This raises an issue about the appropriate disciplinary focus for a review. While it is generally desirable that reviews take in the range of disciplinary perspectives on a topic, this may not always be appropriate as the aim of the project may be explicitly unidisciplinary. Thirdly, a review might be methodological with its emphasis on assessing the contributions and weaknesses of different research designs used in previous studies. A fourth option is the policy-oriented research review which summarises current knowledge with a view to drawing out the policy implications.

Reviews may also be distinguished by their particular focus. One may have a tight focus on recent material, or may explicitly address issues from an historical perspective, either through an interest in patterns of change or to establish enduring patterns and relationships which are not specific to any historical period. To meet the particular purpose required by the research design a review may take a particular cultural or national perspective or it might require a cross-cultural or comparative international focus. Within a general topic area the focus may be on material relating to only some actors, certain settings, particular policies or practices.

In sum the purpose of the review must be clarified in relation to the aim, objectives and overall design of the research. This requires a rationale statement that addresses the following questions:

- What is the contribution of the review to achieving the overall aim of the research?
- What is the primary focus of the review?
- Where is the review positioned in the various stages of the research process?
- How will the outputs from the review be integrated into the outputs from the research as a whole?

As an essential part of research design, this written rationale for the literature review should ideally be included in any initial research proposal. It certainly should be developed in the early stages of the research design.

Step Two: Planning a Systematic Approach

Equipped with the rationale statement as a specification, the second step is to plan the literature review. This requires as much attention as any other aspect of the research design and should result in a blueprint document that can be used as a guide throughout the carrying out of the review. To the rationale document's answer to the questions 'why' and 'what', the blueprint adds 'how'. It sets out in detail the activities that have to be undertaken, the resources required, the timetable and the various tangible outputs to be achieved. Inevitably, the aspirations of any research project are tempered by what is feasible within existing resources and so it is important to be clear what time, personnel and financial resources are available for the review. The blueprint document therefore should provide the research team with a comprehensive plan for searching, reviewing and reporting, all drawn from an explicit rationale for the review. The plan should make it explicit who is required to do what, within what time frame and in what format. To help with the latter the blueprint should include two proformas. The first of these should specify the criteria on which an item will be included for review. This serves as a mechanism for sifting all items identified on an 'in' or 'out' basis at step three, and is described more fully below. The proforma should also include categories covering the type and availability of the item, which can be used for basic annotation of the selected items. The second proforma should specify the criteria for a critical examination of the individual studies at the fourth step.

In considering personnel to be involved in the review, it is important to decide how many people are required. There may even be a case for having the review carried out by researchers other than those responsible for the project as a whole. It is necessary to have an idea of what is expected of those undertaking the review to ensure that they have the necessary knowledge, skills and experience. This will of course vary according to the goals of the review. In some cases an understanding of policy or practice debates will be more important than statistical expertise, while in others the reverse will be the case. Matching staff to requirements may be ensured through recruitment or through tailoring of the review to the strengths of existing personnel. There is also the option of 'skilling up' through a short training or instruction period focused on research design, statistics or the substantive area of interest, just as required.

In drawing up the blueprint it is helpful to work back from the projected final sixth step and the associated outputs. These can vary a great deal in content, format, style and presentation as dictated by the purpose assigned to the review. While it is reasonable to expect that the content of the final output will cover the various dimensions of a topic (existing data, methodology, historical, policy and practice) it may not. It is important that this is clarified as it will determine what approach is planned for in step five: producing an integrated review. Attention should also be given to the expected format in which the review will be reported as it too will have a bearing on the approach taken to the aggregated review. Generally the review will be completed in a way that allows for it to be easily edited into a chapter for the final project report, but it may be more useful to regard it as a free-standing document that could be disseminated in its own right as well as being used to inform the research project as required. Looking back to the previous step—step four: selecting and reviewing individual items—a proforma for extracting information should be developed which is compatible with the approach to be taken in aggregating the individual reviews. The proforma is necessary to ensure standardised and comprehensive coverage of studies. It is important that it reflects the selection strategy that led to the particular set of individual items being included in step three. That strategy has to include both explicit inclusion criteria and a set procedure for sifting the items identified in the search.

In order to search in a systematic fashion, identification criteria need to be established and a procedure for conducting the search set out. There are three basic types of literature—books, journals and 'grey literature'—and three approaches to unearthing items of literature—electronic, manual and word of mouth. An effective search strategy will use a combination of the three approaches and cover all three types of literature. The strategy should name the databases and other sources of abstracts and bibliographies that will be searched, along with key individuals to be approached for advice. Details of the specific criteria on which searching will be done should be given. If it is necessary to restrict the search according to language or sources, this should also be stated. What is important is that the strategy adopted at the search stage is planned for and specified in the requirements of the selection and individual review stage that follows it.

All of these issues must be considered in planning, and recorded within the blueprint. Additionally it may be important at this juncture to hold a meeting bringing together key individuals involved in the review to gain a final endorsement of the blueprint from all concerned. This will primarily involve the research team but can be extended, if appropriate, to other stakeholders such as funders and members of steering or support groups. Whoever is in attendance, the meeting should provide an opportunity to discuss the rationale and plans as laid out in the blueprint document, as well as an opportunity to discuss and agree a division of labour and allocation of responsibilities. If the meeting has involved others beyond the core research team, the opportunity should be taken to agree the frequency and scope of any further meetings or supplementary help—for example, commenting on outputs such as the annotated lists or the reviews of individual items.

Step Three: Conducting a Search

The purpose of this third step, which will have determined the search strategy set out in the blueprint, is to achieve a comprehensive, focused literature search which will determine the scope and extent of material in the area of interest. A preliminary assessment of the extent of the research that is available, and the degree to which it can be used to answer the particular review questions, is always helpful. This may even be done as part of the previous planning step in order to establish the volume of research in the review area so that resources and the time required for the review can be gauged. There may be other reviews in the field of interest that have previously been published or are currently in progress and these are often a useful first port of call. This can be done relatively quickly, through database searches and by looking at the numbers of references cited in published review articles.

Access to relevant hard data, such as earlier surveys, is constantly improving, especially as the deposit of both old and new data sets in data archives are becoming established practice. Secondary analysis is greatly assisted by the increasing number of statistical and other compendia produced by international bodies (such as the United Nations and International Labour Organisation), academics, the proliferation of guides to particular sources of data and their research uses, and focused reviews of research techniques and scales used.

Ensuring a comprehensive search depends on the volume of information obtained, and so the search for references needs to be extensive even if many of the identified titles are later discarded. It is also essential to ensure that the process of identifying references is not biased, minimising the possibility of the review's conclusions being weakened through publication bias (Easterbrook *et al.*, 1991). Unbiased reference retrieval can only be guaranteed in areas where prospective comprehensive registers are maintained, as only such registers provide the opportunity to identify material uninfluenced by findings (Simes, 1986, 1987). In other circumstances identification of references may depend on where, when and how they are published.

Material may be missed if written in certain languages, depending on the resources available for translation. However, it is possible that such restrictions may introduce bias, and where feasible all suitable papers should be included, regardless of language. Because models of health and social care differ across countries, the inclusion of research from around the world can offer important insights. It is important that reviewers are aware of potential publication biases, and rely on a variety of search methods, both computerised and manual, to attempt to ensure comprehensive and unbiased study identification and selection.

Electronic databases such as OCLC First Search with access to Medline, Sociological Abstracts, Journal Articles and Reports to Education (ERIC) and a range of others; Bath Information and Data Services (BIDS) provide coverage of the literature in many areas relevant to child care, but do not record all publications from all journals. These databases contain bibliographic details and frequently abstracts of published articles. As no database is complete it is often necessary to search several databases in order to maximise coverage. In addition, many resources and special collections are now being made available via the Internet which can prove invaluable. Useful packages are found in the form of CD-ROM which can be less expensive than on-line searches. Where cost is a concern it is important to remember that spending time on-line is expensive. Examples relevant to child care are the National Children's Bureau Child Data CD-ROM and Psychlit. Scanning the reference lists of articles found and retrieved through database searches may identify further studies for consideration. Additionally, the bibliographies of review articles may cite other studies and broaden the scope for retrieval of further relevant literature of different types.

Use of electronic means to search greatly enhances the capacity to achieve high recall, but it is worth noting that this may be matched by low precision, through the retrieval of a large number of inappropriate items. These problems can be partly minimised by skilled adaptation of search strategies and knowledge of the relevant indexing terms, such as MeSH headings which are used frequently in medical search packages. However, it is advisable to balance high recall rates and high precision to ensure that while a search is relatively comprehensive it does not result in a senseless volume of unsuitable references. Information on the indexing of relevant articles can be found by consulting indexing manuals, or by identifying appropriate articles and noting the manner in which they have been indexed.

Electronic methods should not be relied on exclusively and, where possible, key journals in a field should be hand searched to identify articles which have been missed in the database searches. It is always possible that appropriate articles have been overlooked through inaccurate or incomplete indexing in the literature databases. The manual approach is also the main way of identifying very recent publications which have yet to be cited or entered and indexed on the electronic databases.

It has already been noted that alongside books and journals it is necessary to include 'grey literature' in any comprehensive search. Important results may have been published in reports, booklets, conference proceedings, technical reports, discussion papers or other formats which are not indexed on the main databases. Comprehensive identification of such 'grey literature' is, by definition, difficult to achieve, but some of it is indexed on databases such as SIGLE (System for Information on Grey Literature), NTIS (National Technical Information Service), DHSS-Data, and British Reports, Translations and Theses, which are received by the BLDSC (British Library Document Supply Centre).

Current research projects may also be identified through research registers, including the NHS National Research Register and records of charities and agencies who fund studies. It may be possible to include interim results from studies still in progress if written permission is obtained.

Conference proceedings can be a particularly useful way of overviewing a field of interest in addition to providing detailed information on research in progress as well as recently completed work. Conference proceedings are recorded in several databases, including the Index of Scientific and Technical Proceedings, available via the Bath Information and Data Services noted earlier, the Conference Papers Index (available via Dialogue) and in printed forms such as the Index of Conference Proceedings received by the BLDSC. However, remember that abstracts in conference proceedings can be an unreliable source of data and attempts should be made to acquire reports of the studies from the authors before such data are included in a review. The libraries of specialist research centres, research organisations and professional societies may provide another useful source of 'grey literature'. It is in these institutions too that invaluable personal contacts can be made. As noted earlier, word of mouth is the third very important means of searching. It is particularly useful at the start of a search and then at its end. When a comprehensive list of studies that meet the inclusion criteria has been constructed, it should be sent to those familiar with the subject. They may be members of the support group or a consultant to the research project, or simply other experts in the field. These people should be asked to check the list for completeness, and whether they are aware of any additional material which could be included or mentioned in the review.

The comprehensive list of references should be annotated to provide information on type of material (book/journal/'grey') focus of interest for review (methods/theory/findings/descriptive/prescriptive) location and availability. All this information can be easily managed with the help of bibliographic software packages such as Reference Manager and Procite or retrieval databases such as Idealist, and Cardbox. These packages have the added advantage of being able to produce reference lists for reports and papers as required.

Step Four: Selecting and Reviewing Individual Items

The purpose of the fourth step is to produce reviews of individual studies which provide the basis for the integrated review. This requires, first, selecting the studies most appropriate to the research

questions with which the review is concerned and retrieving comparable information from them all. The studies located in the search have to
be sorted through in order to identify those articles which report research that helps to answer one or more questions. This selection of
articles has to be free from 'selection' or 'reviewer' bias which occurs
when the decisions to include certain studies are affected by such
factors as their results or simply their availability, for it is at this point
that actual copies of material have to be retrieved and made available
for the assessment. It is essential, therefore, that decisions about the
inclusion of studies are made according to predetermined written criteria stated in the blueprint document.

An inclusion criterion as detailed in the blueprint document should
be used to select the studies. Details should be given about the way in
which decisions concerning the inclusion of individual items will be
made, such as the number of independent assessors who will make
these judgements, together with the procedures that will be followed
when disagreements occur. Selection criteria which have been spelt out
typically define particular aspects of the area of interest and key factors
such as the settings and the relevant groups of people concerned, e.g.
type of service provider or user. These details should follow logically
from the overall aim of the research and have been identified in the
original rationale document.

The criteria should be piloted on a few studies to check that they
are reliably interpreted and that they classify the studies appropriately.
Additional inclusion criteria will specify the types of study design
which will be included in the analysis. This should reflect the degree to
which different study designs are likely to be susceptible to bias and
the availability of reliable study designs in the literature. There may
also be restrictions according to other criteria relating to validity. For
example, studies to be included may be limited to those above a stated
minimum sample size or to studies which carried out a long-term
follow-up. As the inclusion criteria ultimately determine which studies
will be reviewed, it is inevitable that debate and discussion will take
place as to how broad or narrow these criteria should be. Even when
explicit inclusion criteria have been specified, the decisions concerning
inclusion of individual studies remain relatively subjective and susceptible to 'reviewer bias'. The validity of this decision process is increased
if all papers are independently assessed by more than one reviewer,
and the decisions shown to be reliable. It may be prudent to have a
mixture of subject and methodological specialists in assessing inclusion, as they will bring different perspectives to the decisions.

Listed below are a series of questions identified by Globerman (1993)
for use in evaluating a research study. Although they must also be

informed by the particular focus of the review, they do provide a useful guide.

1. *Politics of Research/Author's Perspective*
    (a) Who defines the problem?
    (b) How is the problem defined?
    (c) Who does the research?
    (d) What are the aims of the research?
    (e) What are the assumptions and values behind the research?
    (f) Who funds the research?
    (g) Where is the article published?

2. *The Problem Formulation and Literature Review*
    (a) Is there a clearly articulated problem or issue?
    (b) What is the relationship between the perspectives of the authors and the problem formulation?
    (c) Is literature utilised in conceptualising the problem?
    (d) Is the research question clear?
    (e) Do the literature reviews develop an argument for conducting the study?
    (f) Do literature reviews define or delineate concepts?
    (g) Is the concept formulation, or lack thereof, appropriate to the perspective of the study?
    (h) Is the literature critically analysed?

3. *The Research Methodology*
    (a) Is the design explained, and does it fit the research approach?
    (b) Can the design be inferred according to the formulation of the question?
    (c) Is the study clearly exploratory? or
    (d) Descriptive?
    (e) Experimental?
    (f) Is the study consistent with the argument developed in the literature review?
    (g) Are methods appropriate to carry out the research?
        If 'Yes':
        • Are independent and dependent variables identified?
        • Are concepts operationalised with description scales?
        • Are sampling strategies explained and defended?
        • Is bias discussed?
        • Are ethics/culture/gender considered and are they appropriate?

4. *The Data Collection*
    (a) What are defined as the data?
    (b) Are data sources delineated?

(c) Are procedures clearly described?
(d) Are measures selected appropriately
(e) Is reliable/valid information presented?
5. *The Data Analysis*
    (a) Are data consistent with author's approach?
    (b) Have data analysis procedures been specified, and are they appropriate?
    (c) Can the reader follow, understand and assess the data analysis?
    (d) Are procedures and results clearly defined?
    (e) Are limitations of method acknowledged?
6. *The Results*
    (a) What are the key findings?
    (b) Are these significant, according to the aims of the study?
7. *The Discussion and Implications*
    (a) Were research objectives accomplished?
    (b) Does discussion link to initial problem formulation and the research question?
    (c) Are conclusions discussed? Are they limited to the findings?
    (d) Are the conclusions consistent with the analysis?
    (e) Do the authors claim the study contributes to knowledge and how responsible is this claim?
    (f) Are findings generalised? Is this appropriate?

The data sources used in the studies accepted for inclusion in the review should be carefully checked to avoid including multiple publications based on the same data. It is important to take account of the fact that authors often produce several publications from one piece of work, and in particular it may be difficult to spot serial publications where papers report accumulating numbers of participants or increasing length of follow-up. The question of data validity raised by Globerman (Question 4(e)) should also be stressed. Studies need to be graded according to the reliability of their results, so that they can be given appropriate weight in the later integrated review. Ideally a review will concentrate on studies which provide the strongest evidence, but where only a few good studies are available, weaker designs may have to be considered.

Step Five: Producing an Integrated Review

The aim of step five is to draw together and synthesise the results of the studies to produce a single integrated review document. The tradition of achieving this through a narrative based on the knowledge, insight and ingenuity of the reviewer was noted earlier. Even using the very explicit methodical approach being described here, it is highly likely that at this stage there will be a need to integrate the range of material individually reviewed using a discursive account based on themes. These themes should have been prefigured by the aim and objectives of the review set out in the original rationale document. Also the sources of the material being linked by the themes will be apparent and so judgements can be made about how well-grounded the reviewer's account is. In addition, the reliability and validity of the sources will also be apparent. Inclusion or exclusion of a given study should be done according to pre-set criteria and shown to be reproducible. Moreover, judgement about the comparability and the weight to be attached to different pieces of evidence should be made explicit. This means that the larger and highest quality studies should be given more weight than the smaller and lower quality studies. These factors, together with characteristics and results of the studies, should be displayed in tabular form.

Step Six: Making Use of the Review

The aim of the integrated review document is to communicate clearly the purpose, methods, results and implications of the review. Each subject area presents unique challenges and, as was stressed earlier, every review has it own contribution to make in the context of a particular research project. Accordingly, specific tailoring of the review or aspects of it may be necessary if it is to provide the information required. However, in general, the review document should be structured with separate sections for: review objectives; the quantity, subject range and type of references found; selection of material; information extraction; integration of material; and conclusions. The need for the report should be justified by clearly describing each of the research questions that the review addresses and its links to the overall aim of the research project. The methods used in the review should be described as set out in each of the previous five steps, including: the search strategy; sifting and information extraction by the proformas; and how the integration of the individual reviews was achieved, taking into account the differences between studies. Weaknesses in the methods used and suggestions for improvements should be shared. An assessment of the main messages and their relevance to the research questions should end the review.

It is likely to be helpful to have a table of the individual items of literature included in the review displaying the important characteristics of each one. These should include details of the study results and the study design, and other aspects of study quality and validity should also be given. Sufficient information should be provided to allow replication of the analysis. In order to demonstrate how comprehensive yet selective the review was, a list of studies excluded from the review should be added and, where possible, reasons for each exclusion given.

FUTURE DEVELOPMENTS

While it is being suggested that the six steps outlined above represent an explicit and methodical approach to literature reviewing whatever the context, it is immediately apparent that they may be more feasible for use in some child care reviews than in others. However, this should not be taken as a reason for avoiding the challenge from this approach to make explicit and increase the rigour of the process that is being followed in any review. For if that challenge is not taken up, there is a far greater one emerging which addresses not only reviewing but also the long running debate as to what constitutes research worth having. A topical means of illustrating that challenge is to draw attention to the technique of meta-analysis used within systematic review, which raises the deeper issue about the status of randomised control trials (RCT) as a 'gold standard' of research methodology against which all other approaches should be measured.

The techniques of meta-analysis were developed mainly in the field of psychology where the studies reviewed were typically controlled experiments, but in any case produce quantitative data which are subjected to statistical analysis. They have also been used and developed within the medical field to synthesise the results of clinical trials. The aim of meta-analysis is to provide an integrated and quantified summary of research results on a specific question, with particular relevance to statistical significance and effect size. Statistical methods of meta-analysis pool the results of individual studies to produce a weighted average which gives more weight to the more informative studies (studies with large sample sizes and precise estimates of treatment effects) and less weight to the least informative studies (studies with small sample sizes and imprecise estimates of treatment effects).

In evaluating the status of studies from which data are being drawn, meta-analysis assumes a hierarchy of research design. The first division that can be made is between experimental and observational studies. In experimental studies the investigator attempts to control the way in which participants are allocated to the various groups, while in observational studies treatment allocation is left as a random mixture of many unknown elements, such as client or practitioner preference. Determining that differences observed between groups of clients in observational studies are the effect of the interventions is a far more complex exercise than it is in experimental studies. In addition, a hierarchy exists among experimental studies according to the precise instrument which is used to allocate interventions. The most reliable method involves unknown random allocation; pseudo-random methods, such as alternate allocation, allocation by birth date or allocation by case note number or other identifier are less reliable, as the investigator is aware of each participant's possible allocation preceding entry into the trial.

Observational studies also follow a hierarchy. Cohort studies, in which groups receiving the various interventions being compared are evaluated concurrently, are considered more valid than studies which make comparisons with 'historical' controls. This reflects a proclivity for there to be more differences between two groups separated in time, than there are between two groups at the same point in time. Studies which are arranged in advance and undertaken prospectively are also less likely to be biased than those undertaken retrospectively. Data collection in prospective studies is planned and therefore liable to be complete and uniformly reliable. Furthermore, in direct comparison to retrospective studies, it is impossible for the selection of the participants in prospective studies to be influenced by their outcomes. Case-control studies are prone to many extra biases, and therefore fall below cohort studies in their ranking.

Before-and-after studies constitute the third grouping, where the same subjects are studied before and after an intervention with no additional comparator or 'control' group. The comparison is made within the single group of subjects. In these cases it is often very difficult to determine that the observed differences are peculiar to the intervention. For example, in child behaviour interventions it is often difficult to attribute success to the intervention as other confounding variables are introduced by almost every other aspect of a child's life in the period between the before-and-after points. However, there are some cases when large differences witnessed in before-and-after studies provide quite convincing evidence of the efficacy of an intervention, sometimes when randomised controlled trials are not feasible. These circumstances are usually experimental where it is less likely that other factors have caused the variation.

The standard study designs can, on the basis of these considerations of validity, be ranked into a hierarchy of decreasing strength of evidence (see Box 1). This can be referred to when selecting primary studies and when analysing and interpreting the results. However, a wise caveat is that care should be taken when using a hierarchy of study designs, since the validity not only depends on the type of study but on how well it was designed, carried out and analysed (CRD, 1996). Box 1 is an example of a hierarchy of evidence, which clearly privileges randomised control trials. At present, many studies pertaining to child care, based within many of the relevant disciplines, fall at the lower end of the hierarchy.

- **Well-designed randomised controlled trials**
- **Other types of trial**
Well-designed controlled trial with pseudo-randomisation
Well-designed controlled trials with no randomisation
- **Cohort studies**
Well-designed cohort (prospective study) with concurrent controls
Well-designed cohort (prospective study) with historical controls
Well-designed cohort (retrospective study) with concurrent controls
Well-designed case-control (retrospective) study
- **Descriptive studies**
- **Opinions of respected authorities based on clinical experience and reports of expert committees**

Box 1: Table derived from the CRD guidelines for systematic review.

SUMMARY

This chapter has argued for the need to go beyond the existing general agreement within child care research that literature reviews are done as a matter of course in the early phase of any study. It was suggested that this fails to recognise the potential contribution of reviews to all stages of research. There has also been a lack of attention to the detail of how to undertake reviews in a methodical and rigorous fashion that aims for the same objectivity as expected of other parts of the research process. It was noted that the 'science of systematic review' development within other fields of research provides an example and spur to exploring the possibilities of more explicit and methodical approaches to literature reviewing. At the same time it was noted that the specific approaches used in other fields may not be feasible for the present stage of development in child care research and, indeed, may not be fully appropriate.

As a contribution to the development of more rigorous literature reviewing, a six-step approach derived from the work of the NHS Centre for Reviews and Dissemination at the University of York was then set out in detail. It was suggested that this approach makes the process of reviewing more systematic and objective, without pre-empting differences in research aims, methodologies and forms of analysis and reporting. To the contrary, it is likely that the approach suggested will bring such difference more sharply into focus and, in so doing, will provide the opportunity for exploring and finding consensus on what is an appropriate and acceptable method for undertaking reviews within the child care field at this time.

In order to register the important advances being made towards developing 'a science of reviewing' in other areas of research, the detailed six-step approach was followed by an outline of 'meta-analysis' as an impressive example of these advances. This was also done to show how this method privileges randomised control trials as the 'gold standard' of research methodologies, thereby making the point that there is an important relationship between views on what constitutes worthwhile research and the way in which reviews are carried out. As already noted, meta-analysis may be inappropriate for reviewing much of the existing body of child care research and is unlikely to be the sole basis on which the necessary advance can be made. However, both meta-analysis and, by association, the status of randomised controlled trials must be part of the debate as to how to improve literature reviewing in the child care field. In literature reviewing, as in any aspect of the research process, the most creative and useful advance is likely to come through making explicit what is actually being done at present and encouraging dialogue based on the range of experiences that will emerge.

REFERENCES

CRD (1996). *Guidelines for those Carrying out or Commissioning Reviews*. University of York Centre for Review and Dissemination York: Report 4.

Easterbrook, P. J., Berlin, J., Gopalan, R. & Matthews, D. (1991). Publication bias in clinical research. *Lancet*, **337**, 867–972.

Globerman, J. (1993). Teaching critical appraisal of the social work literature. *Journal of Teaching in Social Work*, **7**, 2, 63–80.

Hakim, C. (1987). *Research Design*. London: Unwin Hyman.

Simes, R. (1986). Publication bias: the case for an international registry of clinical trials. *Journal of Clinical Oncology*, **4**, 1529–1541.

Simes, R. (1987). Confronting publication bias: a cohort design for meta analysis. *Statistics in Medicine*, **6**, 11–29.

Wood, P. (1995). Meta-analysis. In G. Breakwell, S. Hammond & C. Fyfe-Shaw: *Research Methods in Psychology*. London: Sage.

6

THE IMPORTANCE OF AND DIFFICULTIES WITH OFFICIAL STATISTICS: A CASE STUDY OF CHILD CARE DATA

Valleri Switzer

Chapter Outline

INTRODUCTION

AN EVIDENCE-BASED SOCIETY

OFFICIAL STATISTICS
- What Are They?
- A Critique
- Making More Use of Official Statistics
- Using Official Statistics

A CASE STUDY: THE USE OF RESIDENTIAL CARE, FOSTER CARE AND HOME IN CARE ON A REGIONAL LEVEL — NORTHERN IRELAND AND ENGLAND
- Background
- Northern Ireland
- England
- Comparison of Northern Irish Figures with English Figures

SUMMARY

Making Research Work: Promoting Child Care Policy and Practice
Edited by D. Iwaniec and J. Pinkerton
© 1998 John Wiley & Sons Ltd

INTRODUCTION

> Florence Nightingale believed—and in all the actions of her life
> acted upon that belief—that the administrator could only be successful if
> he were guided by statistical knowledge. The legislator—to say nothing
> of the politician—too often failed for want of this knowledge. Nay,
> she went further: she held that the universe—including human
> communities—was evolved in accordance with a divine plan . . . But to
> understand God's thoughts, she held we must study statistics, for these
> are the measure of his purpose. Thus the study of statistics was for her a
> religious duty.
> (Karl Pearson quoted in Smith, 1996, p. 380)

This chapter seeks to examine the importance of and difficulties with
official statistics concluding with a case study of child care data. Initially the background scene is set with a discussion from a historical
and theoretical perspective on the role in society of something a little
broader than official statistics, perhaps better termed as facts, knowledge or information. This deliberation becomes more focused in the
context of an evidence-based society. Within this frame of reference, the
examination of official statistics begins by addressing the question of
what official statistics actually are, progressing to a critique of official
statistics which takes the reader through various debates on their
respective merits and limitations. The discussion on official statistics
is drawn to a close with a look of how more use can be made of
these statistics and some points on using them. The second half of this
chapter is an illustration of the use of official statistics—a case study of
child care data.

AN EVIDENCE-BASED SOCIETY

Today, we are living and working in what may be referred to as an
evidence-based society, where informed quantitative reasoning is the
dominant modality in public debate, as well as in the decision-making
processes of government, business and individuals (Smith, 1996).
Smith posits that statistics has a crucial role to play in such a society,
as disciplinarian and guide to all forms of quantitative investigatory
procedure.

   Galileo said that the book of nature is written in the language of
mathematics and Newton argued that the whole business of science
was to explain all the other phenomena in terms of matter and motion,
treated mathematically. In the nineteenth and twentieth centuries,

social sciences developed most dramatically, beginning with distinct programmes of research on the political economy of 'labour' and welfare studies of the 'poor'. The list of social sciences in our own period is long, covering all aspects of social data, including demography, sociology, consumer research, psephology, scientific management, operational research, general systems theory, epidemiology, public health and games theory. Quantitative methods have now permeated every aspect of society.

A positivist conception of science was accepted in the late eighteenth and nineteenth centuries by the advocates of a science of society (Keat, 1979). Positivists invoke the primacy of the observable to distinguish science from non-science and the use of scientific knowledge for prediction and control. An important and specific role is therefore assigned to statistical data. A number of alternatives to positivism have emerged as a result of the perceived inadequacies of the system; for example, realism acknowledges that it is sometimes necessary to postulate the existence of unobservable entities, and theories are seen as attempts to characterise the nature and mode of operation of such entities. The view that some form of empirical testing is an essential element in assessment of scientific theories is retained.

The evidence-based approach originated as a result of disappointment with the level of real effectiveness of medical services and the mismatch between the resources employed and health status outcomes achieved (Smith, 1996). A similar sense of disappointment can be said to apply to the level of real effectiveness of social services and the mismatch between resources employed and the well-being status outcomes achieved. The well-developed discipline of epidemiology has been contrasted with social care, with the latter clearly at a primitive stage, yet to develop a strong knowledge base and a culture of systematic analysis (Bamford, 1996). Design and execution of practice, policy and procedures in the absence of data makes it impossible to set sensible targets or measure success. It amounts to faking, defined in the Oxford dictionary as 'contriving with poor material' (Sutton & Maynard, 1993).

Positivism is now regarded as crude and misguided (Reid, 1987). Unfortunately, quantitative social science has been too closely associated with positivism and what has resulted is a backlash against the methods of statistical quantification, which may have gone too far. The distinction is made between quantitative or statistical research and positivistic social science, where the former does not imply a belief in some determinist view of history but implies a belief in the usefulness of statistics when attempting to order and comprehend the complexities of substantial bodies of data.

Krige (1979) describes 'facts' as having evaluative implications and comprising reasons for or against particular points of view, which they accordingly buttress or discredit. Young (1979) remarks that our ideas of objectivity and factual accuracy, and the basic place of numbering or quantification in our world-view, are historical products rather than eternal principles of analysis. Stress has been placed on these as part of an experimental, investigative methodology only since the late sixteenth and seventeenth centuries.

OFFICIAL STATISTICS

Against this backdrop of debate and argument, there are lies, damned lies and 'official' statistics, to revise a well-known phrase by Benjamin Disraeli. Miles and Irvine (1979) have written much on the subject of official statistics and posit that the state is the only institution in modern society with both the economic resources and political mandate needed to generate data in large quantities on a national scale, as represented by official statistics. Slattery (1986) has made significant contributions to the area of quantification in the social sciences and he describes the officials of the government statistical service as the high priests of a religion, whereby official statistics are regarded by some as true pearls of wisdom, the hardest of data, indisputable facts, totally reliable, valid and impartial. Whatever 'religious' views one might purport, official statistics are the life blood of modern bureaucracy, the very food of official thought and the diet of official planning. Slattery (1986) also remarks that official statistics are far from the end of the search for truth—in fact they are only the beginning.

What Are They?

The word 'statistics' itself derives from the Latin status or political state, and the German Statistik or state-istic, facts and figures for the use of the state (Slattery, 1986). By the end of the 1840s Britain was active in producing social statistics, where such information was explicitly related to issues of law and policy making (Reid, 1987). The monitoring of social life through the collection and production of social statistics has become a government industry and authors on official statistics remark on the striking increase in the scope and volume of such statistics in the last few decades (Thomas, 1996; Miles & Irvine, 1979).

The main sources of official statistics, as outlined by Bulmer (1980) and Slattery (1986), are:

- the population census;
- the registration and administrative procedures of a variety of government departments like the Registrar General;
- official sample surveys.

Slattery (1986) also draws attention to non-official sources of statistics comprising semi-official, unofficial and private statistics produced by business, local authorities, market research companies, self-help groups, pressure groups, radical organisations and academic institutions. These sources help to fill in the gaps left by official statistics and provide alternative statistics that highlight weaknesses in official data and form the basis for critical analysis.

Official statistics are vital information inputs into administrative, policy-making and planning processes for private industry as much as for the state itself (Miles & Irvine, 1979). Using official social statistics exposes the researcher to a wealth of available information on a wide range of economic, social and political issues. Official statistics allow for examination of trends over time, comparisons between social groups and geographical regions, and 'before and after' studies, enabling sociologists to examine the effects of legislation for example (Slattery, 1986). They provide that quantitative link so often missing from social research and can give weight to and complement findings from qualitative methods. But to use official statistics critically, it is necessary to be aware of their limitations.

A Critique

Evandrou (1991) writes that poor statistics lead to poor government in the following ways:

- it restricts the government's ability to monitor the effectiveness of its policies;
- it limits the extent to which the government can track changes in society;
- it curbs the public's ability to assess government performance and is therefore crucial to the freedom of information debate.

Criticisms of official statistics which emerge in the literature centre around their subjective nature, gaps and discontinuities in the figures, problems around definitions, and difficulties in access. Each of these will be discussed in turn.

The Subjective Nature

Miles and Irvine (1979) remark that the state possesses a near-monopoly on both the production and dissemination of official statistics and power is wielded according to a particular structure of political interests. Slattery (1986) contends that, despite their appearance of political neutrality and impartiality, even official statistics are a key source of political power. Statistical data are neither produced nor utilised in a social vacuum, free of interests, values, prejudices and pressures of human actors (Reid, 1987). Official statistics are produced in specific organisational contexts and involve in their production the active interpretation of events as well as their simple recording in terms of officially defined categories. They are therefore not objective reflections of social reality, but their production involves a host of decisions about the objects, techniques and methods involved (Miles & Irvine, 1979).

Gaps and Discontinuities

Miles and Irvine (1979) describe the specific and restricted, sometimes 'out of focus', view of society presented by official statistics, because of the state's need for only certain forms of data and use of particular forms of statistical categories and techniques. Slattery (1986) comments that statistics are collected for official, administrative and political purposes, and therefore do not always cover areas of particular interest to social science. Thomas (1996) believes that where an imbalance of available statistical information exists, there needs to be an investigation that would produce statistics to counterbalance influence exerted by that statistical information which is available—for example, the formal economy, which is defined by economic statistics, versus the informal economy, on which information is fragmented and of little value. Evandrou (1991) remarks that efforts to accurately monitor changes in society are severely hampered when an existing series of data is no longer published on a regular basis. A further difficulty occurs when no nationally representative figures are available on particular issues or areas such as language literacy.

Definitions

Authors on official statistics have identified several problems which exist around definitions used, additional to the issue of their subjective nature referred to above. Slattery (1986), as a sociologist, believes that official definitions are often 'non-sociological'; that is to say, they are of a different nature to definitions used within the disciplines of social science, the latter typically being products of a theoretical process. Evandrou (1991) posits that there is an issue around changes in definitions of variables or measures, which require appropriate adjustments to be made in order to enable a single time series to be produced. The suggestion has been made to overlap the old with the new definition or method of measurement within the same survey. Attempts have been made in recent years to remedy such inconsistencies; for instance, the publication by the Government Statistical Service (GSS) in 1995 of the booklet *Harmonised Questions for Government Social Surveys* (Roberts, 1997).

Inaccessibility

Inaccessibility of official data is cited by Slattery (1986) as a further disadvantage of official statistics, whether this be due to the cost involved or political reasons. Evandrou (1991) also mentions problems of accessibility around data which exists, but is not available for analysis in the public domain. The manner in which data are presented in published tables often makes breakdown into simpler formats problematic.

Making More Use of Official Statistics

The Social Science Forum (SSF) has been engaged in gathering concrete evidence of some of the difficulties and inadequacies of official statistics, in an effort to bring to the fore the limitations of certain practices and to demonstrate the constructive contribution which users of statistics can make to their development, improvement and general accessibility. The SSF (1989) has outlined principles which it believes should guide the collection and use of official statistics:

- In addition to the current concerns of government, an informed society should determine decisions about which data are collected.
- All statistics and data sets collected with public funds should be in the public domain.
- Where they exist, Britain should conform to international definitions and standards for the collection and analysis of statistics.
- A national statistics council or similar body should be created to provide a mechanism for interested parties to contribute to decisions about the content and status of official statistics.

Evandrou (1991) purports that further progress could be made by encouraging the forming of statistical users groups specialising in particular fields, as this would enable individual users with similar interests to meet up and discuss their concerns as well as communicating them to the relevant government departments. It is important to seize the opportunity made available by the recent opening of channels of communication with government departments by taking up offers made by government departments and civil servants of contacting them with future questions and concerns on official statistics.

A distinction is made between the witting and unwitting testimony given by statistics (Thomas, 1996). Using statistics, either critically or uncritically, is to attend to the witting testimony given by statistics, while attending to the unwitting testimony is to attend to the assumptions, motivations and functions associated with statistical systems. The purpose of attending to this unwitting testimony is to identify the nature of a statistical system and explore what it tells us about society and about the influence it has on society. The message given to the social sciences is that statistics should not be neglected because of the misrepresentations which they sometimes give, but that these misrepresentations should be examined and laid bare (Thomas, 1996).

The relatively little interest in the potentialities of official statistics for the field of social sciences has been attributed to an unfortunate disinclination to undertake large-scale empirical research, an exaggerated suspicion of social measurement and an excessive distrust of officially produced data (Bulmer, 1980). Objections are made from a number of viewpoints. Firstly, it is stated that there is no logical reason why awareness of possible serious sources of error in official data should lead to their rejection for research purposes; rather it should point to the need for methodological work to secure their improvement. Secondly, problems around validity and reliability of official statistics are more pertinent to some fields of social science than to others, such as suicide and crime. Thirdly, cases of extensive use of official data do not suggest that those who use them are unaware of the possible pitfalls. Fourthly, some critiques of official statistics are undoubtedly simply special cases of the rejection of a place for any empirical evidence in social science. Fifthly, the gulf between the common-sense assumptions of statisticians and the theoretical constructs of social science may not be quite as wide as is sometimes supposed. Despite the theoretical divergence between official statisticians and social scientists, there is a striking empirical convergence in the sense of agreement that differences demonstrated in official statistics of social class are 'real' and socially significant (Bulmer, 1980).

It has been argued that while, previously, resource planning was made difficult due to the lack of information, there are now figures available though these have not received due attention (Corby, 1990). Statistics can and should be used to develop policy and practice, but in so doing caution must be exercised in their interpretation and use. Corby (1990), in his analysis of child protection statistics, argues that they provide an ideal opportunity for constructive policy making and practice which should not be missed. While there is a need for refinement of the data, if handled with care, the statistics can be used constructively to analyse practice in the field of child protection.

Using Official Statistics

It has been argued that social scientists should critically examine the categorisations used and data-creation procedures involved in the production of statistics, in addition to investigating the social processes which lie behind most kinds of statistics (Thomas, 1996). Reference is made to such issues as the necessity of examining the small print accompanying statistics (Dale *et al.*, 1986, and Stewart & Kamins, 1993, both in Thomas, 1996); the importance of attending to the conceptual means of their production (Hindess, 1973, in Thomas, 1996); and the fact that systematic production of official statistics does not necessarily mean that they are scientific.

Confronted with any statistical material, Reid (1987) believes that the following must be addressed:

- Who produced it and when?
- Why was it produced?
- How was it produced?
- What is actually being presented?
- What does this material mean?

If the context of the statistics cannot provide answers to those questions, it is only correct to be suspicious of their meaning. In his guidelines to using statistics, Slattery (1986) cautions that the source of the statistics should be checked: why they were collected and how they are to be used should be ascertained. He also advises that the statistics themselves should be examined for error or distortion, the reliability and validity of the measuring instrument should be investigated and interpretations and conclusions which are reached should be reasonable and logical and not mere opinion or conjecture.

What follows is an illustration of the use of child care statistics. This is a descriptive exercise which attempts to illustrate the kind of issues that arise when working with a set of official statistics. Examination of this set of statistics needs to begin by addressing the questions raised above, such as: Who produced it and when? How and why it was produced? The data to be discussed are part of routine returns which are made by local trusts to the Department of Health and Social Services (DHSS) in Northern Ireland, and by local authorities to the Department of Health (DoH) in England on an annual basis. It therefore falls into the category of official statistics which are produced as a result of registration and administrative procedures of a government department. The time period covered is the decade from 1985 to 1995, which in Northern Ireland represents the decade prior to the introduction of a new piece of child care legislation, the Children (NI) Order 1995.

In the light of the above discussion on using official statistics, the question of what is actually being presented here also needs to be addressed. The returns covered are the figures for residential care, foster care and home in care. The geographical regions covered are Northern Ireland and England. In the case of Northern Ireland the data have been obtained by direct request to the information and policy branch of the DHSS, while in the case of England they have been taken from publications of the DoH. Data will be presented in both tabular and graphical form. The use of tables will allow accurate and precise presentation of detail and the use of graphs will complement that by presenting trend information and changes over time. The question of what does this material mean is more extensive and will be addressed throughout the discussion.

A CASE STUDY: THE USE OF RESIDENTIAL CARE, FOSTER CARE AND HOME IN CARE ON A REGIONAL LEVEL—NORTHERN IRELAND AND ENGLAND

Background

Having established the importance of examining data within context and not in isolation, it is necessary to sketch the legal and administrative background to the figures being discussed here. The United Kingdom is made up of England, Wales, Scotland and Northern Ireland. Each region has its own legislation and administration within a framework agreed by the UK government in London, and therefore its own structures for decision making. Policies in the 1980s and the outcome of recent referenda have increasingly brought about the devolution of power to the areas of Scotland and Wales and the establishment of separate assemblies. Different circumstances in Northern Ireland have meant that the region does not share in this direction of change. As a result of civil unrest, direct rule from London has replaced the provincial government since 1974 (Bullock, 1993). However, historical talks are currently underway which will no doubt have a far-reaching impact on how Northern Ireland will be governed in the future.

This analysis will concentrate on data from Northern Ireland and England. New child care legislation has been introduced into both regions in recent years: the Children (NI) Order 1995 referred to above, and the Children Act England and Wales 1989. A separate discussion on residential care, foster care and home in care data from each region is followed by a comparative analysis. Such a comparative analysis allows investigation of how similar the two child care systems are and indeed whether two different pieces of legislation are necessary.

Northern Ireland

How Data on Children in Care are Categorised

Table 1 gives details about how data on children in care by accommodation are categorised in Northern Ireland and England. A detailed description of how data are categorised is essential to answer Reid's (1987) question of: What does the material mean? In Northern Ireland, a change in the collection system took place in 1989 (Switzer, 1997). 'Boarded out' has since been broken down into subcategories of 'relative' and 'foster parents'. Data on residential care has been collected in less detail from 1989 onwards, with the reduction of five categories to three. 'Voluntary home' has been retained while 'under charge of parent, guardian, relative or friend' has been rephrased as 'under care of parent, relative, etc., including wards of court at home'. Department of Health and Social Services' (DHSS) figures for children in care by accommodation for 1989 are presented with the caveat that 'data is not directly comparable with information for previous years; it relates to children in care by all legal routes'.

A further change from 1989 onwards is that snapshots of numbers in care were taken on 31 March rather than on 31 December, reflecting the shift from calendar year to financial year. The change in the system of data collection means that no data were collected for 1988. (*Source:* Department of Health and Social Services, Northern Ireland.)

Table 1: Categorisation of children in care by accommodation in Northern Ireland and England

	Northern Ireland pre-1989	Northern Ireland post-1989	England
Residential care	(a) Lodgings or residential employment (b) Children's homes provided by any Board (c) Voluntary home (d) Accommodation for children ascertained to be handicapped (e) Hostels for working boys and girls	(a) Statutory home (b) Voluntary home (c) Training school	(a) In lodgings or residential employment (b) In community homes (c) With observation and assessment facilities (d) With educational facilities (e) Voluntary homes and hostels (f) Youth treatment centres (g) Schools and hostels for children with special educational needs
Foster care	Boarded out	(a) Boarded out with a relative (b) Boarded out with foster parents	Foster placements
Home in care	Under charge of parent, guardian, relative or friend	Under care of parent, relative etc. (including wards of court at home)	Under charge and control (up to 1991), replaced by placement with parents (from 1992). Placed for adoption (from 1987)
Mixed			
Other	Other accommodation	Other accommodation	Other accommodation

The Numbers of Children in Care

Table 2 shows the number of children in care in Northern Ireland by placement over the ten-year period 1985–95. Simple time trend analysis of these data is thwarted by the changes in the system of data collection as described above. Let us begin by examining the trends evident over the six-year period 1989–95, following the changes in collection. The use of percentages to express the extent of increase or decrease in a set of figures over time provides an indication of the magnitude of change taking place and allows comparison of such changes across groups of figures.

Although the total number of children in care increased by 3.3% from 1989 to 1991, this was followed by a decline of 7.6% in the years 1991 to 1993. The 1994 figure saw an increase of only 2 children on the previous year, while the 1995 figure showed a further drop to 2,624. The numbers of children accommodated in voluntary homes show an overall decline of 9.7%, while the numbers in statutory homes show a larger fall of some 34%. A drop of 30.7% is evident for the numbers boarded out with relatives, in contrast to the numbers boarded out with foster parents which have increased consistently by 16.7% from 1989 to 1995. The numbers under care of parent, guardian, relative or friend have declined by more than a third, while the numbers in training schools have risen by 65.4%. In the category of other accommodation, the 1995 figure is more than five times the figure for 1989. Trends showing an increase are therefore evident only for the categories of boarded out with foster parents, training schools and other accommodation, with the remaining placements all showing a fall in numbers.

In addition to looking at changes in absolute figures over time, it is also worth while to focus on changes in proportions across the various categories. Shifts in the percentage distribution across categories tells something of how the use of each of these categories is changing. In 1989, boarded out with foster parents represented 45% of children in care and this percentage had risen to 55.6% in 1995, indicating greater use of this type of accommodation. Children under care of parent, relative and others made up the next largest proportion in 1989, and although this was still the case in 1995, the proportion had fallen from 27.4% to 18.7%. The proportion represented by children placed in statutory homes fell from 11.2% to 7.9%, while that represented by children boarded out with a relative fell from 10.4% to 7.6%. The proportion of children in voluntary homes fell only slightly, from 4.4% to 4.2%, while that for training schools rose from 0.9% to 1.6%. Other accommodation made up 0.7% of the total figure in 1989 and 4.3% in 1995.

Table 2: Children in care/looked after in Northern Ireland at 31 December or 31 March respectively, by placement

	1985	1986	1987	1988	1989	1990	1991	1992	1993	1994	1995
All children	2,512	2,577	2,604		2,783	2,850	2,876	2,660	2,658	2,660	2,624
Boarded out	1,296	1,313	1,407								
Lodgings or residential employment	1	1	4								
Children's homes provided by any Board	354	333	287		123	114	122	124	118	115	111
Voluntary homes	180	144	139	Changes in data collection system							
Accommodation for children ascertained to be handicapped	4	5	7								
Hostels for working boys and girls	20	18	12								
Under charge of parent, guardian, relative or friend	629	737	726								
Other accommodation	28	26	22		20	62	19	13	45	75	113
Boarded out with relative					289	305	274	229	197	186	200
Boarded out with foster parents					1,251	1,297	1,373	1,392	1,418	1,425	1,460
Under care of parent, relative, etc.					762	721	728	585	595	621	491
Statutory homes					312	320	325	261	232	205	206
Training schools					26	31	35	56	53	33	43

(1) Figures for 1985–87 are at 31 December, figures for 1989–95 are at 31 March. Due to the change in the collection system, no figures were recorded for 1988.
(2) Revised categories appear from 1989 onwards but still include 'voluntary homes' and 'other accommodation'. (Old categories are written in italics.)

Comparing Trends Evident under the Old Collection System to Those Evident under the New

Comparison of trends under the old collection system to those under the new involves comparing percentage changes over two different time periods and hence derived from a different number of figures: three figures for the time period 1985–87 and seven figures for the time period 1989–95. A look at the trends for the period 1985–87 under the previous collection system shows an increase of 3.6% in the total number of children in care, which corresponds to the 5.7% increase over the slightly longer time period 1989–95 following the changes in data collection. The numbers 'boarded out' rise from 1985 to 1987, by approximately 8.6% and if one collapses 'boarded out with relative' and 'boarded out with foster parents' in the years following 1989, there is an equivalent increase of 7.8%. A 22.8% decline in the numbers placed in voluntary homes between 1985 and 1987 is set against a 9.7% decline in the years 1989–95.

By contrast, although the numbers under charge of parent, guardian, relative or friend showed a increase of 15.4% in the years before 1989, from 1989 to 1995 there was an overall decrease of some 35.6% in the numbers under care of parent, relative and other. A fall of 18.9% in numbers in children's homes provided by any board is set against a drop of 34% in the numbers in statutory homes under the new collection system. The numbers of children placed in hostels for working boys and girls decreased from 1985 to 1987, while the numbers in lodgings or residential employment and accommodation for children ascertained to be handicapped are very small.

Although the information collected pre-1989 is not directly comparable to that collected post-1989, one can look at certain trends, as has been attempted above. While this analysis comes with a cautionary note, it goes some way towards informing us about what was happening in the child care system over the decade 1985–95.

England

How Data on Children in Care are Categorised

Categorisation of children in care by accommodation in England has already been presented in Table 1. 'Placed for adoption' figures are available from 1987 onwards; however, children in this situation may be in residential or foster care placements. 'Under charge and control' figures are replaced by 'placement with parents' figures following the implementation of the Children Act England and Wales 1989. (*Source:* Department of Health, Personal Social Services.) The Children Act 1989 was implemented in October 1991 and made considerable changes to the framework under which children can be looked after by a local authority, which has affected comparisons with earlier years (DoH, 1996). With the exception of 'under charge and control', the categories under which local authority statistics are collated have not changed. 'Snapshot' data are recorded at 31 March each year.

The Numbers of Children in Care

Table 3 presents data for the number of children in care in England from 1985 to 1995.

Let us first examine the trends evident in the children in care figures over the ten-year time period. The number of children in care recorded at 31 March has fallen every year from 1985 through to 1995 to give an overall decrease of 30%.

A downward trend of 11.5% can be seen for 'foster placements', with the largest drop (6%) in the year 1991–92 following the implementation of the Children Act 1989. While the numbers of children in lodgings or residential employment show both increases and decreases over the ten-year period, there has been an overall decline of 29.4%. The transition year, 1991 to 1992, saw an increase of 28% in the numbers in lodgings or residential employment.

The category 'community homes' can be subdivided into those with observation and assessment facilities, those with educational facilities and others. As with 'foster placements', the numbers in 'community homes' have fallen each year with the result that the 1995 figure was less than half that for 1985. The greatest drop was in the numbers placed in 'community homes with observation and assessment facilities', with the 1995 figure a quarter what it was ten years previously. Figures for 'community homes' with 'educational facilities' and other community homes show a 63.2% and 53.7% decline · respectively.

A significant drop of 60.1% in the numbers placed in 'voluntary homes and hostels' is also evident. While the numbers in 'youth treatment centres' increased and decreased in the years up to the implementation of the Children Act in 1991, the numbers fell from 39 children to 20 in that year. The year 1994–95 saw an increase from 20 to 30 children in this category. Downward trends are also in evidence for the numbers in 'schools and hostels for children with special educational needs', although this category does come with the caveat 'from 1992 other

Table 3:   Children in care/looked after in England at 31 March by placement

	1985	1986	1987	1988	1989	1990	1991	1992	1993	1994	1995
All children	69,550	67,326	65,768	64,352	62,148	60,532	59,834	56,200	52,600	49,900	48,800
Foster placements	35,010	35,116	35,040	34,926	34,160	34,548	34,766	32,700	31,900	31,200	31,000
In lodgings or residential employment	1,982	1,947	2,030	2,081	2,003	1,733	1,719	2,200	2,000	1,600	1,400
In community homes*	14,794	13,855	13,207	12,302	11,014	10,507	9,710	7,900	7,000	6,400	6,000
With observation and assessment facilities	2,899	2,858	2,769	2,497	2,262	2,176	2,029	1,200	890	770	700
With educational facilities	2,174	1,862	1,801	1,259	1,342	1,178	1,059	980	880	840	800
Others	9,721	9,135	8,637	8,546	7,410	7,153	6,622	5,800	5,200	4,800	4,500
Voluntary homes and hostels	1,478	1,285	1,273	1,032	980	943	854	780	740	630	590
Youth treatment centres	50	36	43	39	34	46	39	20	20	20	30
Schools and hostels for children with special educational needs**	1,786	1,652	1,651	1,367	1,231	1,174	1,050	860	820	710	770
Placed for adoption			935	1,172	1,561	1,583	1,885	2,900	2,600	2,400	2,300
Under charge and control	11,329	10,305	9,037	8,810	8,797	7,740	7,297	Child Care Act 1989			
Placement with parents	Child Care Act 1980							6,500	5,200	4,600	4,300
Other accommodation	3,121	3,130	2,552	2,623	2,368	2,258	2,514	2,300	2,300	2,300	2,400

* Prior to the implementation of the Children Act 1989 these were provided under the Child Care Act 1980.
** From 1992 other types of independent school were separately identified and this may affect comparisons with earlier years.

types of independent school were separately identified and this may affect comparisons with earlier years' (DoH, 1996). A 41.2% decrease took place in the years up to the implementation of the Act and this continued, though at a slower rate, 10.5%.

Between 1987 and 1992 the number of children placed for adoption more than trebled, but this upward trend has reversed since 1992 with numbers falling by 20.7%. Figures for both 'under charge and control' (prior to the Children Act 1989) and 'placement with parents' (its post Children Act 1989 equivalent) have fallen over the years. A decline of 35.6% in the numbers 'under charge and control' corresponds to a decline of 33.8% in the numbers placed with parents. Finally, the numbers of children placed in 'other accommodation' have fallen by 23.1%, from 3,121 to 2,400.

To conclude, a look at the time trends of these data shows a considerable drop in the numbers of children in care. This trend is reflected in decreases in the numbers in all placement categories, with the exception of 'placed for adoption', where the numbers of children actually increased. What the changes in these figures clearly demonstrate is the importance of such information for the purposes of policy and planning.

With regard to proportion, half (50.3%) of the children in care were in 'foster placements' in 1985 and this had risen to 63% by 1995. Although the actual numbers in 'foster placements' fell over the time, the proportion has increased. Over a quarter (28%) were placed in 'lodgings or residential employment' and while this proportion rose to 39% in 1992, it had returned to 28% by 1995. The fall in the numbers of children placed in 'community homes' is echoed in a drop in proportion from 21.3% in 1985 to 12.3% in 1995. A very similar drop has taken place in the proportion of children placed in 'voluntary homes and hostels' from 21.3% to 12.1%.

The percentage of children in care 'under charge and control' has also decreased from 16.3% in 1985 to 13% in 1991, followed by a drop in the percentage in 'placement with parents' from 11.6% in 1985 to 8.8% in 1995. The proportion placed in 'schools and hostels for children with special educational needs' is small (2.5% in 1995), as is that for 'placed for adoption'. However, the percentage figure for the latter category has increased from 1.4% in 1985 to 4.7% in 1995. The numbers in 'youth treatment centres' have continued to make up only a very small percentage of children in care, 0.07% in 1985 and 0.06% in 1995. In the same way that time trend analyses described above have important implications for policy and planning, so too do the shifts which have taken place across categories of accommodation.

Comparison of Northern Irish Figures with English Figures

The existence of almost twice as many categories for the English figures attests to the difficulty involved in comparing by manner of accommodation. For example, while breakdown of foster care into the subcategories of 'relative' and 'foster parents' is provided for the Northern Irish figures, this is not the case for the English statistics. Conversely, while a more detailed breakdown of the different types of residential accommodation is available for England, such as 'with observation and assessment facilities', this is not so for Northern Ireland. While one may risk comparing the rate per 1,000 of children in care in 'voluntary homes and hostels' in England with the rate per 1,000 of children in care in 'voluntary homes' in Northern Ireland, differences in policy and practice between the two regions may make this comparison very crude. However, it is clear that any comparison on a regional level is, by its very nature, crude.

For the purpose of this analysis, categories will be regrouped as residential care, foster care and home in care. This will be done as follows:

- residential care in Northern Ireland post-1989 = voluntary home + statutory homes + training schools;
- prior to 1989 = lodgings or residential employment + children's homes provided by any board + voluntary homes + accommodation for children ascertained to be handicapped + hostels for working boys and girls;
- residential care in England = in lodgings or residential employment + in community homes + in voluntary homes and hostels + youth treatment centres + schools and hostels for children with special educational needs;
- foster care in Northern Ireland post-1989 = with relative + with non-relative;
- foster care in Northern Ireland prior to 1989 = boarded out;
- foster care in England = foster placements;
- home in care in Northern Ireland post-1989 = under care of parent, guardian, relative or friend;
- home in care in Northern Ireland prior to 1989 = under charge of parent, guardian, relative or friend;
- home in care in England post-1992 = placement with parents;
- home in care in England prior to 1992 = under charge and control.

Figures for 'placed for adoption' under the English system have to be
excluded from this analysis as these children may be placed in either
residential or foster care. When compared to figures for residential and
foster care as a whole, the figures for 'placed for adoption' are extremely small and their exclusion is not likely to have any great effect.

This approach minimises problems around the discrepancies between the two systems of categorisation and allows an approximate
comparison on a broader level. The rate per 1,000 of children in care
will be taken as the unit of comparison. The size of the child
populations in Northern Ireland and England are very different, hence
the use of absolute figures in this context is meaningless. It is necessary
that the figures be converted to a common unit and rate per 1,000
represents an ideal unit for such analysis. Before looking at breakdown
by accommodation, let us first examine the total number of children in
care in Northern Ireland compared to England, expressed as rate per
1,000 of the child population.

All Children in Care

The data discussed here are presented in Table 4 and Figure 6.

While the rate per 1,000 of the child population for children in care
was higher in England than in Northern Ireland in 1985 (6.23 compared
to 5.18), this had reversed by 1995 so that there was a higher rate of
children in care in Northern Ireland (5.62 compared to 4.36).

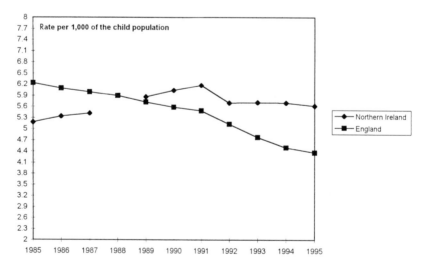

Figure 6:   Children in care in Northern Ireland and England 1985 to 1995

The intervening decade saw a consistent decline in the figures for England. This was coupled with an initial increase in the figures for Northern Ireland until 1991, followed by decrease in 1992 and a levelling off in the next three years. Over the ten years, the rate for children in care in England decreased from 6.23 per 1,000 of the child population to 4.36, while the rate for Northern Ireland increased from 5.18 per 1,000 to 5.62. A greater shift in the rate per 1,000 is evident for the English data when compared with those for Northern Ireland. In 1989 both sets of data converged, with the figure for England at 5.72 and that for Northern Ireland at 5.86. Since then the rates have diverged to leave a considerable gap in 1995.

Residential Care

The rate per 1,000 in the residential care, foster care and home in care sections refers to the rate per 1,000 of the children in care population, whereas the rate per 1,000 described above under 'all children in care' is derived from the child population as a whole. The data discussed here are presented in Table 4 and Figure 7. Throughout the decade 1985–95, the rate per 1,000 of children in residential care showed a downward trend in both England and Northern Ireland. The rate for Northern Ireland fell from 222.53 per 1,000 of children in care to 137.20, while that for England dropped from 288.86 per 1,000 to 180.12. Whether the two sets of data show a linear association may be tested statistically by calculating the correlation coefficient. The resulting co-efficient is 0.887, which is significant at the 0.01 level, indicating a linear relationship between the two sets of data. Statistical significance provides evidence that one's descriptive findings are not merely due to chance, thereby strengthening one's arguments. Whenever data are suitable for analysis and meet the required assumptions, the appropriate test should be applied.

Although the rate for Northern Ireland has been at a consistently lower level than that for England, the actual figures are not that dissimilar, e.g. a rate of 180.12 per 1,000 in England in 1995 compares to a rate of 137.20 in Northern Ireland, while a rate of 288.86 in England in 1985 compares to a rate of 222.53 in Northern Ireland. A look at the differences between the data from the two different regions shows a converging trend in more recent years. The gap between the rates became wider in 1986 and 1987 (differences of 84.45 and 104.36 respectively) but closed thereafter, so that in 1995 it was at its narrowest (42.93).

From this analysis, it is evident that both sets of data show a similar downward trend over the decade 1985–95. In both regions, there is an

Table 4:   The rate per 1,000 of children in care in Northern Ireland and England by placement: residential care, foster care and home in care

	1985	1986	1987	1988	1989	1990	1991	1992	1993	1994	1995
Northern Ireland											
All children—rate per 1,000 of the child population	5.18	5.34	5.42	5.89	5.86	6.03	6.17	5.70	5.71	5.70	5.62
Residential care	222.53	194.41	172.43	—	165.65	163.16	167.59	165.79	151.62	132.71	137.20
Foster care	515.92	509.51	540.32	—	553.36	562.11	572.67	609.40	607.60	605.64	632.62
Home in care	250.40	285.99	278.80	—	273.81	252.98	253.13	219.92	223.85	233.46	187.12
England											
All children—rate per 1,000 of the child population	6.23	6.09	5.99	5.89	5.72	5.58	5.49	5.13	4.78	4.50	4.36
Residential care	288.86	278.87	276.79	261.39	245.58	237.94	223.48	209.25	201.14	187.58	180.12
Foster care	503.38	521.58	532.78	542.73	549.66	570.74	581.04	581.85	606.46	625.25	635.25
Home in care	162.89	153.06	137.41	136.90	141.55	127.87	121.95	115.66	98.86	92.18	88.11
Differences											
Residential care	66.33	84.45	104.36	—	79.93	74.78	55.89	43.46	49.52	54.87	42.93
Foster care	12.54	12.07	7.54	—	3.7	8.63	8.37	27.55	1.14	19.61	2.62
Home in care	87.51	132.93	141.39	—	132.26	125.12	131.18	104.27	124.99	141.27	99

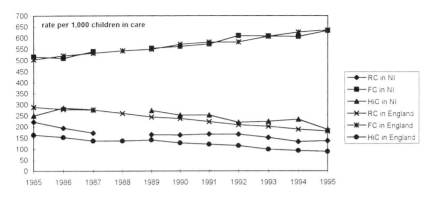

Figure 7:   Children in care in Northern Ireland and England by type of placement, 1985 to 1995

increasingly smaller number of children being looked after in residential accommodation. What the data also show is that the rate per 1,000
of children in care placed in residential placements in Northern Ireland
has been consistently lower than that for England. Such analysis has
considerable implications for policy and practice. While these findings
cannot be described as hard facts, they are certainly more than impres-
sionistic and should be used to inform the processes of policy and
practice.

Foster Care

The data discussed here are presented in Table 4 and Figure 7. It is
interesting to note how closely the data for foster care converge for the
two regions. Both sets of data show a gradual increase over the decade
1985–95 and both sets of figures are very similar—for instance, there
were 632.62 per 1,000 children in care in Northern Ireland in 1995 who
were placed in foster care, which compares to a figure of 635.25 per
1,000 in England for that same year.

A look at changes in the differences between the two rates over the
time period in question shows the largest gap in 1992 (27.55) and the
narrowest gap immediately thereafter (1.14) in 1993. It can also be seen
that, for some years, Northern Ireland had the higher rate per 1,000
(1985, 1987, 1989, 1992, 1993), while in other years the rate for England
was higher (1986, 1990, 1991, 1994, 1995). In Northern Ireland, the rate
per 1,000 increased from 515.92 in 1985 to 632.62 in 1995, while in
England it increased from 503.38 per 1,000 in 1985 to 635.25 in 1995.
The linear relationship between the two sets of data suggested by the

upward trend for both, is statistically significant at the 0.01 level (r = 0.951).

This analysis shows that the rate per 1,000 of children in care in foster care in both Northern Ireland and England shows rising and converging trends when viewed over a ten-year period. The increasing trend indicates that, in both regions, more children are in care in foster placements, while the converging trend suggests that the two systems are similar with respect to their use of foster care as a placement.

Home in Care

The data discussed here are presented in Table 4 and Figure 7. Of the three types of accommodation, the figures for home in care show the greatest discrepancies between the two regions. However, as with residential and foster care, an overall decline in the rate per 1,000 in home in care placements for both Northern Ireland and England can be seen. In 1985, 250.40 per 1,000 of children in care in Northern Ireland were in care at home, and by 1995 this had fallen to 187.12 per 1,000. In 1985, 162.89 per 1,000 of children in care in England were in care at home, and by 1995 the rate was 88.11 per 1,000.

As with the data for residential and foster care, the common trend in the rates for Northern Ireland and England would suggest a linear association between the two sets of data for home in care. Calculation of a correlation coefficient (0.794) provides statistical evidence for this relationship at a significance level of 0.01. The rate per 1,000 of children in home in care placements in England was consistently and considerably lower than that for Northern Ireland for the ten-year period 1985–95. The differences between data for the two regions vary over time, being at their largest in 1987 and 1994 (141.39 and 141.27 respectively) and at their smallest in 1985 and 1995 (87.51 and 99 respectively). No consistent converging or diverging trends can be seen.

The falling rates per 1,000 of children in care at home for both Northern Ireland and England over the time period 1985–95, suggest that an increasingly smaller number of children are in home in care placements. A higher rate in Northern Ireland indicates greater use of home in care placements than in England.

What May be Concluded from this Analysis?

To conclude, the following similarities and differences between the two child care systems can be noted:

- The data for the total number of children in care makes the two systems look very dissimilar—the number of children in care expressed as rate per 1,000 of the child population has shown considerable decline in England over the decade 1985–95, but has increased in Northern Ireland.

- The rate per 1,000 of children in residential and home in care placements has decreased over the time period 1985–95 in Northern Ireland and England.
- The rate per 1,000 of children in foster care placements is on the increase over the time period 1985–95 in Northern Ireland and England.
- Approximately the same rate per 1,000 of children in care are in foster placements in Northern Ireland and England.
- A higher rate per 1,000 of children in care are in residential care in England when compared with Northern Ireland.
- A higher rate per 1,000 of children in care are in home in care placements in Northern Ireland when compared with England.
- In Northern Ireland the rates per 1,000 of children in care from the highest to the lowest are ordered as foster care, home in care and residential care, whereas in England the rates per 1,000 of children in care from the highest to the lowest are ordered as: foster care, residential care and home in care.

While both child care systems show a strong reliance on foster care, there appears to be more use of residential care in England than in Northern Ireland, and conversely more use of home in care in Northern Ireland than in England. Both systems show common trends over time when broken down by manner of accommodation. However, opposite trends are evident when one looks at the total number of children in care expressed as a rate per 1,000 of the child population.

The essential similarity of the two child care systems is certainly in evidence, and indeed begs the question, posed earlier, of whether in fact two different pieces of legislation are necessary for the regions of Northern Ireland and England. For a state such as the United Kingdom, made up of several different regions, the importance of regional comparative analysis is highlighted by this question. The advantage of approaches which utilise regionally available aggregate data is that it is possible to identify broad trends and draw equally broad conclusions, though the remaining gaps in the data can be frustratingly large. While it is not always clear whether the data are strictly comparable, comparative work based on aggregate statistics produce a useful starting point, raising important questions in addition to offering conclusions (Cochrane & Clarke, 1993).

This case study of child care statistics shows how analysis of official statistics can be used to monitor the effectiveness of government policies, particularly where a change has occurred in the legislation, as with the introduction of the Children Act England and Wales 1989. Analysis of the figures for Northern Ireland for the decade preceding the introduction of the Children (NI) Order 1995, provides a baseline against which to compare the changes which will take place in the child care system following the introduction of the Order in November 1996 and the accompanying changes in policy and practice. Good quality official statistics allow the tracking of such changes in society and the dissemination of resulting findings enhances the public's ability to assess government performance as outlined by Evandrou (1991).

The child care data reviewed in this case study can also be seen in the context of the Social Science Forum's (1989) principles for guiding the collection and use of official statistics. Dissemination of official data on children in care by accommodation is necessary for interest groups such as voluntary organisations working with children or academic researchers, in order that they might contribute to the decision-making process about what data are collected and how. Representatives of such groups on a national statistics council would do much to enhance an opportunity to contribute to decisions on the content and status of official statistics in the context of the child care system. Dissemination of these data is all part of making statistics and data sets compiled with state funds available to the public, be they in the form of annual publications or meeting a particular request made over the phone. The two data sets used in this case study were obtained in each of these ways. This case study attests to the fact that there is room for greater conformity to international definitions and standards, as evidenced by the diversity which exists between such aspects of the data from two different regions within one state. Perhaps, as the role of official statistics attains greater importance for an increasing range of groups in society, such improvements in quality and status will automatically take place as part of the upgrading of official data.

SUMMARY

The second part of this chapter constituted the practical part, the completion of an exercise in working with official statistics. It illustrated how routinely collected statistical data can be used to appraise quantitatively and compare two child care systems. Time trends in the data have provided some indication of what has been happening in the Northern Irish and English child care systems over a ten-year period, such as the shift in focus in the different types of accommodation. What can be gleaned from these data has been hampered by such complicating factors as changes in the ways in which data are collected and the idiosyncrasies particular to each system. These mitigating factors represent one of the limitations in working with official statistics. These limitations should form part of the debate and not be the basis for rejection of empirical evidence in the field of child care.

What is required is that greater use be made of official statistics, coupled with the active participation and involvement of the users of such data in the polemic surrounding their collection and application. Such a culture would do much to foster a healthy appreciation of and sturdy belief in the use of official data, facilitating the operationalisation of its undeniable role in an evidence-based society. The quantitative procedure has evolved from the writings of the earliest scientists, matured through the dialectic of later schools of thought and emerged somewhat scathed, though revised and refined, into the twentieth century. Official statistics form a crucial component of the quantitative procedure and, when used correctly and critically, can provide a dimension of measurement to any argument or deliberation.

REFERENCES

Bamford, T. (1996). Information driven decision making: fact or fantasy? In A. Kerslake & N. Gould (eds) *Information Management in Social Services*. Aldershot: Avebury.

Bullock, R. (1993). The United Kingdom. In M. Colton & W. Hellinckx, *Child Care in the EC*. England: Arena.

Bulmer, M. (1980). Why don't sociologists make more use of official statistics? *Sociology*, **14**, 505–523.

Cochrane, A. & Clarke, J. (eds) (1993). *Comparing Welfare States: Britain in International Context*. London: Sage.

Corby, B. (1990). Making use of child protection statistics. *Children and Society*, **4**, 3, 304–314.

DoH (1996). Children looked after by local authorities—year ending 31 March 1995 England. England: Department of Health.

Evandrou, M. (ed.) (1991). *Improving Government Statistics: Gaps and Discontinuities in Official Statistics*. London: Social Science Forum.

Keat, R. (1979). Positivism and statistics in social science. In J. Irvine, I. Miles & J. Evans (eds) *Demystifying Social Statistics*. England: Pluto Press.

Krige, J. (1979). What's so great about facts? In J. Irvine, I. Miles & J. Evans (eds) *Demystifying Social Statistics*. England: Pluto Press.

Miles, I. & Irvine, J. (1979). The critique of official statistics. In J. Irvine, I. Miles & J. Evans (eds) *Demystifying Social Statistics*. England: Pluto Press.

Reid, S. (1987). *Working with Statistics*. England: Polity Press.

Roberts, D. (1997). Harmonisation of statistical definitions. *Journal of the Royal Statistical Society*, A, **160**, 1, 1–4.

Slattery, M. (1986). *Official Statistics*. London: Tavistock.

Smith, A. (1996). Mad cows and ecstasy: chance and choice in an evidence-based society. *Journal of the Royal Statistical Society, A,* **159**, 3, 367–383.

Social Science Forum (1989). *Official Statistics: A Statement of Principle for their Collection and Use.* London: Social Science Forum.

Sutton, M. & Maynard, A. (1993). Are drug policies based on 'fake' statistics? *Addiction,* **88**, 455–458.

Switzer, V. (1997). *Child Care Statistics in Northern Ireland: The Last Decade (1985–1995).* Belfast: Centre for Child Care Research, The Queen's University of Belfast.

Thomas, R. (1996). Statistics as organisational products. *Sociological Research Online,* **1**, 3, <http://www.socresonline.org.uk/socresonline/1/3/5.html>.

Young, R. (1979). Why are figures so significant? The role and critique of quantification. In J. Irvine, I. Miles & J. Evans (eds) *Demystifying Social Statistics.* England: Pluto Press.

7

RESEARCHING HIDDEN POPULATIONS

Kathryn Higgins

INTRODUCTION

A challenge shared by researchers within the child welfare field and those from other disciplines is that there are certain populations central to their range of interest which remain 'hidden', 'elusive', 'special' or 'hard to reach' for various reasons. To illustrate the point, a topical example within the field of child welfare are the populations compris-

Making Research Work: Promoting Child Care Policy and Practice
Edited by D. Iwaniec and J. Pinkerton
© 1998 John Wiley & Sons Ltd

ing 'children in need'. This spans a vast array of children, ranging from those with a disability through to children who are neglected or abused. Although we have a certain degree of information about these populations, what we do not have is a true estimate of their size or detail about many of their characteristics. The inherent difficulties in researching, and indeed at times the lack of awareness of the need to do so, has resulted in many hidden populations being overlooked to date in child care research. Similar difficulties have been encountered by other disciplines and a browse through the methodological literature reveals that the study of hidden populations is not a new phenomenon. Indeed, researching such populations seems to have arisen in the modern sense in the nineteenth century and has since developed as a veritable industry involving disciplines from A to Z: anthropology, criminology, epidemiology, journalism, mathematics, sociology, zoology (Hartnoll, 1992). Within this list of disciplines researchers have produced a range of methodological innovations in response to technical problems they have encountered in researching varied hidden populations and social activities (Caplan, 1982). However, much of this highly relevant material is buried in the methodological literature and is by its nature spread across a range of substantive fields (Lee, 1995).

Although it is unlikely that totally new methods remain to be discovered, the accumulation of knowledge and advances in technology mean that new applications and developments of existing methods may be fruitful. It is by now generally accepted that there is no 'best' method for researching hidden populations, but rather, that diversity is a strength and that different approaches can and should be complementary. However, the question remains of how to best combine or interface these different approaches. In addition, there is considerable scope for these methods to be transferred to disciplines which have not yet fully explored their application, such as the field of child care.

This chapter aims to assemble material from a range of sources and disciplines in order to introduce and explore strategies for researching hidden populations. It will begin by examining some important definitions followed by a brief outline of the reasons for studying hidden populations in general. Methods for estimating the size of hidden populations, notably capture–recapture, will then be discussed. This will be followed by looking at strategies for sampling hidden populations and then the process of accessing such populations will be explored. Although the chapter will draw on material from a host of studies representing a range of disciplines, the focus is on the potential application of these methods to the field of child care.

WHAT ARE HIDDEN POPULATIONS?

The terms 'hidden', 'elusive', 'special,' 'hard to reach' or 'rare populations' are often used as if their meaning were self-explanatory. In reality, they are rather broad and ill-defined concepts that span a range of situations. Heckthorn (1997) posits that a population is 'hidden' when no sampling frame exists and/or public acknowledgement of being part of the population is potentially threatening, for example, due to formal and informal law enforcement. Hartnoll (1992) provides more detail and catalogues five general definitions which cover the range from 'hidden' to 'rare'. Hartnoll's categories are as follows:

- those in a population not known to formal institutions or agencies;
- those known to individual institutions/agencies but information is not passed on;
- socially marginal/deviant groups;
- private populations;
- openly visible populations on whom nobody has bothered to collect data.

The definitions provided by Hartnoll (1992) cover the situations pertinent to the child care field. For the purposes of this chapter the term 'hidden' population will be used.

WHY STUDY HIDDEN POPULATIONS?

There are various reasons for wishing to study both the characteristics of hidden populations and to have an estimate of their size. Firstly, it is important that data are obtained to provide a more complete and accurate scientific account of hidden social activities. This assists in presenting a balanced descriptive picture as a basis for making and evaluating policy and to counter distorted or sensational claims. Additionally, research into such populations provides a necessary basis for planning and resource allocation, for treatments or interventions, general service delivery, health education and risk reduction in its various forms. Sound research is also important as a way to develop and strengthen an advocacy role on behalf of hidden populations. In most instances, two or more of these reasons are combined when a special study on these populations is conducted (Garretson, 1992).

METHODS FOR ESTIMATING THE SIZE OF HIDDEN POPULATIONS

The previous section highlighted why the study of hidden populations is important. Assuming that it has been decided that a population is worthy of study, a sensible approach may be to begin by trying to gain an estimate of its size. As noted, it is of necessity that policy makers and service providers are informed about the size of particular populations or the prevalence of certain activities in areas for which they have responsibility. Naturally research plays a crucial role in providing such data, and to this end there are two key questions which require exploration.

1. How have researchers attempted to get an estimate of the prevalence of specific activities or to make judgements about the size of certain populations?
2. Have these methods proved adequate?

In answering the first question, the range of methods already in use, some standard and others innovative, for estimating the size of specific populations or the prevalence of certain activities will be discussed. The second question will be addressed by drawing out the inherent deficiencies of the approaches and in doing so will highlight the possibilities of more effective and innovative techniques. An example of the 'indicator method' used in drug research will be provided as illustration.

Population Surveys

Firstly, there is a need to consider national population surveys and their use in attempting to estimate the size of hidden populations. Such surveys refer to representative studies of the general population or of specific sections of it. Although improving the design of surveys may ameliorate some of the difficulties, the very nature of general population surveys renders them problematic in researching hidden populations for a number of reasons. In the first place, these surveys do not give direct measures of activities such as drug use in young people or crimes committed. Intervening between the reality of activities such as crime or drug abuse and survey data are the subject, the interviewer and the actual interview. All of these are being influenced by surrounding cultural attitudes and historical context (Hartnoll, 1992). There are a host of examples in the burgeoning literature on survey methods and empirical studies which demonstrate how the process and the context of measurement can greatly affect the results obtained (Haw, Olszewski & Lewis, 1994). The sampling frames used in survey research tend to vary and can impact upon the results. The choice of sample design, for example quota or probabilistic, is also a contributory factor to the results obtained. Additionally, the exclusion of certain groups is problematic, such as the homeless and those institutionalised. There are also the added issues of mobility, non-residents, commuters and temporary residents. Questionnaire design is also crucial, as well as choice of the method, be it self-completion or interviewer administered. Interviewer and respondent gender and ethnicity match and mismatch can also impact upon results obtained. Response rate is a major concern and few surveys are truly representative of the general population. Many fail to deal adequately with the problem of non-response. In addition there are questions around validity of survey data as these are susceptible to public attitudes and the context of the interview. Willingness to report an activity often decreases in inverse proportion to the perceived deviance of the activity. In sum, survey data should be viewed as indirect measures: 'to be interpreted like other indirect indicators, in terms of their sampling and selection bias, measurement error, validity and context' (Hartnoll, 1992, p. 5). Although improving the design of surveys may improve on some of the difficulties, it would be almost impossible to overcome them all.

Official Statistics

It has been demonstrated that population surveys are not very successful at tapping into hidden populations, but what about using official statistics? The utilisation of official statistics is not as simple as at first appears as this source of information has serious limitations (see Chapter 6 for a fuller discussion). These limitations are exacerbated when this source is put to use in researching hidden populations. This point has been highlighted by research in various fields: crime (Downes & Rock, 1988), child sexual abuse (La Fountaine, 1990), drug use (Haw, Olszewski & Lewis, 1994) and homelessness (Shaw et al., 1996). The production of official statistics by state agencies gives rise to what has been called a 'dark figure', that part of what the statistics purport to measure but which goes unreported or unrecorded. Official statistics notoriously underestimate the size of hidden populations and the prevalence of certain activities (Lee, 1995). Taking the example of child sexual abuse, La Fountaine (1990) has outlined some of the difficulties which arise in the case of judicial statistics. She highlights that in England and Wales statistics are given for offences and convictions but not for offenders. Therefore, it is impossible to discern from these statistics something as basic as the number of individuals who have committed sexual offences against children. Furthermore, La Fountaine adds that in cases of child sexual abuse, gaining convictions can be difficult and therefore even offences may not be recorded.

Other difficulties abound; to begin with, the size of the prevalence estimate depends on case definition—in other words, how researchers chose to define what it is they are measuring. In child abuse prevalence estimates may vary due to differences in the definitions of abuse used (Hertzberger, 1990). It is also imperative to distinguish clearly between measurement of 'incidence' and that of 'prevalence'. Incidence is the number of new cases coming to attention in a specific population, as opposed to prevalence which is the total number of cases in a given time period. There is a further problem which is highly relevant to child care. This centres on what should be regarded as a case when counting occurrences of a phenomenon. This is not always self-evident. In the case of many issues pertaining to child care it is difficult to know exactly what is a case; the individual child or the family? This point is illustrated by what happened in Cleveland in relation to sexual abuse. La Fountaine (1990) has pointed out that the number of children taken into care numbered 160, while the number of families involved was only 44. Significantly different impressions could be derived depending on what figure is taken. Official statistics are hampered by the issues of reportability, visibility and recordability. These issues are pertinent in the study of crime, illegal drug use and many other social phenomena relevant to child care.

Nomination Techniques

Clearly there are problems with surveys and official statistics; however, there are strategies that attempt to improve these sources and may even lead to resolving some of the inherent problems with their use. One of these is the nomination technique which has been used to estimate the size of hidden populations. This technique involves inviting individuals who are known to the researcher from the population being studied to list individuals who they know to be in their population. Taking the example of drug users, typically they are contacted either through field work or through service agencies (Rigby & Bennet, 1990) and are invited to list drug users known to them, giving age and sex of nominees together with a range of other details. The major advantage of the nomination technique is that it expands the size of the sample without having to interview all the individuals. However, the accuracy of the information provided is questionable, unless restricted to very close personal contacts, which defeats the purpose of the technique in the first place. Bringing child care research into frame once more, the same technique could be applied to the study of aspects of child care.

Multiplier Methods

If the relationship between the size of a particular indicator and the total population has been established, then the size of the total population can be calculated using a multiplier formula. Multiplier methods have been applied in the field of drug research. On the basis of their work in two London Boroughs between 1980 and 1982, Hartnoll and colleagues (1985) tentatively suggested that there were five regular users of heroin and similar drugs in the population for each user notified by the Home Office as an addict. Another variation on this technique is to link the number of drug-related deaths to the prevalence of drug use. If the death rate of drug users is known, or can be fairly reliably estimated, the number of deaths in a specified year multiplied by the annual mortality rate can theoretically be used to give an annual prevalence. This method, as with any, has a number of shortcomings but nonetheless can be useful in providing some sort of estimate of the size of a given hidden population.

Capture–Recapture

One of the most useful techniques developed to date is that of capture–recapture. These methods are based on procedures developed by ethologists for estimating the size of a population of animals in their natural habitat (Blower, Cook & Bishop, 1981). Animal scientists have been aware for many years that complete counting of an animal population is impossible. Instead they have developed 'intuitive estimators' of populations based upon incomplete sampling, or capture–recapture as it has come to be known (La Porte, 1994). In simple terms, this involves capturing a sample of animals, marking them in some way and releasing them back into the wild. Later a second sample is caught and the ratio of marked to unmarked animals is recorded. The following conditions have to be met when using this technique: marked and unmarked animals must be similar in behaviour, they must intermingle freely, and there must be no addition to the population between the time points at which the samples are taken. If the two samples are independent random samples of the total population, the size of that population can be estimated from the following equation:

$$P_i = \frac{n_i(n_i+1)}{m_i + 1}$$

where P_i = the population size at time i
          n_i = animals captured, marked and released at time i
          $n_i + 1$ = number of animals in sample taken at time $i + 1$
          $m_i + 1$ = number of recaptured marked animals in the second
                       sample.

(Blower, Cook & Bishop, 1981, p. 29)

Social scientists in the United States were the first to recognise that data from two indirect indicators or lists could be regarded as equivalent to the incomplete sampling strategy employed by the ecologists (Green, 1979). Providing that named or attributable data are available to allow unique cases to be identified, and the overlap between indicators determined, then the same principle can be applied to human populations as can be used with animals. The method allows for the production of a prevalence figure complete with confidence intervals (see Gardner and Altman (1995) for calculation of confidence intervals). Recently there has been substantial use of capture–recapture methods to estimate prevalence for a range of welfare and clinical problems, the success of which would encourage their application to the field of child care. Indeed, in a recent editorial in the *British Medical Journal*, La Porte (1994) has suggested that capture–recapture methodology may bring about a paradigm shift in how counting is done in all the disciplines that assess human populations.

La Porte (1994) researched applications of the method to the estimation of disease prevalence. It has also been used to correct for underreporting of spina bifida (Hook, Albright & Cross, 1980) and cancer (Robles *et al.*, 1988; Schouten *et al.*, 1994). Applications of the two-sample capture–recapture methods have been used in a series of studies of local prevalence of drug use (Hartnoll *et al.*, 1985; Parker H. *et al.*, 1987). One fundamental limitation of the basic two-sample method is the assumption that the two samples are independent, which is often not valid. For example, if data on drug users in receipt of treatment form one sample and persons arrested for drugs offences the other, independence between the samples cannot be necessarily assumed. A problem drug user who is charged with drugs offences is usually advised to seek treatment to support his claim that he is drug dependent and so will appear in both samples. These problems of nonindependence led to the development of a multi-sample method which enables both the evaluation and control of dependencies between samples (La Porte, 1994). If data on individuals from three or more samples are organised into a contingency table based on their presence or absence in one or more of the samples, the value for one cell representing cases which are absent from all samples is missing. This value is equivalent to the hidden population. Using log-linear analysis, a model can then be fitted to the data which best describes the dependencies between samples. This can then be used to estimate the value for the missing cell and the confidence interval for the total population. This inclusion of log-linear models to assess dependence between three or more samples greatly increases its suitability in epidemiological studies (Cormack, 1989).

The three-sample, or more, capture–recapture has two advantages over the two-sample approach. As mentioned above, the assumption of independence need not be met as there is sufficient information to describe the dependencies between samples, which can then be accounted for in the prevalence calculation. In addition, complete equivalence in geographical coverage of all samples is unnecessary. The three or four-sample capture–recapture method has been utilised in a number of countries to estimate the size of drug-injecting populations (Davoli et al., 1992) and HIV populations (Drucker & Vermund, 1989; Gaudino et al., 1991, Mastro et al., 1992). It was first used in the UK by Frischer to estimate the number of injecting drug users in Glasgow (Frischer, 1992; Frischer et al., 1991, 1993). It has also been used to estimate the general prevalence of drug use (Hay & McKeaganey, 1996). In addition, it has been applied in a study of local prevalence of street prostitution (Bloor et al., 1991) and more recently work has commenced on estimating the prevalence of problem drinking as well as on studies of the prevalence of homelessness (Fisher et al., 1994; Shaw et al., 1996). A review of the issues that arise in applying the method in the public health field have been reviewed by Watts, Zwi and Foster (1995).

As with any method, there are advantages and drawbacks to the use of capture–recapture. Taking advantages first, the method is economical in that it utilises existing data collection systems, the calculation of confidence intervals for estimates permits firmer grounding for service planning decisions—although, as Shaw et al. (1996) highlight, there are some often overlooked technical difficulties in constructing valid intervals. The method also allows flexibility in the estimation of different subpopulations—for example, those differentiated by age or gender. This method can also facilitate extension over time to produce trend data. Finally, the method allows the use of scored screening instruments which scale the severity of the problems' manifestation in a given instance. This enables prevalence estimates to be calculated based on different policy or conceptual definitions of the issue covered by the research. The disadvantages of the method, on the other hand, arise from problems in meeting the conditions discussed earlier. Firstly, taking the example of a study using agency data, it often cannot be guaranteed that the samples used are independent, and there may be problems of ensuring that data are collected over the same period. As attributable identifying data are required, it may produce problems of confidentiality. Methods are becoming more sophisticated by increasing the number of samples included in the analysis, which provide more information about dependencies between samples and produce a more accurate estimate with tighter confidence intervals. Cormack (1993) suggests that the optimal number of samples is six. However, when translated into social research, it is imperative that a balance is provided between the desire to increase the precision of the population estimate, by increasing the number of samples, with caution about the introduction of error caused by problems of ascertainment or overlap between samples.

Applications of the method in the field of child care research can readily be imagined where counting problems are in evidence and where existing lists are likely to be incomplete. Examples which are immediately apparent are in the estimation of the prevalence of children and young people with a disability or other groups of 'children in need'. This can be extended to examine the completeness of the relevant registers pertaining to categories of children in need, such as the register for child abuse and that for children with a disability. The cost-effectiveness and flexible nature of the method, which relies on already existing material, renders it a practical option which is appealing to researchers and policy makers alike. The method is not without its difficulties which are technical, conceptual and practical. There also remains the very real restriction that centres on the efficacy of existing information systems relevant to the field of child care, as discussed by Switzer in Chapter 6. Some of these issues are only partly resolvable and there would remain some degree of uncertainty as well as some level of imprecision. Nevertheless, in many areas the idea of capture–recapture represents a potentially viable, flexible and economic alternative complementary to traditional methods.

Piecing the Methods Together

An interesting means by which many of the above methods were brought together is one derived from the field of drug research. The 'drug indicator method', as it is known, has as its central tenet the assumption that information on drug use could be collected from a wide range of sources or indicators and pieced together like a jigsaw to provide an overall picture. Three main kinds of indicators were identified: routine/official statistics, information obtained directly from agencies and, finally, information derived from groups and individuals in the community. This mass of data collected from numerous sources could then be used in a variety of ways:

- to enumerate individuals, in this case, drug users in contact with official agencies;
- to enumerate individuals located through fieldwork studies or through population surveys in order to estimate prevalence from a particular indicator using a multiplier formula;
- to estimate prevalence using data on the overlap of cases between two or more indicators, capture–recapture;
- to estimate the size of an 'unknown' population by using nomination techniques;
- as a way to monitor trends over time.

A major advantage of this method is its speed and economy and the broad range of instruments used. As always, limitations abound and centre on the ability to identify error created by the use of a particular indicator or research instrument. In addition, it cannot be assumed that the use of a broad range of indicators and instruments will necessarily correct for errors in one given set of data. Other problems associated with the methods identified have already been discussed. However, the transferability of this model, where appropriate and feasible to other disciplines such as child care, is worthy of serious consideration, particularly with regard to 'children in need'.

CONTEMPORARY DEVELOPMENTS IN SAMPLING HIDDEN POPULATIONS

Once an estimate of the size of a population has been achieved, the next hurdle is to obtain a sample of the population in question. Accordingly, the aim of this section is to discuss the issues surrounding the sampling of hidden populations. These populations have two distinctive characteristics. Firstly, no sampling frame exists, so the size and boundaries of the population are unknown. Secondly, there are strong concerns around privacy, as membership often, though not always, involves stigmatised or illegal behaviour. This leads individuals to refuse to co-operate or to provide inaccurate answers to protect their privacy. As discussed in the preceding section, traditional methods such as household surveys fail to produce reliable samples and are inefficient because most or many hidden populations are rare. There are several major strategies which can be used singly or in combination in sampling hidden populations. These are list sampling, screening, multi-purposing, outcropping, networking, advertising and servicing. (For detailed information on these sampling methods see Lee (1995).) At present, the study of hidden populations is dominated by three sampling methods, which are all forms of networking. The three are: snowball sampling and other forms of chain referral samples, key informant sampling and targeted sampling. This section will concentrate on the issues surrounding these methods.

Perhaps the best-known form of sampling hidden populations is snowball sampling. Erickson describes the method as follows:

> It starts from a first sample whose individuals are asked to name their acquaintances who at their turn will constitute the second wave of people interviewed; to these again the same questions will be asked in order to set the third wave and so on. (Erickson, 1979, p. 276)

Some authors (Goodman, 1961) assume that the initial sample is a random sample of subjects of a target population. There is also a defined number of individuals named by each interviewee that is kept constant in each of the sampling waves. In order to improve efficiency, other authors do not start from a random sample nor do they keep constant the number of nominees (Biernacki & Waldorf, 1981).

Avico et al. (1988) argued that the level of generalisation is likely to be strengthened by large sample sizes and the replication of results. The size of the initial group being of great importance for the accuracy of the final estimate has been endorsed by Snijders (1992). She advised that 'the initial sample size of a one wave snowball sample should not be much smaller than the square root of the population size in order to make precise statistical inferences from snowball samples' (Snijders, 1992, p. 62). The more homogeneous the population, the more likely that random and non-random samples will manifest similar characteristics and results (Biernacki & Waldorf, 1981; Van Meter, 1990).

However most hidden populations are far from homogeneous groups and it is necessary to take into account differences in probability that various groups will be represented in the initial sample. For example, there is a higher chance of individuals well known to relevant agencies being included than those less well or not known. Other studies select only one or two of the nominees named by each interviewed person and extend indefinitely the chains until they break up, when no further contacts are made, keeping the mean length of each chain very low (Kaplan Korff & Sterk, 1987; Avico *et al.*, 1988).

Schmeidler and Horvarth (1990) proposed a weighting strategy based both on selection probabilities and the characteristics of the sample that was actually obtained. Thus the sample can be weighted to the known or estimated distributions of variables in the population stratum by stratum. This weighting is liable to, but may not, increase representativeness (Ten Houten, 1992). An alternative solution to the problem of representativeness of snowball samples is presented by Ten Houten (1992) in the field of drug research and centres on sites of recruitment. He produced a typology of six sites. Zone (residential/ commercial), place (inside/outside) and time (day/night). The typology and parts thereof, often referred to as multi-site sampling, is applicable to the sampling of all hidden populations.

The theoretical problems of sampling hidden populations are well documented. However, Biernacki and Waldorf (1981) note that most textbooks on qualitative methods and their analysis have been remiss in their attention to the procedures or problems entailed in the use of snowball sampling. They identified five particular problems:

- finding respondents and getting the reference chain started;
- verifying the eligibility of potential respondents;
- engaging respondents as research assistants;
- controlling the types of chains and a number of cases in any chain;
- pacing and monitoring of the chains and the quality of the data.

Two additional methods have been developed to overcome the difficulties with snowball samples—'key informant' and 'targeted sampling'. Key informant sampling (Deaux & Callaghan, 1985) is designed to overcome response biases by selecting especially knowledgeable respondents and asking them about the behaviour of others, rather than their own. For example, researchers may ask social workers or counsellors to report on patterns of child abuse, drug use or some other behaviour. This method is fraught with biases ranging from lack of detailed knowledge to professional interests and impartiality. A further variation in certain circumstances is that the subjects—for example, drug users—are used to conduct interviews with fellow drug users (sometimes referred to as privileged access interviews—Griffiths *et al.*, 1993) or, indeed, engaging respondents as research assistants (Biernacki & Waldorf, 1981). If sufficient informants can be taken on, a large sample of population in question can be contacted in a range of locations and social backgrounds over a relatively short period of time.

Therefore, large samples can be accrued quickly by this method. However, because it relies on interviewers contacting and subsequently interviewing close friends and associates, several kinds of problems can arise. Firstly, there is a very real threat to confidentiality. Secondly, respondents may be less likely to disclose sensitive data to someone known to them and this raises serious questions concerning reliability and validity. Finally, as it is less easy to follow up respondents, falsification of interview data is potentially more of an issue.

Targeted sampling (Waters & Biernacki, 1989) is a widely employed response to the deficiencies of chain referral models (Heckthorn, 1997, p. 175). It consists of two basic steps. Firstly, the field researcher maps a target population to the extent that they succeed in penetrating the local networks linking potential respondents; this prevents the undersampling that traditional approaches would produce. Secondly, the field researchers recruit a pre-specified number of subjects at sites identified by the ethnographic mapping, ensuring that subjects from different areas and subgroups will appear in the sample. The adequacy or otherwise of targeted sampling depends on the ethnographic mapping which is often far from perfect and takes a long time to construct.

Increasing recognition of the limitations of targeted sampling, and the absence of new sampling strategies, have resulted in an increasing interest in snowball and other chain referral models. Studies of social networks have shown the potential power of such methods. Refinements of chain referral sampling includes a method for estimating the size of hidden populations using a one-wave snowball sample developed by Frank and Snijders (1994). They select a diverse set of initial subjects, each of whom in turn lists all members of the target population known to them. The size of the hidden population is then estimated, based on the amount of overlap among the members listed. In the same vein Klovdahl (1989) proposes a 'random walk' approach for analysing network structure, using a snowball sample in which each wave consists of only one subject. The results reveal structural features of the network connecting members of the hidden population. Furthermore, Spreen and Zwaagstra (1994) present a combination of snowball and targeted sampling, termed 'targeted personal network sampling', which uses ethnographic mapping to locate an initial sample which becomes the basis for network sampling.

Despite the refinements, some problems remain unsolved. 'The central question in the methodological discussion about sampling and analysing hidden populations is basically "how to draw a random (initial) sample"' (Spreen, 1992, p. 49). This question is key, as it generally has to be assumed that however many waves the chain referral sampling may contain, it necessarily must reflect the biases in the primary sample. In an attempt to overcome some of these difficulties Heckthorn (1997) describes a new form of chain referral sampling, which he terms 'respondent driven sampling', developed within the context of health outreach to drug users. He contends that this approach to both accessing and sampling hidden populations is revolutionary in the sense that it is designed to reduce several of the deficiencies of traditional forms of chain referral sampling. The deficiencies Heckthorn's approach attempts to overcome are as follows. Firstly, it is assumed that inferences about individuals must rely mainly on the initial sample, since additional individuals found by tracing chains are never to be found randomly or even with understood biases. If, however, the sampling process is allowed to continue through enough waves to reach equilibrium, its composition will be independent of the initial subjects. A second problem afflicting chain referral samples is that such samples tend to be biased towards more co-operative respondents. Heckthorn argues that this problem can be reduced because dual recruitment incentives are offered; they offer a primary reward for being interviewed plus a reward for recruiting others to the study. Individuals who resist researchers' appeals may be more amenable to their peers. A third problem is that chain referral samples tend to be biased by subjects protecting friends through not referring them. This problem can be minimised because recruitment incentives weaken the reluctance to approach reserved peers. Finally, chain referral samples may be biased towards subjects with large social networks. Heckthorn argues that there are a number of ways in which this problem can be approached: by weighting samples based on network sizes, saturating targeted areas, or using steering incentives to increase recruitment of subjects with traits associated with small personal networks. In sum, what makes respondent-driven sampling different is that it produces samples that are independent of the initial subjects from which sampling begins and, as a result, it doesn't matter whether the initial sample has been drawn randomly. The range of methods as outlined above have immediate appeal in terms of their transferability to researching hidden populations, and imaginative use of sampling strategies could be applied when researching more difficult populations in the field of child care.

GAINING ACCESS TO HIDDEN POPULATIONS

The previous sections dealt with contemporary developments in the sampling of hidden populations which inevitably leads the discussion on to exploring how researchers gain access to these populations. Some of the relevant material has been touched upon in the previous sections where some sampling strategies by their nature cover elements of the access process, as demonstrated by Heckthorn (1997).

In essence, the two ways for a researcher to gain access to a hidden population is through people and through location. Considering people first, snowball sampling by its nature attempts to move from known to unknown research subjects with the dual purpose of creating a sample and solving the access issue. Similarly, privileged access interviews, as well as generating a sample, also resolve the access issue. A further variation is the use of known members of the population to act as first point of contact. That individual then spots, approaches, initially assesses eligibility and finally introduces the researcher to other members of his population (Haw & Higgins, 1996). These new contacts may be known or unknown to that person. This approach once again avoids the issue of cold approaching by the researcher, although it is not without its problems. Respondent-driven sampling, as discussed by Heckthorn (1997), acts as a strategy for both sampling and gaining access and attempts to limit some of the difficulties with accessing hidden populations.

More traditional means of gaining access can be through location. This can be via an agency or shop where members of the population in question gather. This approach has been used in studies of drug use where the first point of contact is a pharmacist dispensing prescriptions or a nurse or counsellor from a drug-related agency. Contact from a familiar figure provides the initial introduction and affords some common ground for researched and researcher.

The more general consideration for location-based field observation research, as distinct from the types of research outlined above, is that negotiating access to less public locations requires a different set of conventions and codes. In some of the most successful instances of ethnographic research, access flowed from a contact within the locality over many years such as a social worker or a neighbourhood worker (Preble & Casey, 1969; Feldman, 1968). There is often a key contact who acts as a sponsor to the research and who facilitates access (Williams, 1989).

Ethnographic methods employed in the field of drug research and female prostitution (McKeaganey & Barnard, 1992) are based on field observations in a range of settings—youth clubs, schools, streetwork, pharmacy shops—and offer an unusual degree of detail in terms of the contexts of recorded incidents and conversations. Gaining access in these circumstances is a slow process and is not without its ethical problems (Power, 1989). It requires means of access which are both realistic and safe for observers and observed alike. There is the danger of 'going native' in such situations, through getting too close to subjects and the researcher becoming at risk.

In considering all access strategies described above, it is important to attend to the questions of selectiveness, sampling and possibilities for generalisation. Attention must also be paid to the possibility of subjectivity in data collection and interpretation. Once again the issues of gaining access are applicable to the child care field and caution around the various means of gaining access to the population under study must be attended to.

SUMMARY

This chapter has set out on a foray into the research of hidden populations. Some definitions of hidden populations were provided and reasons why it is important that researchers include such populations in their studies were also considered. The various strategies employed by researchers for estimating size, sampling and gaining access were then recounted, accompanied by the advantages and drawbacks associated with their use. Attention was paid to the potential application of such methods to the field of child care research and it was suggested that the success of their use in other disciplines augurs well for adapting them to the field of child care. Implicit throughout has been the acknowledgement that there is a very real restriction which centres on the efficacy of existing information systems relevant to the field of child care.

The Children Act (1989) and similar legislation in Scotland (1995) and in Northern Ireland (1995) call for increased intersectoral and multidisciplinary working. Success in achieving this could see a more co-ordinated approach to information systems which would result in a higher likelihood that the methods described above could be utilised successfully. The increasing profile and general recognition of the importance of research, as outlined by Iwaniec in Chapter 1, as well as the propensity towards evidence-based research and practice, adds further strength to the argument for tackling research issues which are by their nature more difficult. A further welcome development in research is that the 'researched' are increasingly expecting and gaining success in having their voices heard. Researchers enter co-operative relationships with, and on behalf of, powerless or marginalised groups and, as a result, act as a conduit for voicing their views and concerns. These relationships are not without their difficulties and add to the challenge

of researching such populations. All of these developments add up to
the need for innovative research strategies. Researching these populations, as Lee (1995) suggests, requires an imaginative cast of mind.
Technical competence in research skill, even of the highest quality,
needs to be, in Lee's words, 'leavened by imagination'.

REFERENCES

Avico, U., Kaplan, C., Korczak D. & van Meter, K. (1988). *Cocaine Epidemiology
in Three European Communities*. A Pilot Study Using a Snowball Sampling
Methodology. Rotterdam: IVO.

Biernacki, P. & Waldorf, D. (1981). Snowball sampling: problems and methods
of chain referral sampling. *Sociological Methods and Research*, **10**, 141–161.

Bloor, M., Leyland, A., Barnard, M. & McKeaganey, N. (1991). Estimating
hidden populations: a new method of calculating the prevalence of drug
injecting and non-injecting female street prostitution. *British Journal of
Addiction*, **86**, 11, 1477–1483.

Blower, J., Cook, L. & Bishop, J. (1981). *Estimating the Size of Animal Populations*.
London: Allen & Unwin.

Caplan, A. (1982). On privacy and confidentiality in social science research. In
T. Beauchamp, R. R. Faden, R. J. Wallace & L. Waters (eds) *Ethical Issues in
Social Science Research*. Baltimore: John Hopkins University Press.

Cormack, R. M. (1989). Log linear models for capture–recapture. *Biometrics*, **45**,
395–413.

Cormack, R. M. (1993). In S. Haw, D. Olszewski & R. Lewis (1994) *Estimating the
Prevalence of Illicit Drug Use—A Review of Methods*. Edinburgh: Centre for
HIV/AIDS and Drug Studies.

Davoli, M., Arca, M., Spadea, T., Abeni, D., Forastiere, F. & Perucci, C. (1992).
Estimating the Number of Drug Injectors. A Crucial Step in Predicting the
HIV/AIDS Incidence. Presentation 8th International Conference on AIDS,
Amsterdam (July).

Deaux, E. & Callaghan, J. (1985). Key informant versus self-report estimates of
health behaviour. *Evaluation Review*, **9**, 365–368.

Downes, D. & Rock, P. (1988). *Understanding Deviance* (2nd edition). Oxford:
Clarendon Press.

Drucker, E. & Vermund, S. (1989). Estimating population prevalence of human
immunodeficiency virus infection in urban areas with high rates of intravenous drug use: a model of the Bronx 1988. *American Journal of Epidemiology*,
130, 1, 133–142.

Erickson, B. H. (1979). Some problems of inference from chain data. *Sociological
Methodology*, **10**, 276–302.

Feldman, H. W. (1968). Ideological supports to becoming and remaining a
heroin addict. *Journal of Health and Social Behaviour*, **9**, 131–139.

Fisher, N., Turner, S., Pugh, R. & Taylor, C. (1994). Estimating numbers of
homeless mentally ill people in North East Westminster by using capture–
recapture analysis. *British Medical Journal*, **308**, 27–30.

Frank, O. & Snijders, T. (1994). Estimating the size of hidden populations using
snowball sampling. *Journal of Official Statistics*, **10**, 53–67.

Frischer, M., Bloor, M., Finlay, A., Goldberg, D., Green, S., Haw, S., McKeaganey, N. & Platt, S. (1991). A new method for estimating prevalence of injecting drug use in an urban population: results from Scottish city. *International Journal of Epidemiology*, **20**, 4, 997–1000.

Frischer, M. (1992). Estimated prevalence of injecting drug users in Glasgow. *British Journal of Addiction*, **87**, 235–243.

Frischer, M., Leyland, A., Cormack, R., Goldberg, D., Bloor, M., Green, S., Taylor, A., Covell R., McKeaganey, N. & Platt, S. (1993). Estimating the prevalence of injecting drug use and infection with HIV among injection drug users in Glasgow, Scotland. *American Journal of Epidemiology*, **138**, 3, 170–180.

Gardner, J. & Altman, D. (1995). *Statistics with Confidence*. London: BMJ.

Garretson, H. (1992). Conclusions. Invited Expert Meeting on Illegal Drug Use. *Research Methods for Hidden Populations*, Chapter 6. Rotterdam: NIAD.

Gaudino, J., Reardon, J., Ruiz, J. M., Lemp, G. F. & Wilson, M. J. (1991). Estimating the Number of HIV Infected Intravenous Drug Users in Nine Countries of the San Francisco Bay Area. Presentation 7th International Conference on AIDS, Florence, June (Abstract WC 3062).

Goodman, L. (1961). Snowball sampling. *Annals of Mathematical Statistics*, **32**, 148–170.

Green, J. (1979). *A Method for Monitoring Local Drug Abuse Trends and Prevalence Estimation*. Forecasting Branch Administrative Report. Maryland, USA: NIDA.

Griffiths, P., Gossop, M., Powis, B. & Strang, J. (1993). Reaching hidden populations of drug users by privileged access interviewers: methodological and practical issues. *Addiction Research*, **88**, 1617–1627.

Hartnoll, R. (1992). Critical overview of existing methods. NIDA Research Monograph: *Research Methods for Hidden Populations*, Proceedings from an Invited Expert Meeting in Illegal Drug Use.

Hartnoll, R., Mitcheson, M., Lewis, R. & Bryer, S. (1985). Estimating the prevalence of opiate dependence. *The Lancet*, 26 Jan., 203–205.

Haw, S. & Higgins, K. (1996) *Dundee Behavioural and Prevalence Study*. Final Report to Chief Scientists Office. Scottish Office Home and Health Department, March.

Haw, S., Olszewski, D. & Lewis, R. (1994). *Estimating the Prevalence of Illicit Drug Use—A Review of Methods*. Edinburgh: Centre for HIV/AIDS and Drug Studies.

Hay, G. & McKeaganey, N. (1996). Estimating the prevalence of drug misuse in Dundee, Scotland: an application of capture recapture methods. *Journal of Epidemiology and Community Health*, **50**, 4, 469–472.

Heckthorn, D. (1997). Respondent driven sampling: a new approach to the study of hidden populations. *Social Problems*, **44**, 2.

Hertzberger, S. (1990). The cyclical pattern of child abuse: a study in research methodology. *American Behavioral Science*, **33**, 529–545.

Hook, E., Albright, S. & Cross, P. (1980). The use of Bernoulli census and log linear methods for estimating the prevalence of spina bifida in live births and the completeness of vital records in New York State. *American Journal of Epidemiology*, **112**, 750–758.

Kaplan, C., Korff, D. & Sterk, C. (1987). Temporal and social contexts of heroin using populations: an illustration of the snowball sampling technique. *Journal of Nervous and Mental Disease*, **175**, 566–574.

Klovdahl, A. (1989). Urban social networks: some methodological problems and possibilities. In M. Kochen (ed.) *The Small World*. Norwood, NJ: Ablex.

La Fountaine, J. (1990). *Child Sexual Abuse*. Cambridge: Polity Press.

La Porte, R. (1994). Assessing the human condition: capture–recapture methods. *British Medical Journal*, **308**, 5–6.

Lee, R. (1995). *Doing Research on Sensitive Topics*. London: Sage.

Mastro, T., Kitayapoon, D., Weniger, B., Vanichseni, S., Laosunthorn, V., Uneklabh, T., Choopanya, K. & Uneklabh, C. (1992). Estimate of the number of HIV infected injecting drug users in Bangkok using capture–recapture method. Presentation 8th International Conference on AIDS. Amsterdam, July (Abstract POL 4075).

McKeaganey, N., Barnard, M., Bloor, M. & Leyland, A. (1990). Injecting drug use and female street working prostitution in Glasgow. *AIDS*, **4**, 1153–1155.

McKeaganey, N., Barnard, M., Leyland, A., Coote, I. & Follet, E. (1992). Female street working prostitution and HIV infection in Glasgow. *British Medical Journal*, **305**, 801–804.

Parker, H., Newcombe, R. & Bakx, K. (1987). The new heroin users: prevalence and characteristics in wirral, Merseyside. *British Journal of Addiction*, **82**, 147–157.

Power, R. (1989). Participant observation and its place in the study of illicit drug abuse. *British Journal of Addiction*, **84**, 43–52.

Preble, E. & Casey, J. (1969). Taking care of business; the heroin users life on the street. *International Journal of Addiction*, **4**, 11–24.

Rigby, K. & Bennet, G. (1990). *Prevalence of Drug Use in East Dorset: A Nomination Study*. Bournemouth: Community Drug Team Royal, Victoria Hospital Bournemouth.

Robles, S. C., Marret, D., Clarke, E. & Risch, H. (1988). An application of capture–recapture methods to the estimation of the completeness of cancer registration. *Journal of Clinical Epidemiology*, **4**, 1495–1501.

Schouten, L., Straatman, H., Kiemmeney, L., Gimbrere, C. & Verbreek, A. (1994). The capture–recapture methods for estimation of cancer registry completeness—a useful tool. *International Journal of Epidemiology*, **23**, 1111–1116.

Schmeidler, A. & Horvarth, W. (1990). Weighting procedures for ethnographic random samples. *Bulletin de Methodologie Sociologique*, **29**, 15–24.

Shaw, I., Bloor, M., Cormack, R. & Williamson, H. (1996). Estimating the prevalence of hard to reach populations the illustration of mark—recapture methods in the study of homelessness. *Social Policy and Administration*, **30**, 69–85.

Snijders, T. (1992). Estimating on the basis of snowball samples—how to weight? *Bulletin de Methodologie Sociologique*, **36**, 59–70.

Spreen, M. (1992). Rare populations, hidden populations and link tracing designs: what and why? *Bulletin de Methodologie Sociologique*, **36**, 34–58.

Spreen, M. & Zwaagstra (1994). Personal network sampling out degree analysis and multi level analysis: introducing the network concept in studies of hidden populations. *International Sociology*, **9**, 475–491.

Ten Houten, W. (1992). Generalisation and statistical inference from snowball samples. *Bulletin de Methodologie Sociologique*, **37**, 25–40.

Van Meter, K. (1990). Methodologies and design issues: methods for assessing the representativeness of snowball samples. In E. Lambert (ed.) *The Collection and Interpretation of Data from Hidden Populations*. NIDA Research Monograph 98. Washington, DC: US Government Printing Office.

Waters, J. & Biernacki, P. (1989). Targeted sampling: options for the study of hidden populations. *Social Problems*, **36**, 4, 416–430.

Watts, C., Zwi, A. & Foster, G. (1995). Using capture–recapture in promoting public health. *Health Policy and Planning*, **10**, 198–203.

Williams, T. (1989). *The Cocaine Kids*. New York: Addison Wesley.

8

CHILD PARTICIPATORY RESEARCH: ETHICAL AND METHODOLOGICAL CONSIDERATIONS

Colette McAuley

Chapter Outline

INTRODUCTION

LEGISLATIVE REFORM AND CHANGING CONCEPTS OF CHILDHOOD

ETHICAL ISSUES IN CHILD PARTICIPATORY RESEARCH
• Children's Consent
• Protection of Child Respondents

METHODOLOGICAL ISSUES IN CHILD PARTICIPATORY RESEARCH

A RESEARCH ILLUSTRATION

SUMMARY

INTRODUCTION

This chapter begins with a brief overview of recent legislative reforms in England and Wales and in Northern Ireland and their consequences for the legal status of children. These reforms are placed in the broader context of the United Nations Convention on the Rights of the Child.

Making Research Work: Promoting Child Care Policy and Practice
Edited by D. Iwaniec and J. Pinkerton
© 1998 John Wiley & Sons Ltd

Changing conceptualisations of childhood, including the emergent sociology of childhood, are discussed with particular reference to their implications for social researchers. Research which actively attempts to promote the participation of children (child participatory research) is then explored in relation to both ethical and methodological issues posed. An illustration of research carried out by the author which focused specifically on the perspectives of children in substitute care is used to draw out some of the issues posed by child participatory research.

LEGISLATIVE REFORM AND CHANGING CONCEPTS OF CHILDHOOD

Children's right to participate in matters affecting their lives is increasingly being recognised within the United Kingdom. In 1991 the UK government ratified the United Nations Convention on the Rights of the Child. Article 12 of the Convention states:

> State parties shall assure to the child who is capable of forming his or her own views the right to express those views freely in all matters affecting the child, the views of the child being given due weight in accordance with the age and maturity of the child.
>
> For this purpose, the child shall in particular be provided the opportunity to be heard in any judicial and administrative proceedings affecting the child, either directly, or through a representative or an appropriate body, in a manner consistent with the procedural rules of national law.

In 1991 the Children Act 1989 was implemented in England and Wales and in 1996 a virtually identical piece of legislation, the Children (NI) Order 1995, was implemented in Northern Ireland. Both of these new statutory instruments represented a major reform of private and public law relating to children in their respective jurisdictions. In fact the former has been referred to as the single most comprehensive reform of children's legislation in living memory. Under this legislation the welfare of the child must be the courts' paramount consideration in all decisions made concerning children coming before them. Of particular interest to us for the purposes of this chapter, is the fact that, in determining the child's welfare, legislation requires the courts to have particular regard to: 'the ascertainable wishes and feelings of the child concerned (considered in the light of his/her age and understanding)' (S. 1(3)(a), Children Act 1989). (The corresponding section of the Children (NI) Order 1995 is Art. 3(3)(a).) This was the first time that the wishes and feelings of children were accorded this status in England and Wales legislation and the first time in Northern Ireland that legislation gave any recognition at all. Under both statutes, the child is entitled to separate legal representation provided he or she is deemed competent to instruct. A central part of the role of the Guardian Ad Litem to the court is to ascertain the wishes and feelings of the child and to present these to the court (DoH, 1995; Howard, 1996). While Panels of Guardians have been established in England since 1984, the implementation of the Children Order in November 1996 established Guardians Ad Litem for the first time in public law cases in Northern Ireland. In an unique development within the United Kingdom, as a special agency within the DHSS, the Northern Ireland Guardian Ad Litem Agency has been established. This agency is independent of the Health and Social Services Trusts and voluntary agencies and is responsible for the provision of all Guardians in adoption and specified proceedings under the Children (NI) Order 1995 (McAuley, 1996a).

As a direct consequence of these legal developments, there is a developing body of literature on methods of communicating with children (formerly found primarily in the field of social work) which is now aimed at children's solicitors and their counsel and Guardians Ad Litem to assist them in their new roles with children (Liddle, 1992; King & Young, 1992; McAuley, 1996b).

However, while recognising that the adoption of the United Nations Convention on the Rights of the Child undoubtedly represents a considerable leap forward in respect of children's rights, Badran, in her preface to the *UK Agenda for Children* (Lansdown & Newell, 1994), cautions that the process of translating those rights into effective change in children's lives will take a little longer. Similarly, new children's legislation in itself does not necessarily bring about changes in practice regarding children being consulted and their views taken seriously. Nevertheless, under these statutes children are now seen as clients potentially competent to instruct legal representatives. The new status of children represents a significant shift in legal thinking and has consequent training implications (Bainham, 1993).

In the area of social research there have also been corresponding developments. Few earlier sociological studies, even where they were concerned with children, had directly interviewed children. Largely this could be attributed to their conceptualisation of children. New developments in social theory (James & Prout, 1990, 1995) and in cross-national accounts of childhood which aim to provide children and childhood with conceptual autonomy (Qvortrup *et al.*, 1994) have led to sociologists questioning their conceptions of childhood. In 1990 a thematic group on the Sociology of Childhood was established by the

International Sociological Association, and several years later the American Sociological Association formed a section on the Sociology of Children. The beginnings of a Sociology of Childhood is now increasingly referred to in UK sociological literature (Jencks, 1996). Such a perspective criticises earlier sociological studies for constructing children merely as objects rather than subjects of research. Social research starting from the position of seeing children as social actors in their own right see them as legitimate research subjects. Research which assumes that children are subjects who, in turn, have the right to participate is immediately faced with a number of ethical and methodological issues.

ETHICAL ISSUES IN CHILD PARTICIPATORY RESEARCH

Children's Consent

Many of the issues posed are not unique to research with children, but the unequal power relationships between adult researchers and child participants are likely to present specific dilemmas (Mayall, 1994). Lansdown (1994) argues that children's vulnerability in relation to adults is due not only to the physical strength, knowledge and experience base of adults but also to their economic and political position in society. The issue of consent of children to participate in research studies remains one of the more difficult dilemmas as it is bound up with our views of the competence of children. Most recent discussions of children's competence refer to the Gillick legal case (Gillick v West Norfolk and Wisbech AHA (1984), 1 All ER 373). Mrs Gillick, a mother of ten children, took her health authority to court in an attempt to ensure that children under 16 years of age should not have the right to access medical treatment or advice, in this case regarding contraception, without the consent of their parents. The case eventually was referred to the House of Lords. The majority ruling was that children under 16 years of age, provided that they are deemed competent, can give consent to medical treatment. In the words of Lord Scarman:

> As a matter of law the parental right to determine whether or not their minor child below the age of 16 will have medical treatment terminates if and when the child achieves a sufficient understanding and intelligence to understand fully what is proposed. (Gillick v Wisbech & West Norfolk AHA (1985), 3 All ER 423).

In what has become known as the Gillick ruling, the legal view of children's competence to consent places emphasis on the individual ability or competence of a child and is less concerned with a stated age of consent. More recent rulings in the Court of Appeal do appear to revoke the child's right to consent, allowing one or both parents to overrule their consent and indicating that the Gillick competent child may be listened to but their wishes overruled.

Alderson (1995) argues that competence to consent should have three characteristics: understanding, wisdom and freedom. The assessment of such competence is crucial. The question of who deems an individual child to be competent and how this is done remains problematic. In the Gillick case regarding medical treatment, the court expects the doctor to decide on competence. A parallel under the Children Act and the Children Order is the expectation of children's solicitors to decide upon the competence of the children to give instructions. This raises the issue of training for professionals invested with such responsibility.

Whoever has the responsibility for making this assessment, the way in which it is carried out would also seem to be important. Efforts need to be made to ensure that the child is not placed in a particularly anxiety-provoking or stressful situation in which he or she may appear less competent than in normal circumstances.

With regard to children's consent to participate in social research, similar issues arise. Do we place emphasis on the individual child's competence rather than consider an arbitrary age level? If so, who will assess the competence of the child to consent, and how? What training would be required? In the interests of an inclusive approach, Alderson (1995) suggests that all school-aged children should be assumed to be competent to consent to participate in research. The onus then would be on proof of incompetence.

Within the context of children's rights, there is a growing awareness of the need to consult with children on decisions affecting their lives and this is now reflected in children's legislation. To learn about children's perspectives we, as researchers, need to ensure that children are consulted, and in an appropriate manner. The issue of consent in legal terms, while initially clarified by the Gillick ruling, appears again to be somewhat unclear following the Court of Appeal hearings. Nevertheless, children's consent to participate in social research should, as a matter of respect for the child, be sought. The issue of assessing whether an individual child is deemed competent to make an informed decision about participation remains a complex one in parallel to the decisions discussed earlier which face doctors and solicitors. The question of training is equally relevant for researchers. While care needs to be taken in this area, the problems are not insurmountable, with due attention from researchers.

Protection of Child Respondents

Emanating from the view that children may not be fully aware of the consequences of agreeing to participate in research, another area of ethical concern frequently addressed in ethical guidelines is the need to protect child research respondents from research. Alderson (1995) advocates a clear analysis of how the research design, aims, methods, presentation and language affect children's status. Morrow and Richards (1997) suggest the inclusion of an Impact on Children Statement at the research proposal stage. The danger, as they suggest, is that an overly protective stance may prevent children from having the opportunity to participate in research. What is particularly welcome is the growth in child participatory studies, which include reflective analysis concerning anxieties posed and constructive suggestions about undertaking this type of research (e.g. Mahon *et al.*, 1996).

METHODOLOGICAL ISSUES IN CHILD PARTICIPATORY RESEARCH

In a bid to reduce the power differential between researcher and child subject, considerable efforts are being made to develop methods to facilitate children's participation in research. The thinking behind this approach is that children have different competencies than adults and that we as researchers should use research methods which relate to these skills.

Hill (1997) provides a useful overview of approaches documented in research studies which directly involved children. This includes the use of self-completion questionnaires (Fletcher, 1993; Part, 1993; Sinclair & Gibbs, 1996), interviews with children/young people usually using semi-structured questionnaires (Hill, Lambert & Triseliotis, 1989; Roberts *et al.*, 1993) and group discussions (Buchanan, Wheal & Coker, 1993; Freeman *et al.*, 1996). The use and limitations of standardised instruments are also discussed, and the development of techniques derived from direct work with children, i.e. use of vignettes, written and picture prompts, use of drawing, role play and use of technology, are well described. The need for attention to factors such as the ethnic background, age and gender of children is appropriately highlighted.

As child participatory research is still a new area, it is particularly helpful to have thoughtful evaluations of methods employed in both individual interviews and focus groups. A small group of such studies are currently emerging (e.g. Hill, Laybourn & Borland, 1996; Mauthner, 1997).

A RESEARCH ILLUSTRATION

What follows is a brief overview of some of the ethical and methodological issues raised in a recent study by the author. The full findings of the study have been reported elsewhere (McAuley, 1996c, 1996d). It was a longitudinal study of children aged 4 to 11 years at the time of placement, during the first two years of planned long-term foster placements. The study examined their emotional and social development over time as well as their perspectives on the fostering process and contact with birth families and significant others. It employed qualitative and quantitative measures. For the purposes of this chapter I am going to concentrate on the research interviews with the children.

The research objectives regarding these interviews were to:

- ascertain the wishes and feelings of children during the early stages of the fostering process;
- explore the children's perspectives on established relationships with birth families and significant others as they progress through the fostering process;
- examine the children's perception of the developing relationships in the foster families over time.

In pursuit of these research objectives a number of ethical issues emerged. These included the following:

- respecting the child's right to information communicated in a way that he or she understands;
- ensuring that the child has appropriate expectations of the research and researcher;
- establishing rapport/trust with the child while recognising that research is time limited;
- respecting the child's wish for confidentiality while ensuring effective protection;
- providing choice for the child while recognising that he or she may have had little choice about participation;

- ensuring effective dissemination while respecting the need for anonymity for the individual child.

It seemed important to the children that they had received a personal letter before coming for interview. Adapting the letters so that they were age appropriate across the age range proved a lot more challenging than first expected. Clarifying issues, such as who the researcher was and why she wanted to speak to them, at the beginning of interviews ensured that the children were less likely to have unrealistic expectations. A lot of effort went into establishing a rapport and trust with the children, especially in the initial interviews. However, building the necessary relationship also had to be set appropriately within the context of a time-limited research exercise with children of this age and at this stage of development.

Confidentiality was another issue which had to be addressed not only with the social services, social workers and foster carers but directly with the child at the outset of the project. It seemed appropriate to assure confidentiality to the child on such sensitive matters, yet it was also necessary to recognise that the situation might arise where a child would disclose that he or she was in a position of danger, requiring adult protection. Experience in this research, as in previous practice, was that it is wisest to be open and honest with the child about this eventuality from the start.

Within the interviews the children were given choices as to the use of data collection methods, such as use of feeling faces, feeling cards or direct responses, but also choices as to whether they wanted to respond to individual questions. This was done not only to empower the children but also, given the sensitive nature of the subject matter, it seemed reasonable to expect that they might choose not to answer particular questions.

Finally, effective dissemination for the improvement of practice was a key consideration when undertaking the study. In Northern Ireland we have a relatively small population of children in care (approximately 2,500) in a population of 2.4 million and hence the children's circumstances could easily be identified. The core finding, therefore, had to be presented in such a way as to draw from the richness of the individual child's response while ensuring that the respective views of each child remained anonymous.

In addition to these ethical issues, there were methodological aspects of undertaking research with this group of children that had to be considered. Among these were the following:

- interview the child alone but with sufficient support;
- location of interviews;

- format of interviews;
- standardised instruments and/or developed measures.

Drawing on previous experience of working in a child psychiatry setting, I chose to interview the children alone but with a trusted adult nearby. The latter was either the child's foster carer or the child's social worker. Given the fact that my objectives were to interview children about sensitive areas, it seemed appropriate to offer them uninterrupted space for such exploration of feelings. My concern was that the children's perspectives were central to this study and that such privacy might not be possible in many of their living situations. Opting for having a trusted adult nearby was an attempt to increase the children's sense of security. This was particularly important on the first interviews, and especially with the younger children who tended to want to check in with the adults occasionally during the interviews. The interviews took place at the University in pleasant child-oriented rooms with no telephone interruptions.

Few major research studies of child care in social work had, or indeed still have, included formal interviews with children concerning their wishes and feelings. In the foster care literature, Rowe's study (1984) was a notable exception. In discussion with her, she confirmed that the research team had carried out face-to-face adult-style interviews, although consideration had been given to the children's age and level of understanding in the formulation of the interview schedules. The fact that the views of the children were given such serious attention 13 years ago commends the study.

My own approach to the interviews with the children was deeply influenced by my previous practice in direct work with children in social services and in child psychiatry. Obviously the areas identified were likely to be highly sensitive for the child and hence needed careful consideration as to the level and nature of questioning. Having decided on the areas which should and could be approached, in the context of the child having the right to respond or not to the research measures/ questions, I searched for available standardised instruments or previously documented materials in the psychological and social work research literature.

Important considerations in this prospective study included the age range of the children during the study (i.e. 4–13 years) and measures/ materials which could be repeated over time. The sensitive nature of the areas for exploration had also to be taken into account. Seeking the children's perspective on birth families from whom they were separated was likely to evoke strong feelings for them. Similarly, seeking their views regarding their new foster families with whom they were currently living was likely to produce avoidance if the questioning was too direct.

In order to seek the views of children on the fostering process and on relationships with their birth families, friends and significant others during that process, what I needed was an appropriate means of facilitating communication. This was an exploratory stage of investigation. Experience of direct work with children had convinced me of the usefulness of incorporating different mediums in interviews to facilitate communication. There was a significant body of social work literature in the United Kingdom on direct work with children, emanating particularly from the preparation of children for permanent care placements (Curtis, 1983a, 1983b; Fahlberg, 1981, 1988; Jewett, 1984; Thom & Macliver, 1986: Aldgate & Simmonds, 1988). The challenge was to select/create materials which would translate into the research context. The use of feeling faces and feeling card responses, alongside direct responses, provided choices for the children, and the former was almost always chosen as the preferred medium. However, it was important to spend time introducing the child to the idea that sometimes it can be easier to communicate difficult feelings with the cards. An integral part of this participatory process was involving the child in creating faces and cards to depict feelings they might want to include. Interestingly, some of the most illuminating responses surrounded the feeling faces and cards requested by the child.

Sometimes a series of questions had been used earlier in research and it seemed useful to compare the responses of the children studied over time and in comparison with children in previous studies. For example, in an early study which focused on the identification of children, Weinstein (1960) used a series of four questions which had been repeated in later research with children in substitute care (Thorpe, 1974). These were:

1. I love . . . most in the world.
2. If I could pick anyone in the whole world to live with, I would pick. . . .
3. I think that . . . loves me most in the world.
4. If I had a trouble or were worried, I would take it to . . . .

The same questions were given at all three time points in this study, but were each illustrated by cartoons which were gender specific to the study child (see McAuley, 1996c, for illustration). Another useful projective technique often used in diagnostic interviews in child psychiatry is the three wishes question (Hill, 1985). A cartoon version of a genie and a lamp was devised to accompany the question and was consistently popular with the children across the age range and at all three time points (see McAuley, 1996c, for illustration).

In contrast, to attempt to measure the children's perceptions of their developing relationships over time, an adapted version of the Family Relations Test (Bene & Anthony, 1957) was used. This test was devised to measure the emotional attitudes of the child to family members and the child's view of family feelings towards him or her. It has been used to examine the emotional perspective of adopted children and children in residential care (Jaffe, 1977; Schwartz, 1970); children experiencing school problems (Lockwood & Frost, 1973); children attending play-groups (Turner 1977, 1982); and children who have been subjected, or are suspected of having been subjected, to abuse and neglect (Geddis, Turner & Eardley, 1977; Turner & Geddis, 1979).

It may be used with very young children as the task is simple. The test material consists of 20 cardboard figures, ambiguously drawn, representing people of various ages from babyhood to old age, with a posting box attached to each. The child is helped to select those which best represent himself or herself and the members of his or her family. An additional character, Mr Nobody, is then added to the selected group.

Two sets of cards are available, one for use with children up to 8 years and a longer one for older children. Each card carries a statement which may be read to, or by, the child. They are asked to 'post' the card into the box appropriate to the person to whom it seems to fit best. If the child feels that it does not fit anyone, it is posted to Mr Nobody. The statements are designed to represent positive and negative emotions, towards and from the child. The relative importance for a child of the various family members is reflected in the numbers of items allocated to each. An overall score for the child's degree of involvement can be obtained and allows comparisons within a group of children to be made.

In this study each child was asked to choose figures to represent everyone in his or her foster family, including the child. This was used to explore the developing relationships in foster families, and the re-search tasks monitored that boundaries were set as to who the figures may represent. Hence this is an adaptation of the measure for the purposes of the study.

Interestingly, it was the only psychological measure of children's perceptions of close relationships which was available at the time of planning the study. This posting exercise proved really popular with the children over time—even with the 13-year-olds! The younger children seemed to enjoy the posting activity. The test allows children choice as to the allocation of feelings. As an indirect way of ascertaining an aspect of the children's relationships with others, it can be much less threatening than the use of direct questions to a child about his or her new substitute carers.

Finally, the overall format of the interviews seemed important. At the beginning of the interviews it was crucial to establish rapport and relax the children as far as possible while also moving towards the focus of the interview. Similarly, at the end of the sessions, and particularly given the sensitive nature of the content, it was equally important to provide a relaxing activity before leaving the session. Painting and drawing were included at both times. At the beginning of the sessions the children were asked to paint/draw the houses where they lived with their new foster carers. As each child described the house and the people in the drawing, it naturally opened up the subject of the research in a less threatening way. The subject of the final painting session was the child's choice. Children chose to take the paintings with them or leave them with the researcher. If they left them, every effort was made to have them available for the next interview. Often they left at least one of the paintings and asked about or referred to them at subsequent interviews.

SUMMARY

In this chapter the United Nations Convention on the Rights of the Child and the introduction of the Children Act 1989 and the Children (NI) Order 1995 are considered to provide the rapidly changing context of the rights of children in the United Kingdom, their legal status and the recognition that they should be consulted on matters affecting their lives. Alongside these developments, sociologists have been examining their conceptions of childhood, and a sociology of childhood appears to be emerging. Social researchers are increasingly seeing children as subjects of research with the right to participate. The challenge for social researchers is how to involve children in research as active participants in a manner which respects their rights. The issues of consent and protection are particularly pertinent for further consideration. A study by the author which attempted to involve younger children has been used to illustrate some of the ethical and methodological issues discussed. Social research with children is moving into a new and exciting era. Legislative imperatives and fresh conceptions of childhood, combined with knowledge from practice, will hopefully give impetus to researchers to develop approaches which ensure the effective participation of children so that their voices may be more clearly heard through research.

REFERENCES

Aldgate, J. & Simmonds, J. (eds) (1988). *Direct Work with Children*. London: Batsford/ BAAF.

Alderson, P. (1995). *Listening to Children: Children, Ethics and Social Research*. Essex: Barnardo's.

Bainham, A. (1993). *Children: The Modern Law, Family Law*. London: Jordan Publishing Co.

Bene, E. & Anthony, E. J. (1957). *Manual for the Family Relations Test*. Bucks: NFER.

Buchanan, A., Wheal, A. & Coker, R. (1993). *Answering Back* (Dolphin Project). Southampton: Department of Social Work Studies, University of Southampton.

Curtis, P. (1983a). Involving children in the placement process. *Adoption and Fostering*, **7**, 45–47.

Curtis, P. (1983b). Communicating through play. *Adoption and Fostering*, **6**, 27–30.

DoH (1995). *Manual of Practice Standards for Guardians Ad Litem and Reporting Officers*. London: HMSO.

Fahlberg, V. (1981). *Helping Children when they Must Move*. London: BAAF.

Fahlberg, V. (1988). *Fitting the Pieces Together*. London: BAAF.

Fletcher, B. (1993). *Not Just a Name: The Views of Young People in Foster and Residential Care*. London: National Consumer Council/Who Cares? Trust.

Freeman, I., Morrison, A., Lockhard, F. & Swanson, M. (1996) Consulting service users: the news of young people. In M. Hill & J. Aldgate (eds) *Child Welfare Services: Developments in Law, Policy, Practice and Research*. London: Jessica Kingsley.

Geddis, D., Turner, I. & Eardley, J. (1977). Diagnostic value of a psychological test in cases of suspected child abuse. *Archives of Disease in Childhood*, **52**, 708–712.

Hill, M. (1997). Participatory research with children. *Child and Family Social Work*, **2**, 71–183.

Hill, M., Lambert, L. & Triseliotis, J. (1989). *Achieving Adoption with Love and Money*. London: National Children's Bureau.

Hill, M., Laybourn, A. & Borland, M. (1996). Engaging with primary aged children about their emotions and feelings: methodological considerations. *Children and Society*, **10**, 129–144.

Hill, P. (1985). The diagnostic interview with the individual child. In M. Rutter and L. Hersov (eds) *Child and Adolescent Psychiatry*. Oxford: Blackwell Scientific Publications.

Howard, S. (1996). Guardians Ad Litem and reporting officers. *Highlight*, **147**. NCB/Barnardo's.

Jaffe, E. (1977). Perception of family relationships by institutionalised and non-institutionalised dependent children. *Child Psychiatry and Human Development*, **8**, 81–83.

James, A. & Prout, A. (eds) (1990). *Constructing and Reconstructing Childhood*. London: Falmer Press.

James, A. & Prout, A. (1995). Hierarchy, boundary and agency: towards a theoretical perspective on childhood. *Sociological Studies of Children*, 77–99.

Jenks, C. (1996). *Childhood*. London: Routledge.

Jewett, C. (1984). *Helping Children Cope with Separation and Loss*. London: BAAF/Batsford.

King, P. & Young, I. (1992). *The Child as Client: A Handbook for Solicitors who Represent Children, Family Law*. Bristol: Jordan & Sons Ltd.

Lansdown, G. (1994). Children's rights. In B. Mayall (ed.) *Children's Childhoods: Observed and Experienced*. London: Falmer Press.

Lansdown, G. & Newell, P. (1994). *UK Agenda for Children*. London: Children's Rights Development Unit.

Liddle, C. (1992). *Acting for Children*. London: The Law Society.

Lockwood, B. & Frost, B. (1973). Studies of family relations test patterns: most mentioned family members and inter-sibling involvement. *Social Behaviour and Personality*, **1**, 2, 137–142.

Mahon, A., Glendinning C., Clarke, K. & Craig, G. (1996). Researching children: methods and ethics. *Children and Society*, **10**, 2, 145–154.

Mauthner, M. (1997). Methodological aspects of collecting data from children: lessons from three research projects. *Children and Society*, **11**, 16–28.

Mayall, B. (ed.) (1994). *Children's Childhoods: Observed and Experienced*. London: Falmer Press.

Morrow, V. & Richards, M. (1997). The ethics of social research with children: an overview. *Children and Society*, **10**, 90–105.

McAuley, C. (1996a). The role of the Guardian Ad Litem under the Children (NI) Order 1995. *Lay Panel Magazine*, **36**, September, 18–20.

McAuley, C. (1996b). *Taking Instructions from Children. Young Bar Association Lectures*. Belfast: SLS Publications, Faculty of Law, The Queen's University of Belfast.

McAuley, C. (1996c). *Children in Long Term Foster Care: Emotional and Social Development*. Aldershot: Avebury.

McAuley, C. (1996d). Children's perspectives on long term foster care. In M. Hill & J. Aldgate (eds) *Child Welfare Services: Developments in Law, Policy, Practice and Research*. London: Jessica Kingsley.

Qvortrup, J., Brady, M., Sgritta, G. & Wintersberger, H. (eds) (1994). *Childhood Matters*. Aldershot: Avebury.

Part, D. (1993). Fostering as seen by the carers' children. *Adoption and Fostering*, **17**, 26–31.

Roberts, J., Taylor, C., Dempster, H., Bonnar, S. & Smith, C. (1993). *Sexually Abused Children and their Families*. Edinburgh: Child and Family Trust.

Rowe, J. (1984). *Long Term Foster Care*. London: BAAF/Batsford.

Schwartz, E. (1970). The family romance fantasy in children adopted in infancy. *Child Welfare*, **49**, 386–391.

Sinclair, I. & Gibbs, I. (1996). *Quality of Care in Children's Homes*. Report to Department of Health. York: University of York.

Thom, M. & Macliver, C. (1986). *Bruce's Story*. London: The Children's Society.

Thorpe, R. (1974). The Social and Psychological Situation of the Long Term Foster Child with Regard to his Natural Parents. Unpublished Thesis. University of Nottingham.

Turner, I. (1977). *Pre-School Playgroups Research and Evaluation Project*. Report to the DHSS, NI. Belfast: The Queen's University of Belfast.

Turner, I. (1982). Pre-school children's perceptions of parental attitudes. *School Psychology International*, **3**, 137–142.

Turner, I. & Geddis, D. (1979). The psychology of family relationships: an aid to diagnosis. *Child Abuse and Neglect*, **3**, 899–901.

Weinstein, E. (1960). *The Self Image of the Foster Child*. London: Russell Sage Foundation.

9

DEVELOPING A STRATEGY FOR DISSEMINATING RESEARCH FINDINGS

Marina Monteith

Chapter Outline

INTRODUCTION

WHAT IS DISSEMINATION?

METHODS OF DISSEMINATION
- The Traditional Methods
- More Innovative Methods

THE TARGET AUDIENCE

PLANNING A STRATEGY FOR DISSEMINATION

SUMMARY

INTRODUCTION

This chapter presents the need for a dissemination strategy which raises the profile of dissemination activities in the role of researchers and in project planning. Dissemination is an essential part of the research project as without a successful dissemination strategy the results may lie unknown and unused for years. If the gap which exists between

---

Making Research Work: Promoting Child Care Policy and Practice
Edited by D. Iwaniec and J. Pinkerton
© 1998 John Wiley & Sons Ltd

research and practice is to be reduced, researchers need to take more responsibility for the active dissemination of their research and to consider how they might help improve the chances of their research findings being used. Traditionally this has been viewed as something that the researcher does at the end of the project to ensure that relevant people know about the research. The aim of any dissemination strategy should be to get the results known and used by those who are able to implement the findings. This chapter examines the role of dissemination in the research project's life cycle. It explores the meaning of dissemination and relevant theory on how individuals make use of new information being provided to them. The chapter begins by considering the nature of dissemination, then discusses various methods of dissemination, the importance of identifying target audiences, and the need to plan a dissemination strategy, and ends with a summary.

WHAT IS DISSEMINATION?

Applied researchers disseminate their research findings in an attempt to get the information used in decision making, in practice or in the formulation of policy. For research findings to be used, research must first be made available in an accessible format. Dissemination, however, is about more than merely making audiences aware of research findings, it is also about encouraging their use (Dunn et al., 1994; Richardson, Jackson & Sykes, 1990). The aim is not simply to 'get the word out, but to get the word used' (Westbrook & Boethel, 1997, p. 2). Research results need to be accessible and useful to key actors (e.g. service providers, policy makers, service users and advocates among others), otherwise research has little impact. The process of dissemination can be seen as the matching of information or knowledge to target audiences using a method appropriate to each audience. It requires an understanding of theory relating to the acquisition of new knowledge as this throws light on the problems associated with dissemination.

Getting research findings used is a complex process and barriers may exist within the target audience. These can include a lack of understanding of the research process, a lack of skill in using research findings, negative attitudes to research or to the researcher, and a lack of awareness about the topic. Westbrook and Boethel (1997) suggested a number of factors which may influence the use of information:

• Information users have individual needs depending on the level at which they might use the information and their own personal interest.

- Individuals are more likely to make use of research findings in practice if they understand what they mean for practice and how they might be implemented.
- Research users are more likely to accept information from researchers whom they view as credible and reliable sources.
- The process of using information is time-consuming and requires a supporting role from the researcher in facilitating debate and the exchange of ideas.

Dissemination activities need to be recognised as a key part of research, and have an appropriate allocation of time and resources. Dissemination of research findings is often unsuccessful because it is poorly planned and not thought through. This may be due to a lack of time or energy, uncertainty about the importance of findings, or difficulties explaining the complexities of the research results to an audience which demands simple answers (Fuller & Petch, 1995). The contract culture associated with academic researchers brings problems for dissemination too, as researchers often are moving on to a new project with a new contract of employment at a time when dissemination should be taking place. This, in effect, removes the person best able to disseminate the findings. The Research and Development Strategy of the Department of Health in England and Wales, the Scottish Office and the Department of Health and Social Services in Northern Ireland aims to overcome this and other problems associated with one-off contract research projects by core funding research centres over longer periods and not just for the life of one project (see fuller discussion of this in Chapter 1). This approach by funders enables research planning to incorporate a dissemination strategy which can be implemented for each project. Research sponsors now want to see that the research findings are effectively disseminated and that policy makers and service providers are making use of them. Research which is not read and used is not good value for money. Many sponsors, including government bodies, charities and others, commit time and resources to dissemination when commissioning research.

The traditional approach to dissemination is that a research report is produced, followed by a book and a few articles in academic or professional journals. The researcher may also give a presentation at a few seminars or a paper at a conference. This approach of producing the findings, and having them peer reviewed, is very much geared towards the academic world. It relies on the expectation that those interested in the research will have the time and the inclination to read research reports and journals. However, for the busy practitioner research may have a much lower priority, and time allocated to reading research papers may be very limited. Therefore, researchers have to move away from the more traditional approach of dissemination and try to find methods which are suitable to audiences other than academics. There is a lack of a tradition among child care practitioners in undertaking research themselves (Bullock & Little, 1995) and researchers need to take account of this lack of research culture when considering ways of disseminating information. The next section discusses more fully the different methods of dissemination. The links between research, policy and practice are by no means simple or straightforward. The child care field is very diverse with different professions, perspectives, agendas and needs. The relationship between producing research findings and getting them used in policy making and in practice is not clear and linear (this relationship is discussed in more detail in Chapter 2). Researchers need to consider how individuals approach the information being disseminated, how they process it, and the context in which it is being provided.

The process of how people acquire knowledge and make sense of it is important to an understanding of how research findings are dealt with by individuals. Adult learning theory can be helpful in understanding how research findings are used. Dissemination is a developmental process—research findings are produced, audiences targeted and a level of awareness developed with the ultimate aim of having findings used. Adult learning theory focuses on the individual, in an empowerment model where individuals have control over their own learning. In the same way it must be recognised that individuals have control over whether or not they explore research findings and make use of them. Adults often need to have a reason to acquire new knowledge—for example, a difficulty in current practice, dissatisfaction expressed by service users, implementing new legislation, or career advancement. Researchers need to understand that those using research can be motivated by a number of reasons. What is important is that, once motivated, adults will participate actively in the learning experience.

Adults do not receive new information in a vacuum, but rather come with a range of life and work experiences. Those designing training programmes try to build on the knowledge which people already have and attempt to build links between new knowledge and previous experiences. Researchers can similarly become familiar with the background of target audiences and the context in which they are disseminating information. Research findings can then be linked to previous knowledge of the topic and discussed in the light of existing experiences. In this way meaningful discussion with child care practitioners can take place. Individuals targeted for dissemination will make sense of the information given based on their own environment, existing knowledge, beliefs and personal experiences. People with similar backgrounds can thus be grouped together to comprise a target audience. Any new information given to individuals will be interpreted by them in the light of their existing mental models or constructions of knowledge (Westbrook & Boethel, 1997). Child care practitioners may use research in highly selective ways. In order to consider new material, old ideas or theories may need to be discarded. Therefore, in dissemination exercises researchers should consider the need to discuss current thinking in relation to the topic. Merely providing information will not necessarily mean a shift in thinking or behaviour unless the practitioners were already dissatisfied with current practice. If this is not the case, dissemination activity may need to facilitate discussion and reflection on current practice and consideration of what the research findings mean in terms of that practice. A simple list of policy and practice implications may not be sufficient to stimulate the use of the research findings.

Kolb (1984, 1995) proposes an individual experiential learning theory for adults which provides a very useful model (see Figure 8). This theory can aid understanding about how individuals make sense of new information. Kolb recognised that individuals have different learning styles and that the learning process is about providing a learning environment where people can use their own preferred method of learning. He felt that individuals need to be able to get involved in new experiences and be able to reflect on these experiences. From these

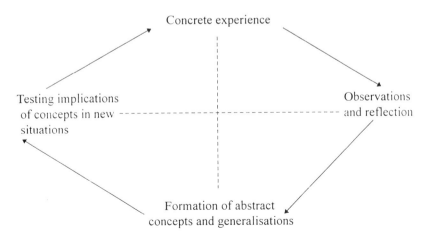

Figure 8:   Kolb's individual experiental learning theory

general observations the person is able to conceptualise the new experience in the light of existing experience. These new concepts can then be used to make decisions and solve problems. Kolb suggested that those involved in learning needed very different skills which express two sets of polar opposites (active and reflective, abstract and concrete) that come into play at different stages of the learning process.

Applying the individual experiential learning theory to the dissemination of research findings, the researcher can start to understand the stages that each person may go through when assimilating research information and attempting to apply it in practice. Different audiences will have varying degrees of concrete experience in the research area which the researcher will have to consider in planning dissemination activities (this is covered in more detail in a later section). For example, an experienced practitioner may come to a dissemination seminar with many years of experience in the child care field and may have particular issues which are currently pertinent. If his or her experience and current practice issues are relevant to the area of research, the dissemination seminar will enable the practitioner to reflect on his or her current practice in light of the research findings. Discussions with the researcher and other members of the audience may enable the practitioner to define a particular problem in his or her practice and establish possible alternative actions. The practitioner can then make decisions about a possible course of action in the light of the knowledge gained from research and commit time and energy to a revised or new method of working.

Researchers hope that the practitioners coming to the seminar will accept their findings and use them to improve or change their practice. However, the process of gaining knowledge and using it indicates that the practitioners must be able to reflect on research findings in the light of existing experiences and then work through identifying problems specific to their own situations and make decisions about the action to take. This process requires many different skills from the practitioners, including the ability to reflect and theorise, and the ability to plan and make decisions. Researchers, in planning a research dissemination activity, need to be aware of what the activity aims to do and the demands this will make on the audience. Is it solely an initial information-giving session where the researchers wish to make an audience aware of their work? Do the researchers hope that some of the participants will go away from the session and actually make some decisions based on the research? If it is the latter (which could be a follow-up to the former session), then the researchers need to facilitate the audience's learning by providing an environment in which they can consider, reflect upon and discuss the research findings in the light of pre-existing knowledge, experience, and beliefs. Adult learning theory suggests that to improve research use the researchers need to focus on the individuals or groups being targeted by the dissemination activities, and the contexts in which they operate.

In addition to considering the actual user of research, those involved in dissemination activities need also to consider the medium or method used, the content of the message being transmitted (i.e. the research findings) and the source from which the message originates (Westbrook & Boethel, 1997). Methods of dissemination and target audiences are discussed further in later sections. Westbrook and Boethel (1997) indicate a number of factors related to the dissemination source (i.e. the researcher) which can influence the use of research:

- the researcher's credibility;
- the researcher's relationship with potential users of research;
- differences between the researcher's values and assumptions and those of potential research users; and
- the perceived expertise and reliability of the researcher.

Considering the content of the information being disseminated, Edwards (1991, p. 61) states that empirical studies have 'found no relationship between research quality and use'. Westbrook and Boethel (1997), however, believe that research which is firmly grounded in the world of practice is more likely to be used. The process of disseminating research findings should take the user from awareness to knowledge and understanding and then to a commitment to use in actual practice or policy formulation.

To summarise, dissemination is more than simply distributing a report or writing a paper. It is a process where a number of dissemination activities are chosen to match the needs, experiences, values and existing knowledge of target audiences with the aim of getting research used in policy making and in practice. Dissemination should encourage reflection and thought about research and enable potential research users to assimilate this new information with existing knowledge and experiences. Researchers need to consider not only the research information they wish to impart but also their own credibility and relationships with potential users, as well as various methods of dissemination and the actual target audiences themselves. The next section examines the various methods of dissemination which can be employed by the researcher.

METHODS OF DISSEMINATION

There are numerous approaches which researchers can adopt to disseminate their research findings, ranging from the traditional approaches, such as the written report, to more innovative approaches, including the use of World Wide Web pages on the Internet. Methods can include both written and oral communication.

The Traditional Methods

The written report is probably the most traditional method of communicating the research findings of a project. The usual format, commonly found in academic reports, includes an introduction, a literature review, the methodology, the findings, discussion of the findings and the conclusions and/or recommendations drawn from them. A person conducting his or her research as part of an academic award will have to adhere to this type of format. Outside of academic research, the formal research report often departs from this traditional format; for example, most funders are only interested in the methodology for quality assurance purposes to ensure that the study's rigour is confirmed. Therefore, the methodology is often found in the appendices with a short, clear summary of the method provided in the introduction. In addition, executive summaries are usually included at the beginning of the report to provide easy access to the key findings as well as clear sign-posting to the rest of the report. Irrespective of the report format chosen, the key issue is clarity.

Producing the final research report can be a daunting task and many useful guides (e.g. Preece, 1994; Jay, 1995; Sussams, 1991; Wolcott, 1990) are available on the subject. Some useful tips (although by no means exhaustive!) include:

- Give careful consideration to the structure of the report prior to any writing.
- Divide the task into meaningful blocks and work systematically through them (this may be proposed chapters or sections of chapters). Do not feel that everything has to be completed at once.
- Plan a writing schedule incorporating these blocks allowing time for redrafting and putting the whole report together.
- Start writing as soon as possible; the purpose and rationale of the study and the review of previous research can be written up before or during data collection.

- Plan a writing schedule allowing time for redrafting.
- Write in a style which comes naturally. Do not try to force a more 'academic' style.
- Avoid jargon and technical terms.
- Make decisions about which findings are to be included in the report. Avoid the temptation to provide detailed analyses of every question asked.
- Consider the ordering of material. Do not be restricted by the format of the research instruments (questionnaires, interview schedules, aide memoires).
- Consider how material is going to be presented, in text, tables or figures. (Graphs, diagrams, simple tables, quotations and text-boxes can be used to highlight key points.)
- Detailed tables can be placed in the appendices with key tables or graphs in the main body of text.
- Avoid the overuse of quotations; use them only to illustrate key points.
- Avoid the temptation to choose quotations that seem to get the most attention as this may be misleading in terms of the actual research findings.
- Provide meaningful summaries which can be used independently of the main report and which give helpful sign-posting to the report's main sections.
- Finally, give some thought to, and get a second opinion on, the final overall 'look' and presentation of the report. Consider investing some resources in getting the report professionally printed.

Although producing the research report is a time-consuming task and includes a great deal of information, it is not always the most successful method of having research findings translated into practice. Often reports are bulky, wordy, extremely long, and time consuming to read. The average practitioner is unlikely to have the time or, indeed, the inclination to digest all the information provided in this type of report. The report, on which the researcher has usually spent many weeks, is often relegated to a bookshelf, unread. The significance of the report is that it is proof to the research funders that the research has indeed been carried out, and that the appropriate amount of resources have been applied to the task. However, in terms of actually getting the research findings used in practice, the task of dissemination has just begun!

The report provides a useful goal for the researcher to reach in terms of analysing and shifting through the wealth of material collected by the research project. Once the main research report is complete, the real dissemination work of the researcher can begin. The researcher can attempt to overcome some of the problems associated with large detailed reports by producing well-written, succinct summary reports and/or producing a series of short reports based on particular topics within the research report. These are more likely to attract readership than very long, detailed and complex reports, and can be distributed at seminars or other dissemination events.

Another traditional mode of dissemination using written communications is the research article. Producing papers for journal articles is particularly important for academic researchers, as this is linked to university research assessment procedures and also brings personal kudos in the academic world. Journals will have their own regulations and conventions which have to be strictly adhered to. These include format, layout, and length as well as the type of research which is accepted by the journal. However, journals have a relatively small readership, which is often limited to the academic world. It is important to know the journal readership if you are aiming to target a particular group. Some of the more journalistic type magazines like *Community Care, Nursery World* and *Professional Social Work* have a wider circulation among the child care profession. There can also be considerable time delay between writing a journal article and finally having it appear in an issue of a journal. Other modes of written communication which can be used for the dissemination of research findings include books, textbooks, and management briefing papers circulated within organisations.

In addition to the written communication of research findings, another traditional approach to dissemination is the oral presentation. This provides an opportunity for two-way communication where the researcher can answer questions and discuss findings with policy makers, service managers and child care practitioners. Types of oral presentations include conferences, seminars, meetings and training sessions. The researcher can make use of a wide variety of aids to help with the presentation, including overheads, slides and slide shows via computer (e.g. using software such as Microsoft PowerPoint). The researcher should select aids carefully and only use them to highlight key points. Visual aids should be clear, of good quality and easy to read. The advances in technology has rendered the hand-written overheads obsolete, and audiences now expect high-quality visual aids. Preparation of visual aids is just as important to the overall impact as the oral presentation prepared.

Oral presentations can also be enhanced by the provision of handouts, or, if a summary report or briefing paper has been produced, these may be given out to those attending. It is important to consider the size of the audience, as this may influence the type of presentation. With a smaller audience a more interactive approach can be taken with much discussion and debate about the research findings. With larger groups, for example a conference which may have a hundred or more participants, a more formal presentation is necessary and question time limited to a few minutes at the end of the presentation or at the end of a session including several presentations.

Apart from oral presentations, the poster display is another traditional mode of dissemination, mainly found at academic conferences. Poster displays use a mix of written and oral communications. The poster summarises the study visually, and the researcher is on hand to answer questions and discuss the research findings.

This review of traditional modes of dissemination has indicated a number of opportunities for disseminating research findings, including research reports, summary reports, journal articles, oral presentations and poster displays. However, there are also an interesting number of more innovative methods coming to the fore which can be used for dissemination purposes. These are outlined briefly below.

More Innovative Methods

One of the greatest advances in communication of recent years has been the Internet, providing world-wide access to masses of information via a computer network. Many researchers are now developing World Wide Web pages on the Internet which provide information about their research projects and give access to summary reports and shorter papers. The experience of the Centre for Child Care Research (CCCR) at The Queen's University of Belfast—as a new venture—found it essential to develop pages which provide information on the work of CCCR, its researchers and the research projects. Summary reports can be accessed by the international research community via these pages (and can be read on screen, printed or downloaded) and information is provided about publications which can be obtained directly from the CCCR. A wealth of information is available via the Internet, and there are many useful sites—too many to mention here. Some are specifically focused on the dissemination of child care research. For example, Childwatch International, in co-operation with UNICEF and UNESCO, provide a database via the World Wide Web recording research and information on children's rights, particularly in relation to the United Nations Convention on the Rights of the Child.

The Joseph Rowntree Foundation Web Site now provides access to their research summaries (called Findings), press releases and publication lists.

Research findings can also be disseminated using the media. The Economic and Social Research Council produce a very useful guide to dealing with the media (ESRC, 1993). It is important that the researchers are clear about what information they wish to make known and who their audiences are when working with the media. Some researchers avoid using the media due to difficulties in controlling how the material is used, but nonetheless the media can be a very powerful tool. If a radio or television broadcast is involved it is advisable to clarify expectations and the topics being covered. It is essential to prepare properly for such occasions, and to remember that television involves both visual and oral communications. If researchers have access to a public relations office within their organisation, it should be approached for advice and guidance.

Other innovative methods include the use of video-tape, audio-tape, Braille, agency newsletters, local and national press items, and summary sheets to help disseminate research findings. For example, Save the Children Fund (SCF) produced a 30-minute video about leaving care based on research conducted by young people (SCF, 1995). The video was targeted at youth workers, managers, decision makers and training colleges who were interested in leaving care issues and the views of young people. The cost of producing a good-quality video may be prohibitive, often making it a less viable option. However, there may be opportunities for sponsorship—the SCF video was sponsored by NatWest. Some researchers have worked with practitioners to develop checklists or guidelines based on their research findings, and in this way the researchers and practitioners are working together and using research findings to improve practice. For example, as part of the dissemination of research on leaving care (Pinkerton & McCrea, 1996), the Centre for Child Care Research is working with the Voice of Young People In Care Ltd (VOYPIC) to produce an easy to use 'A–Z of Leaving Care'. This aims to combine research findings and recommendations with the lived experience of care leavers to produce a guide which is attractive to young people.

THE TARGET AUDIENCE

The previous section outlined a number of methods of dissemination including both written and oral communications. Before selecting an appropriate mode of dissemination, or indeed a number of modes, it is important to consider the target audience. Some methods of dissemination are more suitable to certain audiences than to others. It is essential, therefore, to consider who the researcher is writing for.

- Is the researcher writing for other researchers, social work practitioners, other child care practitioners, academics, policy makers or service managers?
- Are members of the public, or community groups or parents groups likely to be interested in the research?
- How much do the various audiences know already about the research topic?
- What issues are they interested in?

The researcher needs to find out who the potential users of the research are and which methods of dissemination are preferred by different groups.

A research project may have several potential audiences and it is necessary to consider each of them. The research may be of relevance to practitioners if the intention is to either confirm or change current practices. It may also be of interest to policy makers and to both voluntary and statutory child care agencies. The mode of communication should be chosen carefully and matched to each target audience. For example, the research funders may require a detailed research report at various stages of the research project. However, the interim and final reports of the project may be of little use to the busy practitioner or service manager. Well-written, meaningful summaries are essential tools for use with this type of audience.

Researchers must consider the level of knowledge which a particular audience will have about the subject area and make decisions about the complexity of the information to be provided. Individuals will view the research findings in the light of their existing knowledge and experiences and try to make sense of it within that context. Therefore, researchers need to become familiar with their audiences and make decisions in terms of the medium used to provide information (e.g. reports, seminars, papers, discussion, Braille, audio-tape), the language to be used and the level of technical detail. Westbrook and Boethel (1997) suggest that the best way to get to know target audiences is to involve representatives from various groups in the research project from the beginning and to maintain contact with them as the project progresses. If researchers are familiar with their target audiences, it will be much easier to orient the dissemination of findings to their needs and to provide the information in a way which makes the results easy to access and understand. Researchers who have gained insight about potential audiences can then make use of existing networks and resources through linking into these existing systems, such as training programmes or research seminars run by an agency.

In addition, given the 'oral culture' of social work indicated by Smith (1995), it may be more appropriate that research findings are disseminated to this group through seminars or in meetings where results can be discussed in terms of current practices. Obviously running several seminars with lesser numbers may be more costly, in both researcher time and resources, than providing a one-off large group seminar, but the pay-off in terms of getting research findings understood and debated will be much greater. Training courses (before and after qualification) are another method of dissemination which can be used to target practitioners. The researcher can contact agency training personnel about the possibility of using material from the research, or perhaps including a research slot given by the researcher in a training programme. As discussed earlier, the main mode of dissemination for the academic audience will be papers in academic peer-reviewed journals, papers at academic conferences and books. However, much research is of interest to a much wider field, including service users, community organisations and those who provide child care services. The researcher needs to assess possible methods of dissemination in the light of their appropriateness to the various groups who are interested in the research findings.

PLANNING A STRATEGY FOR DISSEMINATION

The previous sections outlined the nature of dissemination, the various methods of dissemination and the need to consider the types of audiences who may be targeted. This section will introduce the need for a strategy for dissemination and explain why this is important. As the researcher's time and resources are both limited, choices will have to be made in terms of how much dissemination activity will take place, who will be targeted and what methods will be used. Discussions about dissemination methods and potential audiences should begin at the outset of the project, when the project proposal is drawn up. It is essential that time and resources are built into the project timetable at an early stage. Time can be set aside at the end of the project and at interim stages, where appropriate, for the purpose of dissemination.

Adequate thought about future dissemination should be given at the preliminary stages of the project design. Where the researcher plans to release findings at the end of each stage of the project in addition to final reporting, time should be set aside for dissemination at these interim points as well as at the end of the project. If sufficient time is not provided in the timetable for dissemination, then any unplanned activity taking place at interim stages will have a detrimental effect on the next stage of the project, using up time originally scheduled for doing research. Where a project consists of several stages this effect can snowball, resulting in the project missing stage deadlines and eventually overall deadlines. It is therefore critical that careful thought is given to dissemination activities at an early stage and that these are included in the project timetable.

Planning for dissemination often does not take place and dissemination is only properly timetabled after the final or interim report has been produced. The process of informing people about the research project, seeking views and opinions regarding the project proposal, and keeping people informed about the project's progress can all be seen as preparation for the dissemination of research findings. From the start of the project through to its completion a network of interested parties will be established who are aware of the project's existence. The researcher should aim to sustain this awareness of the project by reminding those interested in the research (e.g. research advisory groups, contacts in child care service agencies, pressure groups, policy makers) that it is still ongoing. This can be done through discussions, meetings, interim reports and seminars. In this way the researcher can prepare the way for the eventual discussion of research findings and can also help identify potential audiences for the main dissemination activities. These dissemination activities can be planned at key stages of the project and should be outlined in the original project proposal and in project timetables.

As discussed earlier, a final report often helps the researcher make sense of the data and motivates the researcher to complete the necessary analyses. Although many sponsors require a detailed research report as a tangible product to justify the expense of the research, the time employed producing it is often not cost-effective in terms of its actual use. The production of such a report should be seen as only a part of dissemination and definitely not all things to all target audiences. It is rarely possible to meet the needs of all groups through one medium. Many researchers make the mistake of trying to include material of interest to all parties, academics, policy makers, service providers, and service users, in the one research report. An earlier section outlined the different methods of dissemination which could be used. The choice of method will depend on a combination of the audience being targeted, available resources and researcher time. It is important that researchers familiarise themselves with the audiences identified so that informed choices are made. Attention should be paid to the culture of the audience and to the context in which they work.

In summary, researchers need to consider dissemination at a very early stage in the project's life, and to plan activities carefully, taking into account priorities, resources and actual researcher time available (Fuller & Petch, 1995). It is important that researchers are realistic in planning dissemination activities by setting priorities and making choices. It is far too easy to be over-ambitious and attempt to produce the research findings in every possible medium covering all potential interest groups, no matter how diverse. Table 5 sets out a dissemination strategy for the 'Children and Young People with Disabilities in Northern Ireland' research project. This project has four parts completed over a three-year period, and has a number of potential audiences including policy makers, service providers, child care practitioners, service users, voluntary agencies and pressure groups, academics and other researchers. Child care practitioners to whom the research would be of interest include many different professions such as social workers, health visitors, district nurses, doctors and the various professions allied to medicine). As can be seen, the potential audience is extremely diverse. Choices were made about suitable methods of communication for each group and dissemination priorities were identified. Obviously much more dissemination work could be done in addition to that outlined, but this strategy was drawn up given the time frame of the project and the available resources.

As a final point on planning a dissemination strategy, researchers should take responsibility for its execution. In some cases the researchers complete the work and dissemination is carried out by the commissioner of the research, usually in the form of the research report and perhaps a summary paper targeted at the organisation's senior management. The researchers, however, are most familiar with the findings and should be involved in planning and co-ordinating the research dissemination. Researchers may judge that for some activities particular specialist skills are needed, for example, when making a video or incorporating material into training packs. Researchers should involve other professionals with relevant skills in these activities thus enhancing the dissemination product and hopefully increasing the likelihood of the research being used in practice. Those funding child care research should ensure that dissemination is written into the research contract when research is commissioned. Those responsible for commissioning research should not penalise researchers bidding for work who opt to spend more time on dissemination activities, but instead should ensure that an adequate dissemination strategy is a required part of the research bid.

Table 5: A dissemination strategy for a research project: Children and young people with disabilities in Northern Ireland

Project stage	Target audience	Method of dissemination	Timing
Part 1: Overview or service provision prior to the Children (NI) Order 1995	Sponsors (DHSS, Four Health and Social Service Boards and Queen's University of Belfast)	Interim research report and summary report	February 1997
	Academics and Researchers	Interim research report and summary report; seminar	February 1997 May 1997
	Policy Makers	Summary report and training sessions	February–April 1997
	Child Care Practitioners	Summary report seminars/training sessions	February–April 1997
Part 2: The Transition to Adulthood Study (Young People with Disabilities in Northern Ireland and their experiences, needs and aspirations as they move from childhood to adulthood)	Sponsors	Interim report and summary report	February 1998
	Policy makers	Summary report and seminars	March–April 1998
	Child Care Practitioners	Summary report, seminars and discussion groups/training sessions	March–April 1998
	Academics and Researchers	Interim and summary reports, papers in academic journals, conference papers	March 1998–September 1998 (although may appear at later dates in journals)
	Young People with Disabilities and parents/Carers	Informal summary sheet about the research findings (including braille and audio tape versions)	April 1998
Parts 3 and 4: Overview of service provision one year after implementation of the Children (NI) Order 1995 and comparison to Part 1	Sponsors	Interim report and summary report	February 1999
	Policy makers	Summary report and seminars	March–April 1999
	Child Care Practitioners	Summary report, seminars and discussion groups/training sessions	March–April 1999
	Academics and Researchers	Interim and summary reports, papers in academic journals, conference papers	March 1999–September 1999

SUMMARY

Dissemination is a vital component of a research project and as such should be included in project planning and resource allocation. Dissemination activities should be aimed at not only raising awareness of research but also at promoting discussion, debate and reflection about what these findings mean in terms of current policies and practice. This may mean adding to the more traditional methods of dissemination, such as the research report, academic journal articles and conference papers. These methods have their own place and importance, but other methods may have to be adopted to reach particular target audiences and to improve the likelihood that research findings are used in policy and practice. Researchers need to consider carefully the individuals or groups who may be interested in the research findings and match their audience with appropriate dissemination methods. Dissemination is an important and integral part of any research project. It is essential that time and resources are made available for dissemination activities and that these activities are included in the overall planning of the project.

Within child welfare the *raison d'être* for conducting research should be to get the findings used, whether this is to confirm existing practice or policies or to inform policy makers and practitioners about the need for changes. A dissemination strategy should be designed at an early stage in the project's life which commits time and resources to such dissemination activities, thus promoting the usefulness of the research being carried out.

REFERENCES

Bullock, R. & Little, M. (1995). Linking research and development: return home as experienced by separated children. In M. Colton, W. Hellinckx, P. Ghesquiere & M. Williams (eds) *The Art and Science of Child Care*. Aldershot: Arena.

Dunn, E., Norton, P., Stewart, M., Tudiver, F. & Bass, M. (1994). *Disseminating Research/Changing Practice. Research Methods for Primary Care*, Vol. 6. London: Sage.

ESRC (1993). *Pressing Home Your Findings: Media Guidelines for ESRC Researchers*. Swindon: Economic and Social Research Centre.

Edwards, L. (1991). *Using Knowledge and Technology to Improve the Quality of Life of People who have Disabilities: A Prosumer Approach*. Philadelphia: Pennsylvania College of Optometry.

Fuller, R. & Petch A. (1995). *Practitioner Research: The Reflexive Social Worker*. Oxford: OUP.

Jay, R. (1995). *How to Write Proposals and Reports That Get Results*. London: Pitman (for) The Institute of Management.

Kolb, D. A. (1984). *Experiential Learning: Experience as the Source of Learning and Development*. Englewood Cliffs, NJ: Prentice-Hall.

Kolb, D. A. (1995). *Organizational Behavior: An Experiential Approach* (6th edition). Englewood Cliffs, NJ: Prentice-Hall.

Pinkerton, J. & McCrea, R. (1996). *Meeting the Challenge? Young People Leaving the Care of Social Services and Training Schools in Northern Ireland*. Belfast: Centre for Child Care Research, Department of Social Work, The Queen's University of Relfast.

Preece, R. A. (1994). *Starting Research, An Introduction to Academic Research and Dissertation Writing*. London: Pinter Publishers.

Richardson, A., Jackson, C. & Sykes, W. (1990). *Taking Research Seriously: Means of Improving and Assessing the Use and Dissemination of Research*. London: HMSO.

SCF (1995). Does anybody care? Young people's research on leaving care. Video. London: Save the Children Fund.

Smith, J. (1995). *Social Workers as Users and Beneficiaries of Research*. Stirling: Social Work Research Centre.

Sussams, J. E. (1991). *How to Write Effective Reports* (2nd edition). Aldershot: Gower.

Westbrook, J. D. & Boethel, M. (1997). *The Dissemination and Utilization of Disability Research: The National Center for Dissemination of Disability Research Approach*. Internet: http://www.ncddr.org/du/ncddrapproach.html

Wolcott, H. F. (1990). *Writing Up Qualitative Research*. London: Sage.

III

PROMOTING AND SECURING A BASIS FOR RESEARCH

10

PREPARING A RESEARCH PROPOSAL FOR FUNDING PURPOSES

Patrick McCrystal

Chapter Outline

INTRODUCTION

WHAT IS A RESEARCH PROPOSAL?

THE APPLICATION PROCESS

THE RESEARCH PROPOSAL AS PART OF THE RESEARCH PROCESS

THE STEPS IN DEVELOPING A RESEARCH PROPOSAL

OUTLINE OF A RESEARCH PROPOSAL

DEVELOPING A POWERFUL PRESENTATION STYLE

HOW CAN YOU MAKE THE SPONSOR WANT TO SUPPORT THE PROPOSAL?

SOME DO'S AND DON'TS IN THE RESEARCH PROPOSAL PROCESS

SUMMARY

INTRODUCTION

The public assumes that a researcher spends the day dreaming up and trying out creative ideas. In recent times the onus has increasingly fallen on researchers not only to plan and implement their research but

---

Making Research Work: Promoting Child Care Policy and Practice
Edited by D. Iwaniec and J. Pinkerton
© 1998 John Wiley & Sons Ltd

also to obtain the necessary funding required to undertake it. In reality, research proposal development, the process for competing for such funds, is an invisible but critical barrier over which even a good researcher may tumble. A research proposal begins in one of two ways. One is an idea that a researcher wishes to develop and obtain funding in order to pursue it; the other is when a researcher responds to an 'invitation to tender' and develops an idea into a proposal to meet the requirements of the funding agency.

The most successful proposals usually start with an idea which begins the search for funding, rather than funding motivating the search for an idea. Rogers (1970) found a 40% success rate for those who had an idea they wanted to get funded in comparison with only 24% for those who thought up an idea when they became aware that funds were available. But while projects typically start with a good idea, sponsors fund activities, not ideas. Admirable intentions and good ideas are a great start, but sponsors are buying expertise and value for money, it is activities such as the contents of the research proposal that determine whether your project is an effective investment of their resources.

Obtaining research funding has never been easy. It can prove to be a very arduous and stressful task which, in many ways, becomes a job in itself. Today research institutions have individuals who specialise in this work, supported by others with specialist knowledge in the financial details. Academic careers are more dependent on research funding awards than previously. This has become increasingly important since the 1992 Education Act abolished the binary division in Higher Education and provided for a new, integrated method of funding for all universities. Teaching and research have become separately funded and accounted for.

The element of research grant to be made available to universities by the new Higher Education Funding Council (HEFC) will be determined by a formula in which the key variable will be a research rating obtained by each Unit of Assessment (roughly equivalent to a specialised academic field) in the Research Assessment Exercise (RAE) undertaken every four years (1992 and 1996 to date). In this way the HEFC assesses the quality of research outputs among universities in order to establish some principles for the distribution of recurrent grant which will differentiate levels of per capita funding according to the quality of achievements of particular subject groupings in particular universities. All institutions of Higher Education will be treated on the same basis, but differently, according to merit. All merits will be determined by the public record of research output, assessed by both volume and quality.

One important criterion by which merit is judged within the RAE is securing an increased income from external research contracts. These include the European Union (EU), Research and Development (R&D) programmes and the national Research Councils which are now administering large budgets following the transfer of money for 'basic' research (i.e. distinctively new thought and discovery in published form) from the University Funding Council to the Research Councils. For university departments and groups, the practical implication is to win money for research within the university's annual recurrent grant and to increase amounts and sources of external funding. This includes obtaining research funds awarded by the research councils and other private sources of funding for research. Others are largely the charitable trusts such as the Nuffield Foundation. Publications form another important category in the RAE. Research projects enable researchers to develop empirical papers for publication which are then included in the submission as part of the RAE.

As the competition for research funding creates ever-increasing resource demand, the costs associated with funding applications increases (Bolek et al., 1992). To be competitive in this environment, researchers and their institutions will have to develop strategies to improve the probability that research proposals are successful. As it can prove to be very daunting for those undertaking such a task for the first time, this chapter aims not only to ease the anxiety involved in this activity, but also to encourage researchers to be proactive and pursue financial support for research ideas that they may wish to pursue on their own behalf or on behalf of their institutions. An understanding of the role of the research proposal when competing for external funding is essential to be successful in this process. This chapter will describe the process involved in the production of a research proposal drawing on the experience of the Centre for Child Care Research (CCCR).

WHAT IS A RESEARCH PROPOSAL?

Any research application must address a range of issues. For the major grant-awarding bodies (in the UK this includes the Medical Research Council, the Economic and Social Research Council, Department of Health and Social Services and the bigger charitable trusts such as Joseph Rowntree and Leverhulme) these may be addressed by means of the detailed application form which has clear guidelines for submitting the proposal. The guidelines are crucial, and the applicant who fails to conform to them will quite simply not get past the first round.

The exact information sought by the different fund-awarding bodies varies, but a number of headings appear so consistently on the application forms that they are worth using to structure the outline of the research. Even if the applicant is applying to a body that does not have clearly specified application procedures, such headings are worth using in order to impose maximum structure and clarity on the application. Adequate and appropriate presentation of an idea into a detailed research proposal is a skill that can be learned.

> The research proposal is your opportunity to persuade the 'client' that you know what you are talking about. That you have thought through the issues involved and are going to deliver. That it is worthwhile to take the risk and give you licence to get on with it. (Robson, 1995, p. 465)

A research proposal describes a plan of work to learn something of actual or potential significance about an area of interest. It opens up the topic of the proposed research and explains exactly how the research will be carried out—spelling out in precise detail the resources, both personnel and equipment, that the researcher requires for carrying out the research. Its opening problem statement draws the reader into the plan; showing its significance, describing how it builds upon previous work (both substantially and methodologically), and outlining the investigation. The whole plan of action flows from the problem statement: the activities described in the method section, their sequence in the proposed work plan, their feasibility, shown by the availability of the resources in terms of personnel and facilities, and their economic efficiency demonstrated by the costings for the research. It should be a logical presentation with nothing left to speculation; all questions and issues that may arise should be anticipated. This can be helped by asking a colleague to read the proposal and give an objective opinion of it. Any unresolved matter may be seen as a weakness in the proposal and lead to its rejection.

The description of a research proposal makes it clear that the proposal is an integrated chain of reasoning that makes strong logical connections for what is being proposed. Simply, it is a document that represents the case for an idea and details of the steps the researcher proposes to take in order to pursue it. In some ways it can be thought of as a sales document, as it has some of the aspects of such trade. Such an analogy is not so extreme as the financial details, for example, in such a document play a role in the professional life of the researcher who is considering undertaking the research. It is assumed that in a sales document the proposer knows best, and the task of the proposal is to bring the reader around to that way of thinking.

The proposal is a further opportunity for the researcher to present an idea and proposed actions for consideration in a shared decision-making situation between himself or herself and the funding agency, while remembering that the funding agency holds the balance of power in this situation. The proposal is helping the sponsor to see how you view the situation, how the idea fills a need, how it builds on what has been done before, how it will proceed, how pitfalls will be avoided, what the consequences of the research are likely to be, and what significance this will have.

THE APPLICATION PROCESS

It is increasingly common practice for researchers pursuing financial support for their research to participate in an application procedure, in some ways similar to job applications. This can include an advertisement inviting tenders, followed by the submission of the proposal, sometimes on a preconstructed application form. Agencies/researchers will be short-listed from these applications and invited to present their proposal to a panel of experts/reviewers, whose task is to assess the proposal and ask questions on the finer details of the submission before a final decision is made on funding arrangements. In common with applying for a job, researchers can benefit from developing a basic understanding of the rules and expectations governing this process and become knowledgeable about the funding agency to which they are applying. To this end a few hours with funding documents may prove highly profitable. Having identified the appropriate funding agency—possibly from sources such as Fitzherbert, Forrester and Grau (1997) and Brown and Casson (1997)—and the approach for the proposed research, the researchers should now begin to develop the proposal based on the funding agency's requirements/guidelines. It is an obvious part of the professional approach advocated here that any specific rubric suggested by the funding agency should be strictly adhered to. Despite this 'guided' application process, many of the features of the proposal are common to all submissions whether they are speculative applications to charitable trusts or are within the more controlled process of those advertised in the press or academic/ professional journals.

Whatever the source of research funding, an application involves a series of discrete processes. Firstly, upon submission of the proposal the funding agency will check that the proposal matches the formal requirements and funding policies of that body (length of application, total amount of money requested, duration of grant, etc.). Secondly, the application will usually go to referees who will concern themselves with the quality of the science, the adequacy of the case made for the amount of money requested, and the practicalities of the application such as: Is it possible to complete the research in the time proposed?

THE RESEARCH PROPOSAL AS PART OF THE RESEARCH PROCESS

There is a temptation to think of writing the research proposal as merely an irksome formality, a hurdle that has to be jumped before you can get on with the real work of research. Approached like this, it is likely to produce an unconvincing piece of work which will most likely get rejected by the funding agency. It is perhaps more appropriate to view a research proposal as an important and integral part of the research process. An essential component of effective research is the role of planning and organisation of the work to be pursued. It can be very beneficial to the researcher to think of the research proposal as an effective method of planning and organising the proceeding research. This will enable the researcher to gain an overview of what lies ahead and how it will be undertaken; it will also provide the researcher with a plan and timescale in which the research will be tackled—a tool to which he or she can refer when the research is ongoing. This additional role of the research proposal will become clearer as this chapter unfolds.

The proposal is not only a valuable method for organising the research to be undertaken but it can also become the contract between researcher and funder. It is also important to be clear about the funding body's rights and obligations: e.g. can they exert any control over the research process or the publication of findings? It is worth while clarifying the respective roles and responsibilities of each party in the agreement in order to specify respective roles and responsibilities of funder and researcher.

The research proposal as a planning tool is an integral part of project development within the Centre for Child Care Research core research programme. Research proposals are developed for undertaking the core research programme by the research staff for new research programmes which are then submitted to the Strategy and Policy Group who assess the feasibility of the research within the remit and resources of the CCCR. This enables CCCR researchers to develop a research project assessed and supported by parties with a vested interest specifically in the research itself before the project begins.

However, in contrast to the above competitive process it is an attempt to persuade experienced judges that what you are proposing looks interesting and feasible and is within the constraints of resources and time that you have suggested. For many, this process can be the main purpose of the proposal. Such researchers may find they are the ones who have most to lose if the research is a failure. When a funding agency offers its support for a research proposal they are in effect endorsing it because they believe it will be of value to them. In doing so they are expressing confidence in the researchers and their ability.

A useful analogy has been made by several writers between researchers and architects (e.g. Hakim, 1987; Leedy, 1989) where planning is the main link. The architect plans buildings, the researcher draws up plans to investigate issues and solve problems. In each case these plans must say something about structure, about how the task is conceptualised, and about methods to be used in carrying out the plans. For both the researcher and the architect, it is insufficient simply to present the concept of the problem and its suggested mode of solution (tower block or houses; survey or experiment). Factors such as the resources needed to carry out the work, the qualifications and experience of those involved, previous work that has already been carried out by the applicant and others, computer facilities, and the acquisition of any necessary permissions and clearances are all very important. These issues will be discussed in greater detail when outlining the content of a research proposal. It is advisable for researchers to lay out the proposal for inspection and comment by colleagues to get their objective views.

THE STEPS IN DEVELOPING
A RESEARCH PROPOSAL

How do you go about begunning the process? This is essentially the pre-proposal stage, and is particularly problematic for researchers who are producing a proposal for the first time or for those with limited experience. The researcher knows what is expected of him or her in terms of the final outcome—i.e. documenting the completion of a piece of research in advance of its commencement once it is known what needs to be done.

A proposal is often written with one specific funding agency in mind, but this can usually be amended if it is necessary to approach another agency due to a refusal of support in the first instance. It is essential for the researcher to develop a proposal that will address issues of specific interest to the potential sponsor, which means that the researcher must be familiar with the work of the agency he or she will approach for support, in addition to meeting their criteria to be considered for support. This requires a degree of flexibility by the researcher as he or she develops the research idea into a project design that can accommodate his or her own ambitions within the context of the work of the funding agency. When undertaking this, it is essential to spend time thinking through the development of the research. In practice the time spent on this task is sometimes curtailed by the looming submission deadline, as is the whole process of producing the research proposal.

OUTLINE OF A RESEARCH PROPOSAL

While proposals may differ widely, most will include the following sections or some variation on them.

Title Page
Contents
Summary
Background to the Research
Research Objectives
Research Method
Timescale for the Research
Management of the Research
Research Outputs
Costings
References
Appendices

These sections have been included here as they describe the model followed by the CCCR in proposals developed within the Centre.

The outline is the centrepiece of any proposal and its importance cannot be overemphasised. Equally, the researchers should not overlook the value of presentational aspects to a successful research proposal.

Title Page

This is the first piece of the proposal seen by those not associated with its production. The information required here are the proposer (re-

	Research Proposal
Proposer:	Centre for Child Care Research
Client:	Joseph Rowntree Foundation
Proposal:	Evaluating Research Proposals
Duration of Project:	9 months
Date:	July 1998
Contact:	Mr Patrick McCrystal (01232) 335401

Figure 9: Example of a cover page

searcher submitting the proposal), the client (funding agency), the proposal (title of the proposed research), the duration of the project, the date of submission of the project and the contact (the principal researcher). Figure 9 presents an example of a cover page. The most important detail here is the research title upon which the proposal is then structured to meet the requirements.

Contents

A necessary piece for any document. This lays out the order and therefore the structure and organisation of the proposal. This gives a clear structure to the details of the document. A well laid out contents page enhances the overall presentation of the proposal, making clear what is included, as well as adding structure and order to the whole document. In addition, this enables readers to go directly to the aspects of the proposal that may be of particular interest to the funding body, e.g. methodology. When the research is being conducted this will enhance the value of the proposal as a reference document for the researcher carrying out the project. Figure 10 presents an example of a contents page.

Summary

This is written after the proposal is completed, but is the first section read by those who are considering the merits of the proposal. It should be brief, clear, informative and written with extreme care, remembering that it is the first section to be read. It is, in some cases, the only part of the proposal that is read. Information contained within the summary should include:

• what is being proposed;
• why the research is needed;

Contents	
	Page
Summary	
Background to the Research	1
Research Objectives	5
Research Method	6
Timescale for the Project	19
Management of the Research	22
Research Outputs	23
Costings	24
References	25
Appendices	26

Figure 10: Example of a contents page

- how it will be done;
- why it should be of interest to the funding agency;
- what the intended outcomes will be.

Background to the Research

The opening statement should draw the reader into the proposed re-search. This will restate the purpose of the research and set it within its practical and theoretical context by explaining the background and current thinking in the field. It will include a short review of relevant work done by others. You will want to show that there is a gap to be filled, or a next step to be taken, or a concern arising—and that you have a good idea on how this should be addressed. This will show that you are familiar with related developments and are not attempting something which is outdated by other research. State clearly the importance of the research and its relevance. The aim is to lead the reader towards the conclusion you have reached: why this work needs to be done, and the way it will be conducted.

Research Objectives

This section will state the general themes of the research before going on to specify what the research proposes to do. The language here needs to be explicit and concise, precise objectives may be stated in bullet point form listing the objectives in order of importance. At this stage the proposal has set the scene and clearly stated what the research intends to do. The proposed research is beginning to take its own identity and points to previous work in this area. The objectives should translate into the method which will be used to carry out the research. The next section of the proposal sets out in clear terms how the research objectives will be achieved.

Research Method

This is the most important part of the proposed research for several reasons. In this section you go into precise details describing the methods and procedures to be used to achieve the research objectives. It demonstrates that you know how to undertake research. It is considered equally important that the researcher specifies what he or she will do for the funding agencies, specifying what they are getting for their money. For the funding agencies there is too much of their money, time, and effort invested in an approved project for them to rush into it without a clearly defined research design. Nothing is a substitute for explicitly setting both problem and procedures into context (Leedy, 1989). The procedures for undertaking the research must be clearly written into the proposal. Where possible avoid any jargon and explain research terminology which is used; the researchers must not assume that those who will read the research proposal are familiar with the research procedures to be adopted for the research. However, sufficient specialist terminology may be required in order to demonstrate technical know-how, research ability and experience. A number of subheadings expanded upon will help structure this section and clarify its presentation for the reader. When considering each of these elements individually, it must be kept in mind that all of the components of a research project are inextricably linked to one another and should be viewed both in isolation and within the overall framework of the research design. While this may vary from proposal to proposal, in general the following subheadings may clarify this section:

- *Research design and structure.* This describes the approach to the proposed research to be taken including whether this will be quantitative or qualitative, or both, and the kind of samples to be used.
- *Review of the literature.* This states the purpose of the review and its value to the research.
- *Development and application of questionnaire-interview protocol design.* This describes how the data collection instruments will be developed and their application to the research.
- *Samples.* This describes how these will be selected, including their size and justification for their selection procedure.

- *Data collection.* This describes how this will be managed and carried out. The data gathered will determine the types of analysis used.
- *Data analysis.* The kinds of statistical analysis, or other analysis that is appropriate, will be dictated by the data collected which will then determine the kinds of conclusions and implications that might emanate from the research.

It is important to note that this section is not a discussion on research methodologies but a clear demonstration of the researcher's ability to apply appropriate methods to the specific research being proposed.

Timescale for the Research

This is one of the most important parts of the proposal, particularly from the funding agency's perspective as it serves to demonstrate how long the research will take, justifying each stage and showing when the funding will stop. In addition to showing your ability and required experience to plan and organise a research project, you are presenting your deadline. With this in mind, it is important to work out a realistic timescale for the research, one that takes into consideration any potential difficulties. This is particularly relevant when deciding how much time each report, especially the final report, will require. Included in this section will be details of the sequence, and length of time each stage of the research will take to complete. Figure 11 presents an example of how the timescale should be written into the proposal.

Timescale

Outlined below is the timescale for a research project lasting eight months

Timescale	Description of Work
Month 1	Review of the literature
Months 1–3	Develop and pilot questinnaires Develop sampling frame
Months 4–5	Postal questinnaire Interview survey Focus groups
Month 6	Analysis of information collected
Months 7–8	Report writing

Figure 11: Example of a timescale

Management of the Research

The location where the research will be based and its suitability (e.g. university department), facilities, personnel and their experience are specified here, along with any staff that may have to be recruited. This section will also enable the researcher to show how much time he or she will devote to the actual research or what relevant links will be made with other institutions or personnel which may benefit the research. An association with other successful projects and prominent research institutions can impress funding agencies. This section will also include recommendations on the types and nature of communication, where appropriate, between the research sponsors and the research team. This might include the timing and frequency of meetings between both parties to inform the sponsors of progress being made.

It must be remembered that it is not only the idea and action plan that are subject to consideration but also your capacity to carry them through successfully. This is particularly true if the researcher has no previous record of success, or if such success is not known to the reviewer. The proposal is the only evidence the reviewer has of capabilities. Realising this is half the battle; the other half is presenting the researcher adequately and appropriately. The presentation displays ability to assemble the foregoing materials into an internally consistent chain of reasoning. It must be tailored to fit the timescale proposed to facilitate the review process.

Research Outputs

The specific outputs of the proposed research are detailed here. This includes any interim reports and all documents produced as a result of the research, including all proposed dissemination such as seminars, conference papers and publications emanating from the research, such as papers in academic journals. Figure 12 presents an example of a research outputs section.

Costings

This section is of particular interest to the funding agency. There are several points to bear in mind when costing your research. Firstly, if there is a limit to funding available then you must remain within this limit without adversely affecting the quality of the proposed research. Secondly, you must justify all proposed costs. While there may be a tendency to be conservative in your costing of a research project due to financial restrictions or competition from other researchers, the best

---

Research outputs

The following outputs are proposed for the research.

- An interim report will be produced for the research funder after three months of the project. This will report on the findings of the research to this stage.
- A final report will outline the findings when the research is completed.
- The research will be disseminated through a half-day seminar, conference papers and refereed publications produced for academic journals during, and at the completion of, the research.

Figure 12:   Example of research outputs

advice is to be realistic. Research is, by definition, problematic and unforeseen circumstances inevitably tend to increase costs. Cutting corners and skimping when calculating the cost of the research may slightly increase your chances of winning the funding you require (though not necessarily; experienced assessors might regard it as an indication of a lack of professionalism) but it will almost certainly decrease your chances of delivering satisfactorily on time. If you do not have the time or resources to complete the project as envisaged, the situation can be sometimes rescued by 'trading down' to a different design (see Hakim, 1987). All aspects of the research must be considered before this section is complete.

Items to be included in your costings for the project are:

- research and non-research personnel; the desired level of experience required including future salary increases or changes in personnel, salaries of all staff including employee national insurance contributions and, where appropriate, pension contributions;
- equipment, all computer hardware and software, office supplies, tapes, etc.;
- travel costs incurred when carrying out the research, such as driving to interview locations;
- consumables, which includes the costs of, for example, telephone calls, a questionnaire survey and all postage involved in such a survey;
- overheads: in the case of researchers applying from a university, there is often a 40% levy placed on the final cost at which you arrive.

The above list is not exhaustive but gives an idea of the items that need to be costed.

Do not underestimate costs in the hope of enhancing your chances of winning support from the funding agency. Remember, if successful, the researcher must assume responsibility not only for conducting the research but also for the financial management of the project. Funding agencies are familiar with research costs and may conclude that you are badly prepared and/or that you will try to approach them later for the shortfall if this section is not completed accurately. Advice on the costings of a research project can be sought from an appropriate person within your own organisation. For example, most universities have an appointed person with responsibility for calculating such costs. This is a particularly useful resource for researchers with limited experience in costing research projects. Alternatively, discussing the costings with a more experienced researcher may help overcome any difficulties in this section. At this point it is worth noting that the first-time proposer may be advised to consider applying for support for smaller projects and building up a track record before seeking support for relatively large and complex research projects. A final point to note here is to ensure an overall level of consistency throughout the proposal, including the costings. There must be a match between the proposed research and the costings required to undertake it. For example, if you propose to interview 100 child care professionals as part of a study into changing attitudes and practices as a result of new legislation, the costings should include the resources necessary for no more or no less than this number. It is also useful to mention in this subsection that the cost of the research includes the right of the researcher to publish the findings of the project.

There are two aspects of timing that are crucial when costing the research. The first is the total amount of time for which the grant will be held, and the second is the amount of time that the applicant will be able to devote specifically to the project. Obviously the longer the project, the more expensive it is, and so referees are particularly careful to scrutinise the justification for the length of time involved. If applicants are requesting funding for three years, but have not made a good case for this length of time, then referees are likely to advise that the research will simply not be funded, or that funding be awarded for a two-year rather than a three-year period. Referees will also be interested to know how much time the applicant will be able to devote specifically to the actual research, or to the supervision of researchers employed on the award. Figure 13 presents an example of how a costings page should look within the proposal.

References

All references cited in the text should be listed in this section in the same way as you would in reports and publications.

Costing	
(One research assistant and administrative support)	
Description of Work	*(£)*
Research Assistant Grade 1B (9 months)	12,650
Travel and Subsistence	500
Consumables (i.e. postal questionnaire survey)	500
Administrative Support (Grade 3)	1,221
University Overheads @ 40% (where applicable)	7,300
Total	**22,171**

Figure 13:   Example of a costings page

Appendices

This section is included in order to enable the researcher to present details which may not sit neatly in the main text. This includes information such as curriculum vitaes of the researchers and other significant personnel who may be involved in the research or information relating to the researcher's own organisation.

DEVELOPING A POWERFUL PRESENTATION STYLE

The importance of good writing skills when developing the research proposal should not be underestimated. Too often, good research proposals go unfunded because the language of the proposal failed to convince the funding agency of the significance and feasibility of the proposed work. Moreover, sometimes the language gets in the way, resulting in an unclear, imprecise, or incorrect document. Good writing is brief; it is an investment that will pay dividends (Ogden & Goldberg, 1995). If the intended audience for the research proposal reachs the conclusion that not enough care and skill went into the writing and editing process they could take the view that equally poor work might be presented in the project itself. With this in mind it is advisable to be aware that the proposal, when being assessed, may be read by individuals from varying backgrounds who, accordingly, will bring different biases and beliefs, based on their work experiences and responsibilities. The writing style and organisation of the proposal become increasingly important.

Organisation of Information

The organisation of information contained in a research proposal is crucial to its success. Moreover, ideas and facts pertaining to original research usually have to be arranged for clarity and effect before being written into a proposal. One way to begin this task of arrangement is to order the gathered material to meet the reader's needs and expectations. By developing a research proposal according to this organisational scheme, the resulting document will not only appear to build on prior work, but convey a more compelling argument in support of the proposed research. Once an organisational pattern is established, the researchers can then develop the outline.

Writing Style

Proposal writing is a fine balance. The researcher should describe the study in detail so the sponsor is convinced that the problem is worth investigating and that the writer has the ability to handle it. The secret to success is to find the appropriate balance between providing details and leaving issues open to interpretation by the reader. The balance shifts towards detail as the content of the project is clarified to the reader. The researcher should address several questions here:

• Is the organisation of the sections effective and conducive to understanding?
• Is there a sufficient amount of detail within each section?
• Is the material contained in the grant application unified and coherent?

Once these structural issues are attended to, the research proposal must then be evaluated and revised for readability and correctness. If the prose is not conducive to understanding, or if the researcher consistently fails to accede to language conventions, then the effectiveness of the proposal can be undermined. Good 'writing style' within a proposal generally means readability and correctness. A readable proposal contains active verbs, is very concise, and includes language that is clear and precise. If a research proposal is 'correct' linguistically, then the conventions of language such as punctuation, grammar, mechanisms, spelling and usage have been given careful attention. This will improve the general presentation of the research proposal which may ultimately play a role in its succeess.

Does the Proposal Flow Logically from Section to Section?

The title of the research proposal should be chosen so that the project objectives flow from it and seem both important and desirable. The statement of objectives and the method for the research should move beyond the review of the past research, showing how it will add to accomplishments, remedy past failure and so forth. The objectives should translate into research questions, or models to be tested. These, in turn, will suggest the sample and the rest of the research design. The data gathered will determine the kinds of analysis, statistical or other, that is appropriate; and this will determine the kinds of conclusions and implications that will flow from the study. All research studies presenting the case for a generalisation are chains of reasoning.

HOW CAN YOU MAKE THE SPONSOR WANT TO SUPPORT THE PROPOSAL?

As noted earlier—although it may not seem like it when you go hat in hand as an applicant seeking funds—sponsors are as dependent on you as you are on them. If you are a trained child care practitioner for example, you will be in a strong position to know the strengths of your project; therefore, you are in the best position to demonstrate creatively how your project relates to the sponsor's goals. The following are issues which, if addressed, may improve the chances of success for your proposal.

- If the research proposal addresses a problem of concern to the funding agency and you are likely to be able to contribute to the solution, this is the most obvious approach to take.
- You may be able to reach an audience that the funder might not otherwise contact.
- Your project may have important side-effects such as: supporting an organisation that the agency wants to support; pleasing someone in a key position who has been critical of the programme; or gathering additional data on a particular issue, treatment, or research method of interest.
- Your project may have implications of personal interest to particular members of the staff, or to the agency because of past projects supported, or to a particular member of a foundation's board of trustees. (Such implications can be worked into the flow of the

materials so they make logical sense, letting the targeted member discover the material for himself or herself.)

- Because of personnel available to you, you may be able to do the project more competently than others. This may include the help of a prestigious senior researcher whose work would be a credit to the agency. Point out that the agency will get the benefit of such a person's research skills as he or she consults with you or otherwise provides assistance.
- Perhaps you have access to special equipment that gives you an advantage. It need not belong to your own institution; you need only give evidence of your access to it.
- If your institution is willing to partially subsidise your project, this will multiply the power of the sponsor's funds.
- There may be special public relations value in supporting your project. This might result from: a conference, symposium, or publication that is a part of your project; the involvement of a national organisation; or your special relationship with a professional organisation.

This is not an exhaustive list but makes the point that there are many possibilities. You must think of all issues and build them naturally and logically into the proposal so that the funding agency discovers them and draws the conclusion you intend. This requires the researcher to use judgement on how to best incorporate these details into the proposal; they are rarely the basic reasons for funding research but often serve to enhance the overall presentation.

SOME DO'S AND DON'TS IN THE RESEARCH PROPOSAL PROCESS

In attempting to bring together the suggestions for developing a research proposal for submission to a funding agency made in this chapter a number of *do's* and *don'ts* best illustrate the process succinctly.

- DO ask members of your department to show you copies of previously successful applications so that you can get a feel for the required styles and level of detail. When writing the case for support of the research, DO make it clear why the research should be done.
- DO think of a sensible title for your research, and spend some extra time working on the 'short' sections such as 'aims' or 'summary'. It

is these short parts which may help determine the choice of referees for your project, and often these short sections that are copied across to inform other committees and research councils of the range of projects being funded. Create the best, and clearest expression within each of the sections, rather than relying on the support or demystification of an appendix.

- DO begin your case for support with a paragraph or so, introducing the topic which will be comprehensible to academics of *any* discipline. Spell out clearly what you plan to do. A research proposal will be considered weak if it introduces a topic well, but then says little other than 'so we are going to investigate this' instead of substantive details.

- DO mention pilot work that you have conducted, past studies using similar methods, to demonstrate that this methodology can deliver the required results. DON'T assume those assessing your proposal will be familiar with your published past research. If you are relatively inexperienced in research, and cannot demonstrate your own past success with these techniques, consider applying for a small grant in the first instance.

- DON'T under budget in time and money. You will not get credit for offering to carry out 200 interviews in two weeks—you will give the impression of inexperience and poor planning. If assessors think you cannot deliver what was promised in the time, or with the resources requested, they will not risk their funds, however small the sums requested. DON'T over-budget. Travel money and particular conference expenses, for example, need to be justified.

- DO ask experienced researchers within your department to read through your application. Even if they are not familiar with your research area, they may be able to spot ambiguities in your application. Unlike journal articles, where referees routinely request revisions, fund-awarding agencies rarely invite you to improve an application—there are usually too many favourable applications already competing. Take every precaution to ensure that your case is as good as possible first time round. For the same reason, DON'T forget to check very carefully the form and the supporting case for typographical, spelling or numerical errors before you submit it. If an application is sloppy it will create a poor impression of the researchers' attention to detail.

- If your application is unsuccessful, DO make use of whatever feedback is available or obtainable to plan your future course of action. It is unlikely that you will be allowed simply to resubmit the same application again to the same or a different council, but you may be allowed to resubmit a revised application.

SUMMARY

To be competitive in today's research environment, researchers need to develop new strategies to improve the probability that research proposals are approved and funding awarded. Successful researchers report that scientific knowledge is only one element of the funding process. Additional expertise is required to meet the challenges of increased competition and decreased availability of research funds. Understanding the process, including research reviews, strengthening the language of the proposal, presenting well-justified budgets, as well as presenting a compelling scientific argument are all requisite research development skills. Finally, several important points to remember when assessing the merits of your own proposal are that a good proposal is direct and straightforward; it communicates well; and is well organised.

REFERENCES

Bolek, C. S., Bielawski, L., Niemcryk, S., Needle, R. & Baker, S. (1992). Developing a Competitive Research Proposal. *Drugs and Society*, **6**, 1–22.

Brown, P. & Casson, D. (1997). *A Guide to the Major Trusts*, Vol. 2: *A Further 700 Trusts*. London: Directory of Social Change.

CCCR (1996). *Annual Report 1995/96*. Belfast: Centre for Child Care Research, The Queen's University of Belfast.

Fitzherbert, L., Forrester, S. & Grau, J. (1997). *A Guide to the Major Trusts*, Vol. 1: *The Top 300 Trusts*. London: Directory of Social Change.

Hakim, C. (1987). *Research Design, Strategies and Choices in the Design of Social Research*. London: Unwin Hyman.

Leedy, P. D. (1989). *Practical Research. Planning and Design*. New York: Macmillan Publishing Co.

Ogden, T. E. & Goldberg, I. A. (1995). *Research Proposals. A Guide to Success*. New York: Raven Press.

Robson, C. (1995). *Real World Research. A Resource for Social Scientists and Practitioner-Researchers*. Oxford: Blackwell.

Rogers, T. F. (1970). *Small Grant Projects of the Regional Research Program: Final Report*. New York: Bureau of Applied Social Research, Columbia University. (CRIC Document No. ED 0504 074).

11

COMMISSIONING RESEARCH

Marina Monteith

Chapter Outline

INTRODUCTION

DECIDING TO COMMISSION A RESEARCH PROJECT

RECRUITING THE RESEARCH SUPPLIER

- Open Competition
- Closed Competition
- Informal Competition
- Formal Competition
- The Assessment Process

MONITORING THE CONTRACT

THE RESEARCH BUYER–SUPPLIER RELATIONSHIP

SUMMARY

INTRODUCTION

In the current market-testing and competitive-tendering climate of the public sector, researchers and child care managers have become involved in the process of buying research. Researchers or child care practitioners with a research remit find that their job can involve not only doing in-house research, but also managing and co-ordinating research projects where expertise may be bought in for all or part of the project.

Making Research Work: Promoting Child Care Policy and Practice
Edited by D. Iwaniec and J. Pinkerton
© 1998 John Wiley & Sons Ltd

Research is said to be commissioned when applications are made by researchers in response to an invitation from an organisation or an advertisement about a competition being held. Usually this involves a particular project or a number of projects. The organisation concerned will have identified their research needs, the particular areas of interest and perhaps gone some way towards defining the research questions to be investigated. This approach is different to responsive funding where research ideas originate with the researcher who then seeks funding to carry out the research. Government departments, such as the Department of Health (see Chapter 1), fund both commissioned research and responsive research while the large charitable funding bodies (see Chapter 12) such as the Joseph Rowntree Foundation tend to be responsive funders. Government funders with large research budgets usually have well-established mechanisms in place for commissioning research. This chapter is aimed at those researchers and child care practitioners in health trusts (and health and social services trusts in Northern Ireland), local authorities, voluntary organisations and the community sector who may sometimes have to commission research but who may not have the benefit of experience built up through extensive research funding over many years.

The advantages of commissioned research are that it allows organisations to buy in particular expertise when required and enables those who do not have research resources in-house to conduct research of interest to them without the expense of setting up an in-house facility. Some of the pitfalls involved are that a lack of clarity between those commissioning research and those supplying research can result in poor quality research. Lack of experience can also lead to inappropriate suppliers being chosen. In addition, if methods of selection are not carefully considered the selling skills of suppliers may influence buyers more than their research skills. These issues will be explored further throughout the chapter.

Topics discussed here include making the decision to commission research, the recruitment of the research supplier, including types of competitions and the assessment process, monitoring the research contract, and the relationship between the in-house researcher or research buyer and the external consultant or supplier.

DECIDING TO COMMISSION A RESEARCH PROJECT

The first step for any research buyer is to consider the actual project involved. He or she will have to be clear about what is being commissioned in order to provide sufficient information to research suppliers to enable them to cost the project and to ensure that the project being commissioned and ultimately delivered is the one that was required. The buyer will have to identify the research area, the aims and objectives of the study, and the research questions. Other members of the buyer's organisation may need to be consulted to clarify research needs and the project boundaries. The potential budget for the project will also have to be agreed as decisions about the size and scope of the project can only be made in accordance with available resources.

The buyer will have to make decisions about the extent to which he or she wishes to involve external researchers, and for what part of the project. Many buyers commission whole research projects, including research design, fieldwork, data capture, data analysis, reporting and dissemination. Alternatively, for other projects only part of the research project may be purchased—for example, fieldwork and data capture. The buyer will have to consider, firstly, in-house capacity and expertise and then decide whether all or part of the research project will be bought externally. The availability of particular expertise outside the organisation will also influence the decision about what exactly will be commissioned. The buyer will need to consider the potential market for the research project and the likelihood of available expertise. Once the remit of the project has been decided, its associated budget has been agreed, a judgement has been made about capacity of any in-house researchers and the external market considered, the decision should be made about what is to be commissioned. A project specification or brief (discussed further in a later section) can then be written providing details of the background to the research, its aims and objectives, the research questions posed, the expected outputs and information about the requirements for submitting a proposal. A project specification tends to be used in formal tendering and the research supplier submits a tender document in response. Problem-based project briefs specify a format for the structure of proposals and the key issues to be addressed as this makes comparison across project proposals much easier at the assessment stage.

Expected contents may include the proposed methodology, knowledge of the area, expertise and experience of staff, management arrangements, timetabling and pricing information (see Chapter 10 on the issue of how to write a project proposal). It is important that the buyer outlines key information which he or she requires as part of the assessment process so that this is provided within the proposals being submitted. The project brief would also address publication issues, provide information about the expected payment schedule, the proposed timetable and anticipated available funding. It should also give contact details for anyone who wishes to discuss the project further.

Available funding can be identified either as a maximum sum available to a project, or as a range within which bids are expected to fall. Those outside this range can be disregarded as either above what could be afforded or of insufficient quality to fulfil the requirements of the project. Once the project brief has been drawn up, the next step is to identify and recruit a supplier for the research.

RECRUITING THE RESEARCH SUPPLIER

Most research suppliers are recruited through a competition of some sort where researchers or research organisations are invited to tender for a project. They submit a project proposal which includes a total cost and the buyer then makes a decision between the potential suppliers. It is possible to recruit a researcher or research organisation without a competition, but the buyer would need to have a good knowledge of their skills, experience, and track record, as well as being familiar with the research market and current charges. This type of knowledge can be built up through experience of working with various suppliers and gaining knowledge of costings. If the research buyer is less experienced, he or she can try to contact others who commission research and exchange information about buying research. Some research projects require a particular competence or expertise and there may be an obvious choice for the project. In these circumstances there is no need to have a competition. In other cases, the timetable of the project or reasons of continuity (e.g. a further stage in a project) may entail going directly to a particular researcher.

For the majority of projects, however, buyers will hold a competition for a research project. The reasons are that this identifies a range of expertise, enabling new researchers to be included in the pool of potential suppliers, as well as keeping existing suppliers from becoming complacent and ensuring that research costs are competitive. A competition to recruit researchers or research organisations may be open or closed. An open competition is advertised and any researcher may apply. In a closed competition only a limited number of researchers are invited to enter.

Open Competition

This type of competition is open to all and enables a wide selection of researchers and organisations to come forward. In practice, however, it is very difficult to deal with, as the buyer could have many applications and spend a great deal of time evaluating each proposal, thereby increasing the overall cost of the project. The Social Research Association (1994) suggests that good researchers may also be put off by this type of competition which attracts so many other research bids and has a limited chance of success. One of the main arguments for open competition is that it enables new researchers or organisations to apply. In addition, a 1993 EC directive requires open forms of competition for government contracts worth ECU 200,000 or more. This means that research buyers working in the public sector need to advertise projects of this value throughout the European Union. This may mean a more complex commissioning process with the potential for researchers from other countries bidding for the work.

If open competition is adopted, there are two potential ways of limiting the amount of time and expense involved. One method is to advertise the research project and ask those interested to complete an Expression of Interest, outlining briefly their experience and expertise, knowledge of the subject area, key people who would be working on the project, and how they would approach the project. These Expressions of Interest can then be used to shortlist a much smaller number of researchers or organisations who will then be asked to submit full proposals as part of a tender process. There is another method of limiting time-consuming selection activities which is appropriate to larger research buyers. An organisation which commissions research on a regular basis can periodically advertise for inclusion in a Select List of Research Suppliers. The buyers can outline their research interests or forthcoming programme over a particular period and ask researchers to outline briefly their skills, expertise and experience as well as the particular projects and/or types of work they would be interested in undertaking. Those applying can then be included in the Select List if they have the necessary credentials. The Select List can be used for shortlisting potential suppliers for a particular project who are then invited to bid. Both these approaches have the advantage of ensuring that newer researchers are included in the competition but in a way which minimises labour-intensive recruitment activity. The key point is that the length of both Expressions of Interest and Select List applications are kept short with a very specific format and that these are used to aid shortlisting. Only a limited number of detailed proposals should be invited.

Closed Competition

Closed competition involves a small number of known researchers or research organisations who are invited to submit a proposal for a project. This is a much more efficient and cost-effective method of recruitment as many buyers invite between three and six research suppliers to make a bid. Another advantage is that a buyer can build up knowledge about a small number of suppliers and establish relationships with them. The Social Research Association (1994) point out that buyers often include larger numbers on the invitation list in anticipation that some will not submit proposals. Too short a list may mean not enough returned proposals to ensure a competition, but too long a list means a lot more time-consuming work. One solution is to give advance notice of the forthcoming invitation, asking researchers to inform the buyer by a certain date if they do not intend to submit a proposal. This allows time to issue further invitations to other researchers if necessary.

The Social Research Association (1994) estimated that it could cost a researcher between £1,000 and £5,000 at 1994 prices to complete a detailed, fully costed proposal depending on the size and nature of the particular project. Using a mid-range value of £3,000 they calculated that inviting four researchers to submit full proposals would use £12,000 of research resources compared to £30,000 if ten people were invited. Research buyers need to be aware of these costs as ultimately they will be footing this bill. The cost of completing unsuccessful proposals will be re-absorbed into the cost margins of project bids. Those commissioning research should be aware of the expense involved in running a competition. If the research project is quite small and has a budget of a few thousand, it would perhaps be better to consider a more informal type of competition, or perhaps investigate potential research suppliers and approach a single researcher or organisation. Few researchers would consider investing the time and energy involved in a more formal competition for such small gains.

There are limitations to the closed competition involving a small number of research suppliers in that other research expertise can be overlooked and access for newer researchers is non-existent. Also, the regulations of some organisations may mean that research buyers are required to conduct an open competition. If this is the case, then it is best to invite Expressions of Interest for a particular project, or applications for inclusion on a Select List. As discussed earlier, this can be used to shortlist and invite a limited number of researchers to submit detailed proposals. It is good practice to avoid asking for full proposals from candidates until shortlisting is complete, and to be aware of the likely costs of the competition procedures both to those commissioning research and to research suppliers.

Informal Competition

Where a competition is run informally, buyers do not require suppliers to complete detailed proposals in a required format in response to their specification of the research requirements. Instead they may identify a number of potential suppliers either already known to them or by informal investigations of the research market. This will include their experience, areas of expertise and likely costing structures. Discussions about the project may be conducted with a number of suppliers, including their capacity to carry it out, possible ideas about the research and some idea of likely costs.

If an informal approach to research buying is used, it is important that meetings with suppliers include those who will actually be responsible for conducting the research, in addition to the research managers. This will enable the buyer to get a better picture of how the research is likely to be carried out. The number of research suppliers invited for interview will depend on the size of the project and the buyer's knowledge of the market. It is better to keep the numbers small, perhaps four or five, and if the project is small this may be limited further. Inexperienced research buyers may wish to conduct informal interviews with more than five suppliers to become more familiar with the research market. However, where more suppliers are approached the initial interviews should not be too time-consuming, and should be used to help identify a smaller number of organisations, perhaps two or three, who are interested in the research for a further informal interview.

The informal competition is particularly relevant for projects with budgets of a few thousand pounds where the cost of a more formal competition would be prohibitive. However, those commissioning research for public sector organisations may find that their internal regulations and procedures prohibit this type of competition. Where an informal competition is allowed, there are still concerns about public accountability and the ability to portray fairness. The Social Research Association (1994) suggest that this can be overcome by documenting contacts with various researchers to show that competition has taken place and to justify decisions.

Formal Competition

A much more formal approach to buying research is the tendering process, and this is usually the method used by public sector organisations as it is part of their wider purchasing mechanisms and protocols.

The Social Research Association (1994) found it helpful to distinguish between strict tendering, modified tendering and problem-based tendering. Strict tendering requires sealed bids to be made for a pre-specified project. With this approach the buyer needs to draw up a very detailed specification of what is required and suppliers are asked to cost this specification and provide such details by a set time in a sealed envelope which is then stamped with the date and time of return. All tenders are opened after the formal closing date and time for the bids. No further bids can then be accepted. This type of strict tendering requires the buyer to keep suppliers at arm's length, with limited opportunities for discussion of ideas as each supplier needs to be operating on the same level. With strict tendering the contract is usually awarded to the cheapest tender, provided that they meet the minimum criteria specified for the project and can indicate that they are able to complete the work satisfactorily.

Strict tendering is an extremely rigid method of competition which originated from the purchasing of products which can be specified to a particular standard, with little expected variation. The suitability of this method to buying research is questionable. The need for the buyer to provide a very detailed specification which suppliers will then cost means that there is no room for exploring various methods of conducting the research. The nature of strict tendering means that the buyer will have to make decisions about the methodology to be used, and complete much of the research design. Suppliers will then cost this predetermined process and will have minimal involvement in research design. This approach is only suitable if the buyer has the capacity in-house to carry out design work and wants to control the method being used. This approach is sometimes adopted by government research departments conducting survey research using a standardised interview schedule.

The lack of involvement of research suppliers in the design process can be a loss in that fresh ideas and the consideration of alternative approaches may be overlooked. Some buyers attempt to get round this by asking suppliers to suggest an alternative method to the one specified and provide costings for both. This increases the workload for the supplier making a bid and will only be seen as a worthwhile task for larger lucrative projects. In addition, this approach has comparability problems which strict tendering procedures have difficulty coping with. It is more likely that alternative approaches will be judged using the standardised format agreed for the main submissions, and not on their own merit. It is likely, therefore, that the original methods identified in the project specification will be followed and any alternative would need to be very impressive to compete.

Strict tendering is definitely not an approach suitable to inexperienced buyers with limited knowledge of the research process. The need
to tightly specify requirements is best done by an experienced researcher. The limitations placed on free discussions with researchers by
the strict tendering process can make it difficult for the researcher to
obtain a full understanding of the project. This is often only achieved
through ongoing dialogue, which is not usually encouraged under
strict tendering conditions. The reason why some organisations purchase research through strict tendering is that it is imposed by their
purchasing systems or departments in the interests of fairness, equity
and objectivity. However, there are other approaches to tendering
which are less rigid and which fit the research process better. Strict
tendering should only be used where a project is able to be specified to
a high degree and where all the design work is carried out in-house.
This type of tendering is often found where an organisation has an in-
house researcher or research team who contract out part of the research
project, rather than all of it from conception and design through to
reporting and dissemination.

Modified tendering is similar to strict tendering, but some degree of
flexibility and scope for informal discussions with researchers are built
in. Strict tendering is rarely rigidly applied without some modification.
The main departure is that of encouraging dialogue with researchers to
improve the quality of research bids. This enables researchers to discuss the buyers' needs in-depth prior to submitting tenders. Nevertheless, it is still a formal tendering approach and as such tends to limit the
amount of discussion around research design. The design is likely to
have been specified in the project brief, which is also used as the focus
of pre-tender discussions.

The problem-based brief is an alternative to the tightly specified
project brief used in formal tendering. In this case, the project brief
includes details of the project background, aims and objectives and the
likely research questions or problem to be investigated. The research
design is not specified and researchers are invited to make recommendations about an appropriate methodology and submit a fully worked
proposal outlining their approach, including costings. This approach
produces much diversity, as different researchers have different skills,
resources and preferences for particular approaches. The buyer will
then have to make decisions about which proposal best suits the
project, quality issues and value for money. They will have to draw on
their knowledge of research prices and any prior experience of working
with research suppliers to help choose between various proposals.
Buyers can ask suppliers to provide details of particular projects completed previously and to identify other customers who can be ap-

proached about their performance. It is important that the buyer has gained insight into the 'going rate' for particular types of research so that judgements can be made about value for money to enable comparisons across projects. Value for money is not only about keeping prices down but also about ensuring the quality and ultimate use of the research. Research quality should not be sacrificed in the interest of costs. It is better that resources are used to complete a smaller research project to a good standard than to fund a larger, poorly designed and inadequate research project where the findings are of dubious value.

When making decisions about which type of competition to run it is important to keep focused on research needs and in-house capacity. Even with strict tendering, it is important that where possible suppliers are given an opportunity to comment on the specified design of the project and are able to make minor adaptations if necessary. Formal tendering should only be used where the buyer has an in-house capacity to carry out detailed research specifications and design work. If the buyer has to commission all stages of the project, including research design, the problem-based brief is the more suitable approach. Whether formal tendering is used or a problem-based brief is adopted, it is important that some flexibility is built into the process allowing dialogue with research buyers as this will facilitate better understanding of the project.

Where a research project has several stages, or has a pilot or feasibility study, a decision will have to be made about whether one competition should be run for the whole project or whether competitions should be run at different stages. Commissioning a supplier for a major long-running project has risks in that the buyer may not be satisfied with the quality of the work half way through the contract. Commissioning at various stages is time-consuming but does give the buyer a chance to assess performance at earlier stages before making a fuller commitment. The buyer needs to weigh up the potential costs of running several competitions against the hazards of commissioning one researcher for the duration of the project. The buyer's knowledge of the research market and prior experience of working with certain suppliers will influence this decision. It is good practice for research buyers to build up such experience about research costs and the capacity of different suppliers.

The Assessment Process

Where a formal competition takes place—whether open or closed, involving tenders or the submissions of proposals—some form of assessment is needed. This usually this involves a selection panel which evaluates the tenders or proposals using a set of predetermined criteria. It is important that the selection panel includes experienced researchers, as well as those with a vested interest in the research area. Some panels include an external referee in order to ensure peer review. Such a referee should be chosen carefully and not be in competition with those who have submitted tenders or proposals on this occasion. More objectivity may be obtained by selecting an external referee from a different geographical location, who is less likely to be regularly in competition with the current applicants. Obviously, those on the selection panel are not allowed to submit proposals themselves. The selection panel can be involved at both shortlisting stages and at the final assessment. Shortlisting can involve consideration of the Select List or Expressions of Interest prior to inviting formal tenders or full proposals. It can also be used to select a smaller number of proposals (usually three) for final assessment where a larger number of proposals have been invited. The final assessment process can involve an interview with those who have submitted tenders or proposals. The interview is likely to be limited to clarifying particular points if it is a tender process, whereas the remit is much wider with a problem-based approach where a proposal is invited. The interview can involve both clarification and further elaboration and discussion of particular aspects of the submission.

The selection panel, in their final assessment, will consider:

- the relevance of the proposal to the areas identified;
- the analysis of previous studies and literature;
- understanding of the aims and research questions;
- the quality of the proposed research, including appropriate project design, sampling methodology, measurement and analysis;
- adequate quality control mechanisms;
- value for money;
- the ability to generalise from findings;
- the expected benefits;
- the use of resources, including staffing, other costs and timetabling;
- project management arrangements; and
- prior experience in the area of the research.

The criteria will be similar for the formal tendering process, although many of the design features will be predetermined. This means that quality issues will be limited to the researcher's capacity to fulfil the requirements, and value for money will be determined from cost-efficiency. Cost comparisons form an easier part of the assessment process, but more subjective judgements have to be made in terms of research quality, the ability to design questionnaires, interviewing skills, analytical ability, integrity, reliability and the ability to deliver to time and budget.

The selection panel will make a final judgement and will select the successful candidate adhering to such criteria as set out above. Many panels use a scoring system similar to that used in the recruitment of staff, in which each criterion is allocated a number of points. This is helpful as it allows proposals to be more easily compared across a number of dimensions. If this type of selection tool is used, careful thought should be given to the weightings allocated to different criteria. A poorly designed scoring system, like poorly designed research, will be of little help to the selection process, and may overlook important insights which can be gained by a less quantifiable approach. Where proposals have been submitted, the decision to select a particular supplier can be made either unconditionally or with the agreement that certain amendments are made to the original proposal. Candidates should be informed of the outcome of the assessment process in writing. Once the decision is made to award a contract, this can be discussed with the successful applicant and final arrangements made regarding timetabling and any required amendments. After agreement has been reached, a contract can be drawn up and signed by both parties. Most organisations have legal advisers who can help research buyers with the contract details, but if this is not the case it may be worth seeking some formal legal advice at this stage. In most cases, the project specification or brief plus the submitted tender or refined proposal are attached to the contract and referred to in the contract. The contract should also indicate any monitoring mechanisms to be put in place by the buyer, as well as an agreed payment plan. It should identify the project leader on the supplier side and a key contact on the buyer side, both of whom will be responsible for overseeing the project. Once the contract has been signed the research work can begin.

MONITORING THE CONTRACT

The commissioning process does not end with the award of the project. The research buyer must keep in contact with the researcher and monitor progress. This is particularly important with large-scale projects where unexpected problems may occur causing some setbacks. These can be dealt with jointly by the funder and researcher so that appropriate action can be taken to resolve the issues or problems emerging. It is

in the interest of both parties that any hurdles are negotiated successfully. Regular contact is essential, where the researcher can update the
research buyer about progress and discuss any problems. Such policy
enables the researcher to develop a relationship with the client and the
continued dialogue will enable better decisions to be made during the
research.

A Steering Group, which meets regularly with the research supplier
to discuss progress, is often set up for the research project. It is essential
that the overall responsibilities and the remit of the Steering Group are
made clear when the contract is awarded. The Steering Group is usually responsible for ensuring that the research complies with the research proposal, that ethical issues have been considered and that
appropriate procedures are followed. The Steering Group may also
advise on research instruments for data collection and approve them,
as well as give more general advice in relation to the project. If the
Steering Group does not have responsibility for all aspects of the research this should be made clear and an appropriate person identified
for other aspects of the project.

Purchasers of research often set key milestones to be reached with
associated deadlines built into the contract. This provides evidence of
the work that has been completed so far, in terms of quality and the
overall timetable of the project. The buyer can also link stage payments
to these milestones where projects are larger and it would be unreason-
able to wait for the project to be completed before payment is made.
Research is a costly process and few organisations could afford such an
outlay in advance. Most research buyers make payments in stages—for
example, at the end of the design stage, at the end of fieldwork, after
data input and at the completion of the research. These decisions are
made in the light of the particular piece of work and consideration of
when most costs will be incurred. Where survey research is involved,
fieldwork is very resource intensive and may use a substantial amount
of the overall budget. A payment schedule can be agreed at the contract
stage if costing information given in research proposals is broken down
into various components. Some buyers even state a payment schedule
in the project specification or brief.

A final point in terms of monitoring the contract concerns closure. It
is essential that both the buyer and the supplier are clear on when the
project ends and what constitutes a completed project. If dissemination
activities have been built into the commissioning process a clear statement is needed of what form it is going to take. It is advisable to have
agreed tangible products, for example, conducting two regional seminars, producing a research report and a summary paper. Clarity will
avoid misunderstanding and dissatisfaction. Any extra requirements

can then be costed appropriately as additional work to the original agreement. If the buyer has particular expectations about the type of research report required these should be discussed at an early stage in commissioning and indicated in the project brief, so that this work is properly costed. This is particularly important if very detailed reports or additional technical reports are required.

THE RESEARCH BUYER–SUPPLIER RELATIONSHIP

Sharing of information is central to the development of relationships between research buyers and suppliers. Clarity of process is vital so that suppliers know what is expected of them. If a number of researchers are invited to bid for a project, this should be made clear. It is also good practice to inform suppliers whether the competition is open or closed, as this will enable suppliers to make decisions about their chances of success when considering involvement in a competition. The criteria for judging or assessing proposals or tenders should also be accessible. Buyers should provide information on the scale of the project and/or any budget limitations. There is no point in suppliers working up detailed proposals for large, complex studies when finances are only available for a small-scale study. There are a number of ways of giving this information. A budget range can be given or, alternatively, a maximum budget can be set. Another way of indicating the size and scale of the project is to state the expected sample size, geographical location of interviewees, and the length of the questionnaire or interview schedule.

Once a decision has been reached, the successful candidate and all unsuccessful candidates should be notified as soon as possible. Those who were unsuccessful at early stages should be informed at that time as this knowledge is necessary if they are considering bidding for other work. Unsuccessful candidates may seek feedback on their application and it is good practice to give reasons why they did not win the contract. This can help build relationships for future work as well as aiding the development of possible future services.

A crucial aspect of the relationship between buyers and suppliers is the pressure of timetables. Suppliers need to be aware that research buyers are accountable within their organisation for the delivery of the project to the given timescale and within the budget. Similarly, research buyers need to be aware that suppliers also work on other projects. This is particularly relevant when planning the timing of competitions. If the timetable is too tight, suppliers may not have adequate time to prepare proposals. It is frustrating for suppliers to have only a few weeks to prepare a full proposal or tender document and then have to wait months for the outcome. If researchers are given very limited preparation time this will limit the quality of submissions, and some may decide not to accept the invitation to apply. The timescale of competitions should be planned to allow adequate time to complete a proposal or tender document with a reasonable turn-around time for notification of decisions. The Social Research Association (1994) suggests three weeks for the preparation of small-scale project proposals and five to six weeks for larger, more complicated ones. The research buyer should also keep the size of the competition in proportion to the scale of the project. There is little point in a long complicated recruitment process requiring very detailed project proposals from a large number of competitors if the project is small in scale.

Finally, both the research buyer and the supplier need to have a mutual understanding about project pricing. There needs to be clarity about how long a price submitted by a supplier will be valid if the commissioning process is delayed and the project commences much later than scheduled. There should be clarity about what work is included in the pricing and how any additional, unforeseen work is to be dealt with. These points need to be discussed and clarified at the contract stage to avoid later disputes and misunderstandings. Where there are informal competitions, or where only one supplier has been approached, there will need to be some form of price negotiation. If there has been a formal tendering process it is not normally possible to negotiate on price unless all tenders are unsatisfactory and all competitors are able to resubmit costings.

Some buyers attempt to establish long-term relationships with certain suppliers. This approach has the advantage of enabling good working relationships to develop with the suppliers who can also build up expertise in a particular field. This may also keep costs down as less time will be spent by suppliers getting familiar with a research area. The disadvantages in this approach may be that new ideas are overlooked and that suppliers may become complacent about future contracts. It will be difficult for new researchers to break into research areas and established researchers may find themselves restricted to particular areas. Information on past performance and good work can be built into the commissioning process and used when drawing up shortlists and assessing proposals.

One final point on the relationship between buyer and supplier is the recognition of intellectual property rights. It is essential that both parties are clear about how this issue is to be handled. It can pose thorny questions such as how does the buyer deal with the supplier who puts forward some good ideas but does not get the contract? Buyers should respect the source of any ideas. Similarly, researchers need to be aware that they are judged on their ability to produce ideas and to think analytically and these will need to be portrayed to some extent at the proposal stage. However, buyers should not expect major methodological work in advance of a commission, but rather seek outlines or broad approaches. Where a researcher puts forward good ideas but is unsuccessful in the competition, perhaps due to lesser experience, the buyer needs to offer some solution if he or she wishes to use those ideas. It is not reasonable to make use of ideas without discussing it with the researcher concerned. The issue of intellectual property rights is a difficult one but should not be ignored because of the difficulties it poses.

SUMMARY

This chapter has dealt with issues of commissioning research where the research area or problem is initiated by the funder. This is different from responsive funding where the research ideas originate with the researcher who then approaches organisations about potential funding opportunities. Attention was given to a number of decisions which need to be made by the research buyer when commissioning research. These include deciding the area of investigation, the available budget, and whether to use in-house research capacity or go to the external research market, or some combination of both. Once these decisions have been made a project specification or brief can be prepared for use at a later tendering or proposal stage.

It was pointed out that research suppliers are usually recruited through some type of competition, which can be formal or informal, open or closed. The three main types of formal competition, strict tendering, modified tendering and problem-based briefs, were discussed. It was stressed that whether formal tendering or a problem-based brief approach is adopted, it is important to build some flexibility into the process which allows dialogue between the research buyer and the research suppliers. This will facilitate a better understanding of the research area and requirements, and increase the likelihood of the end product being useful.

The forms of assessment required, where a formal competition takes place, were elaborated on. Selection panels were also discussed, with attention given to the use of predetermined criteria and the importance of notifying both successful and unsuccessful potential research suppliers. It was made clear that the commissioning process does not end when the contract is awarded. The research buyer needs to monitor progress and ensure that the supplier delivers the project to the timetable agreed and within budget. Information sharing is critical to the success of the project. The hands-off approach adopted by those using the formal tendering process designed to purchase more tangible products is not conducive to ensuring good-quality research. The commissioning process should be clear and visible to researchers and any expectations outlined. Good communications between the research buyer and the supplier from the early stages of commissioning through to the completion of the actual research was emphasised. This will ensure that the agreed timetable is kept within the allocated budget and will improve the quality of the final product. The aim of any child care research should be to provide knowledge which can be used in policy making and to improve practice. The development of good working relationships between research buyers and suppliers is the best guarantee of achieving that aim.

REFERENCE

Social Research Association (1994). *Commissioning Social Research: A Good Practice Guide.* London: SRA.

12

HOW AND WHO TO APPROACH REGARDING RESEARCH SPONSORING

Patrick McCrystal

Chapter Outline

INTRODUCTION

This chapter aims to give researchers pursuing funding for research in child care information and advice on how to approach funding agencies. The general categories of funding agencies are described and illustrations of each type of funding body is given. The information needed and issues to be aware of when pursuing funding are covered in this chapter. Regardless of how good a research proposal is, it is unlikely to be successful unless you approach a funding agency that

---

offers support in the specific area in which the proposed research is to
be carried out. This is an important part of the planning process. Funding agencies often comment in their information and guidelines to
applicants on the number of submissions they receive which are unsuitable and inappropriate to them. The result is that time is wasted by
both parties, in particular by the researcher who has invested a lot of
time and energy developing a proposal which is not even considered
because of a lack of planning. In order to assist the researcher, this
chapter should be considered as an important addition to the preparation of a proposal detailed in Chapter 10.

Funding agencies fall into several categories. In Great Britain these
include: Government-sponsored research; the Research Councils, who
primarily fund academic research; and the charitable trusts which support specific causes defined by their funder. There are also other agencies, which may be categorised as 'interested associations', such as
voluntary agencies seeking evaluation studies to be carried out. Each
funding agency has a remit within which proposals submitted for
consideration must fall in order to be considered suitable for support.
If these criteria are not met then the proposal will not be considered. It
is important to be aware of the requirements of funding agencies before
submitting a proposal in order to avoid creating the wrong impression
as funders will not be impressed with researchers who have not taken
the time to read their remit and guidelines. The guidelines are there to
assist the researcher to prepare proposals to meet specific requirements
of the agency to which he wishes to submit the proposal. Within these
guidelines there are some common principles which can be seen as
boundaries placed on all proposals.

BOUNDARIES PLACED ON RESEARCH PROPOSALS

When the proposal is completed and the researcher is considering to
whom it should be submitted, he or she must first ask whether the
proposal is within the scope of a specific funder's programme. Sponsors cannot support every area of research if they hope to have an
impact with the resources at their disposal. For most funding agencies
it is particularly important to have an impact as it can affect their
continuing existence and image. Similarly, government agencies are
expected to deliver on the areas of concern inherent in their legal
obligations and policies. Charitable trusts and foundations equally are
bounded by their funder's intent—for example, the Rowntree Founda-

tion was specifically established to support research into social issues. Administrators and trustees interpret the founder's wishes in such a way as to have the greatest impact on their area of special interest or concern. Accordingly, the researcher needs to be aware of the contemporary interpretation of the founder's ideals. In addition there are a number of other boundaries within which the researcher must work in order to have the research considered for support.

Boundaries around the Programme Scope

Since a funding agency concentrates its resources in a limited number of areas, the proposal must be perceived to fall within those boundaries to receive consideration. Most of the large charitable trusts (like The Nuffield Trust) will supply information on guidelines and types of projects funded directly to researchers in order to guide them in developing their research proposal. This will indicate what has to be emphasised in accordance with the modern interpretation of the foundation's stated goals. Most government agencies have application packages with regulations describing research programme goals, and sometimes provide lists of previously funded projects. However, it is not advisable to follow such supplied information, as this can be restrictive, but rather treat it as illustrative, giving sample interpretations of programme guidelines for the types of research projects that are appropriate for funding by the particular source.

Boundaries around the Nature of Applicants

As a rule there are outlines of qualifications required regarding who can apply and can be funded. Sometimes these boundaries are geographical, as some charitable trusts restrict their support to certain regions or government seeks proposals from regions or applicants unfunded in previous funding competitions. On occasions proposals may be restricted to certain types of institutions such as universities. These are known as closed tenders as opposed to open tenders when anyone is invited to submit a proposal (see Chapter 11 for full discussion).

Boundaries around Project Cost

Lists of past projects supported by an agency which are usually available directly from them, will suggest the level of funding that may be available for future projects. This does not mean that they will not exceed this level if a particularly attractive proposal is submitted, but gives the researcher some idea of the level of funding that may be processed by the agency without special scrutiny. This is particularly significant due to the fact that the costings section is the one that may immediately eliminate a proposal from consideration by the agency if it is excessively higher than the levels or suggested ceiling included in the agency's published guidelines.

Boundaries Resulting from Institutional Requirements

Certain requirements of the funding agency may not be acceptable to the institution within which a researcher is based; for example, some funding bodies may require that the research institution share the costs of the proposed research beyond what is their policy, or may restrict its dissemination upon completion. Many universities will not accept research with such restrictions. Each funder makes its own unique demands, and its requirements around these should be checked to see if they fit your particular situation before submitting your proposal, but particularly before accepting such demands.

GUIDANCE FOR RESEARCHERS SUBMITTING PROPOSALS

While funding agencies have a specific remit, researchers very often have specific guidelines within which they must work. Centre for Child Care Research (CCCR, 1997) staff work within the guidelines issued by the Research Management Unit at The Queen's University, Belfast. These guidelines are specific to researchers at The Queen's University but serve as an example of guidelines for researchers in all universities and in other institutions to follow when formulating research proposals for submission to external funders. They include the following which is taken from *Notes on Guidance on Work for External Bodies* produced by the University Administrative Secretary and issued by the Research Management Unit (1996).

1   Apart from the two traditional activities of teaching and academic research, funded mainly from public funds, the University and its staff have long engaged in work for a wide range of other bodies. The University encourages the continuation and substantial extension of this activity providing it satisfies certain criteria, particularly the avoidance of conflict with the traditional activities.

2   The purposes of carrying out work for outside bodies are varied and may include one or more of the following examples:

- extending the range of research;
- increasing the volume of research;
- increasing general University income;
- adding to School/Unit funds;
- providing cash benefits to University staff;
- enhancing the reputation of the University and its staff;
- providing professional experience for staff;
- providing services to industry and commerce;
- acquisition of additional facilities;
- helping the community.

3   The involvement of University staff in activities for external bodies can be classified under two general headings: 'Extra-University work' (i.e. private work, consultancy) and 'Intra-University work' which includes general academic research from which the university may derive cash benefits.

4   The University requires staff to submit a report on all activities for outside bodies which relate to their professional skills or position in the University plus personal and voluntary work which, in aggregate, is of such volume or so timed that it might impinge on the performance of their duties to the University.

5   To facilitate reporting, the Administrative Secretary will issue a simple form to each member of staff annually. Wilful failure to complete and return this form may be regarded as a breach of discipline.

6   Completed forms should be sent to the Director of School/Head of Unit, so that his/her comments may be added. The Director/Head will then forward the forms to the Administrative Secretary's Office, keeping a copy for information.

7   The University will maintain a record of all returns of outside work and summary reports will be prepared. These reports will be part of a process by which School/Unit performance is assessed.

It is clear from the above extract from the 'Notes on Guidance' that the university researcher has certain obligations to his or her institution which must be explicit in the proposal and be agreed by the funding agency that intends to support the research.

TYPES OF FUNDING AGENCIES

The boundaries and guidelines to be observed by researchers when submitting proposals to funding agencies are, to a certain extent, defined by the type of agency prepared to support research. As already noted, there are four major research funding sources within the UK: Government; Research Councils; the charitable trusts and foundations; and 'interest associations'. A brief description of the first three and their role in supporting research will be given, and a more detailed outline of their work will be discussed later in the chapter. This is followed by a description of the role of 'interest associations' with an example of this type of support and resultant research.

Government Agencies

In most Western countries, government agencies are the largest sources of grant money. As a rule they are legally obliged to, or prefer to, make grants to institutions rather than to individuals. Generally this takes the form of commissioned research with the onus on the researchers to market their skills in such a way as to convince this source of funding, and especially key decision makers, that they can complete a programme in an agreed time and produce the expected results.

Research Councils

The main function of the Research Councils is to help university researchers carry out their own research at the forefront of subjects, by awarding financial support to their research projects. The awards are specific projects proposed by the researchers themselves but must fall within the remit of the Council. Proposals to these Councils are appraised by a system of peer review, involving boards/committees/subcommittees composed of the applicants' scientific peers drawn from the academic world. Professional criteria are applied, such as the value and timescales of the research, reputation and ability of the researcher and appropriateness of the resources specified.

Charitable Trusts and Foundations

The charitable trusts range enormously from medical charities, such as the Wellcome Trust, which functions in a manner very similar to the Medical Research Council, to those that may be disbursing small amounts of money on an irregular basis. In addition, some trusts are not interested in research at all and others are more willing to fund buildings to be named after the original benefactor. Researchers are therefore strongly advised to undertake some preliminary research into the various trusts in order that an application for funding is directed to a trust that supports his or her research area. It is impossible to give a detailed list of grant-awarding bodies in this chapter, but a very useful reference has been compiled by Directory of Social Change, *A Guide to the Major Trusts*, Volumes 1 and 2, covering approximately 1,000 foundations and a very up-to-date list of UK charities funding research, including child care research. This source is updated annually.

Interest Associations

In addition to these funding agencies, there are some 'interest associations'. These include voluntary groups which have no connection with research but which may consider commissioning a project if it meets certain criteria appropriate to both the agency and the researcher's institution. An example of this was work carried out by the CCCR for Belfast Central Mission (BCM), a local social work agency. One of its residential homes for young people introduced a competence-based programme for staff and wanted to undertake their own evaluation of the effectiveness of the programme. This type of work falls within the remit of the CCCR, as one of its aims is 'to offer training and consultation on undertaking and applying child care research' (CCCR, 1997) and so a commission was agreed with BCM to provide consultancy and training on how to develop the evaluative measuring instrument, collect and analyse the resultant data.

However, not all funded research will fit so neatly into the remit of the research institution and the funding agency, as was the case in this example. The researcher will have his or her own agenda within which he or she has to work, as will the funding agency. It is, therefore, important if you are considering carrying out research commissioned by an 'interest association' to be aware of such potential restrictions when deciding how best to approach a funder, as well as which funder to approach.

Despite problems with shrinking funds for research, it is useful to be aware that child care research is still being carried out, and successful applicants are being awarded substantial sums of money. For the right projects directed to the right body, money is still available. A number of the major grant-awarding bodies of interest to researchers pursuing funding in the area of child care are well known. This includes various government departments; the Higher Education Funding Council for England, which funds university research; the Economic and Social Research Council and the British Academy and the Humanities Research Board; as well as a number of Charitable Trusts and Foundations. It is important to appreciate the nature of these varied institutions and what follows attempts to provide an introduction to each of them.

THE FUNDING AGENCIES

Government-Funded Research

From April 1998, National Health Service (NHS) Research and Development (R&D) funding will be raised by levies on NHS purchasers. The R&D strategy of the NHS seeks to establish a 'a knowledge-based health service in which clinical, managerial and policy decisions are based on sound information about research findings and scientific developments' (DoH, R&D). The framework for the strategy is based on advice from the Central Research and Development Committee and expert advisory groups. Problems are identified, translated into areas for research and prioritised by advisory groups. Commissioning groups then have responsibility for ensuring that a programme of work is carried out in the priority areas. Calls for outline proposals are made through press and journal advertisements. The commissioning group selects a number of outline proposals and the researchers are invited to submit full proposals. Proposals are assessed against criteria which include 'scientific merit, relevance to NHS priorities, value to the NHS, study design, and methodology', as well as assessments of the costs and duration of the research and the capacity of the researchers to meet the set objectives. The full proposals are subject to a process of external peer review.

Within this strategy is the Policy Research Programme which seeks to 'provide, through high quality research, a knowledge base for health services policy, social services, and central policies directed at the health of the population as a whole'. At any given time, 250 university research contracts are funded under this programme (School of Social Sciences, 1996). Research conducted under the Policy Research Programme has contributed to the formulation of the Health of the Nation strategy. Examples of studies conducted in this programme includes projects examining teenage pregnancies, women's health issues and variations in the health status of minority ethnic groups. The health of children was an area of importance within the Health of the Nation strategy and related research includes the ongoing Childhood Injury Prevention and Promotion of Safety Study. Other research commissioned in relation to children includes evaluation of the Children Act 1989 and studies of residential care and adoption. In addition, studies have been commissioned to monitor and evaluate the mixed economy in social care provision and to examine social work education and training (see Chapter 1 for a full discussion of the government's research and development strategies).

University-Funded Research (Higher Education Funding Council for England)

The Higher Education Funding Council for England (HEFCE) was established in May 1992 under the Further and Higher Education Act 1992 as a non-departmental public body operating within the context of government policy. The HEFCE's main function is to distribute funds provided by the Secretary of State for Education and Employment. The Council funds education and research at 136 universities and higher education colleges in England. It also funds courses at 74 further education colleges, who receive their main funding from the Further Education Funding Council. The HEFCE distributed approximately £3.5 billion in 1996–97 for teaching, research and capital costs.

The HEFCE works closely with other higher education funding bodies in the UK, including the Teacher Training Agency and the Further Education Funding Council. The Council regularly consults with a broad range of institutions' representative bodies and collaborates with them and with other funding bodies on a number of joint initiatives. It also provides advisory services to the Department of Education for Northern Ireland (DENI), the Northern Ireland Higher Education Council (NIHEC) and the Department of Agriculture for Northern Ireland (DANI).

The Research Councils: Economic and Social Research Council

The UK Research Councils were established under Royal Charter to fulfil the objectives set out by Government in the White Paper *Realising our Potential*, dated May 1993. Statutory control of the Councils is exercised by the Department of Trade and Industry, supported by the Director-General of Research Councils, within the Office of Science and Technology. The main concern of the Research Councils is to ensure that satisfactory support for exploitation opportunities is provided and that responsibilities are clearly defined and understood. Much of the initiative for identification, assessment and protection must, and should, come from the principal investigator, Research Directors or equivalent, and the head of department. The Research Councils expect institutions to ensure that opportunities for exploitation in current research programmes are not missed, and to establish the necessary machinery to achieve this. A significant number of mechanisms and independent external advice can be used, such as technology audits to augment internal processes.

There are seven Research Councils with specific remits to promote research in their particular areas. The Council that would interest researchers applying for funding in the area of child care is the Economic Social Research Council (ESRC). An example of an ESRC-funded study is the National Child Development Study, which has been tracking nearly 10,000 people for over 30 years. The ESRC is the UK's largest funding agency for research and postgraduate training into social and economic issues. It was established by Royal Charter in 1965 and has three goals:

- support high-quality research and postgraduate training that will contribute to economic competitiveness, the quality of life and the effectiveness of public services and policy;
- ensure that researchers have the training, resources and infrastructure to continue to make advances, including the necessary datasets and methodologies;
- broaden the public's knowledge and understanding of the contribution that the social sciences can make to policy makers, business and the public at large.

Two-thirds of the ESRC budget is allocated to research and nearly one-third to postgraduate training, with the remainder being used for evaluation, dissemination, forging business links and other activities. Not having 'in-house' researchers, ESRC funds are distributed to academics at universities and other institutes around the UK. Each year around 1,000 researchers throughout Britain are funded by the ESRC. Research is funded through open competitions and grants awarded on the basis of academic excellence.

ESRC funds support academic salaries, the premises and general infrastructure on which institutions can secure research grants; they contribute to the training and education of postgraduates; they support new young researchers who may not yet be in a position to secure research grants; and they also support strategic and basic 'seed corn' research.

The Council allocates research funds selectively, on the basis of quality determined by the outcomes of the 1996 Research Assessment Exercise (RAE). The main criteria affecting changes in funding for 1997–98 are the outcome of the RAE and the introduction of the new research funding method. The Council has acknowledged world-class excellence by providing a funding premium to departments with the highest ratings in the RAE. The Council is distributing £684 million of its research funding to institutions selectively, according to the quality of their research as judged by the RAE. The Council's grants to institutions are conditional on the funds being used for the eligible activities set out in paragraph 65(2) of the Further and Higher Education Act 1992.

There are three main funding schemes.

1. Research centres which investigate long-term issues, typically over a ten-year period, and employ teams of researchers.

2. Research programmes which address medium-term issues that often have a pressing social, commercial or political dimension. The programmes are composed of individual projects at different institutions and co-ordinated by a director.
3. Research grants which fund 'stand alone' projects that are suggested by academics and often explore new areas, providing the 'seed corn' for larger studies.

The third scheme is perhaps the most appropriate for researchers wishing to pursue funding to undertake child care research as it is most in line with the aims and content of this chapter and of Chapter 10, but this should not discourage researchers from pursuing funding through the other two schemes.

ESRC responsive mode schemes (Research Grants, Research Seminars and Fellowships under the Research Grants Board) are open to UK universities, colleges of higher education, and independent institutes approved by the ESRC. Applicants are eligible whether or not they are members of a recognised institution. Applicants for research awards who are not established members of a recognised institution must be accommodated by an institution and provided with appropriate facilities to carry out the research. They and other staff engaged upon the research are normally expected to reside within reasonable travelling distance of the institution when not engaged in fieldwork. For such applicants, the institution must provide a covering statement on the research proposal form to the effect that, in the event of an award, it will provide accommodation and facilities for the applicant similar to that provided for established members of staff.

The applicant should normally be the person undertaking responsibility for directing the research and for the observance of all terms and conditions, as well as being actively involved in carrying it through. The number of hours that the applicant expects to spend on the research, and the extent of other commitments, must be stated on the research proposal. Guidance on the presentation of applications is provided by the ESRC research grants and contracts office. It is noted by ESRC that careful and well-adjusted costings will speed the time taken to issue an award should one be recommended.

The British Academy and the Humanities Research Board

Another agency with a remit to fund research in the general area of child care is the British Academy and the Humanities Research Board. The Academy is the premier society devoted to the promotion of advanced research and scholarship in the humanities and the social sci-

ences. Since the ESRC provides the major share of funding to support
research in the social sciences nationally, researchers may, depending
on the size and methodology of the research, be more appropriately
directed to the ESRC. However, as an alternative source of research
funding in this area it is worth considering the Academy. It is a self-
governing body of Fellows which was founded in 1901 and received a
Royal Charter in 1902. Its primary purpose is to promote research and
scholarship in these areas. It seeks to achieve that purpose in a number
of ways, including research grants and other awards, i.e. the sponsorship of a number of projects and of research institutes overseas.

The bulk of the Academy's income derives from a grant-in-aid that
it receives from the Government, but it also has private funds arising
from gifts and legacies, from contributions made by the Fellows themselves, and from grants made by research donations. A number of
awards are available from the Academy including research grants
awarded to individual scholars, learned bodies and other groups; and
research posts which include postdoctoral fellowships and research
readerships. The Academy produces its own guidelines and conditions
of offer which should be referred to when making applications for
financial support.

Grants are available up to a limit of £5,000 and have to be used as
payment for the following items: research and secretarial assistance
necessary for and directly used for the research project; travel and
maintenance expenses in the UK or in connection with an approved
programme of research; costs of consumable items necessary for and
directly used in the research; costs of preparing for publication.

CHARITABLE TRUSTS AND FOUNDATIONS

The other main sources of research funding are the charitable trusts
and foundations. These trusts are usually founded by a benefactor,
often a wealthy philanthropist, many of whom now have their funds
administered by a board of trustees and a full-time administration
team. A quick-reference guide to some of these funding bodies, their
application and assessment procedures, has been included (see Table
6). Information regarding Trusts and Foundations changes annually
but is updated in a series of publications by the Directory of Social
Change Publication with *A Guide to the Major Trusts*, now consisting of
two volumes covering funding to all areas as well as financial support
to various programmes and innovations in these fields, including support for scholarships, bursaries and studentships (Brown & Casson,

1997; Fitzherbert, Forrester & Grau, 1997). It is only possible to give researchers pursuing funding an indication of such trusts as this chapter can only tap such a source, giving readers a feel for what may be available and worthwhile pursuing. Three examples of the founders of such trusts and foundations will serve this purpose.

Joseph Rowntree Foundation

Joseph Rowntree (1836–1925) was a Quaker and successful businessman who 'believed that he had a responsibility to use his money for the good of others. He was interested in 'discovering the underlying causes of social problems and looking at radical solutions' (Fitzherbert, Forrester & Grau, 1997, p. 222). In 1904, with the consent of his family, he transferred a substantial part of his wealth to three trusts with which his name is associated. The three trusts, the Joseph Rowntree Charitable Trust, the Joseph Rowntree Foundation and the Joseph Rowntree Reform Trust Ltd, are now separate from each other and have no link with the former Rowntree Company. The Joseph Rowntree Foundation supports research and development mainly in the three areas of housing, social care and disability, and social policy. The foundation supports work by both professional researchers and by innovative practitioners.

The Leverhulme Trust

This trust derives from the will of the first Viscount Leverhulme who died in 1925. The income of the trust derives dividends from its shareholding in Unilever plc. It gives grants to institutions and individuals throughout the UK for the purpose of research and education, concentrating on work in the higher and further education sectors. Grants to institutions for research are normally for three years or less.

The Nuffield Foundation

This was founded by Lord Nuffield in 1943 with an endowment of £10 million, consisting of shares in Morris Motors Ltd. At Morris he worked as a repairer and maker of bicycles before founding Morris Motors from which he acquired his great wealth. Grants are given for projects within the foundation's areas of interest which includes education, child protection, family law and mental health. Financial support is given for academic research and to individuals for education and training, ranging from a few hundred pounds to £100,000 over two or three years.

Table 6: Charitable trusts and foundations who support child care research—a quick reference guide

Funder	Particular areas of interest	Guidelines	Submission dates
Leverhulme Trust (£12,610,000 1995)	Responsive funding i.e. not pre-defined in disciplines including humanities and social sciences	Yes	15 November 15 February 15 May 15 September
Nuffield Trust (£6,559,000 1995)	Child protection, family law and justice	Yes	December February May July November
The Joseph Rowntree Foundation (£6,199,000 1995)	Social Policy (i.e. family and parenthood) social care and disability	Yes	Mid December Mid March Mid June Mid September
The FBT Charitable Fund (£1,380,000 1995)	Mental illness, mental disability	No	1 May 1 November
The Sir Halley Stewart Trust (£597,000 1994/95)	Social research	Yes	December April August
Mr and Mrs J.A. Pye's Charitable Settlement (£349,000 1995/96)	Child welfare	No	No date given
Bernard Van Leer Foundation (£311,000 1995)	Education of disadvantaged children	No	No date given

Children's Research Fund (£170,000 1995/96)	Child health research	Yes	March November
The Glover Trust (£218,000 1994)	Children, disability health	Yes	No date given
The Yapp Education and Research Trust (£145,000 1994/95)	Grants to universities, colleges of HE and hospitals	Yes	1 February 1 June 1 October
The Christopher HR Reeves Charitable Trusts (£88,000 1995)	Disability, social welfare	Yes	No date given
The Frognall Trust (£71,000 1994/95)	Children, elderly, blind, disabled	Yes	No date
The Arthur James and Constance Paterson Charitable Trust (£60,000 1994/95)	Medical research, health and welfare of children	No	No date given
European Research Office (US Army) (not known)	Research grants in all disciplines	No	No date given
Roland Harris Educational Trust (not known)	Child psychotherapy research	No	No date given

Table 6 provides information on the names of trusts who support research in the field of child care and whether or not these trusts provide specific guidelines and the submission dates for research proposals. Below the name of each trust is the latest annual amount of financial support and the year this was provided. The table gives an indication of the variation in size of such trusts, which may assist the researcher when considering which trust to approach with his or her proposal. Where no submission date is specified it is assumed that proposals can be submitted on an ongoing basis.

SUMMARY

While there is much competition for research funding, there are many agencies inviting applications for their support for research covering a wide range of areas. If a researcher is to secure support it is necessary to understand not just how to develop a research proposal, but also who to approach as the appropriate funding body for their particular area of research. An understanding of the different categories of funding agency is the first step in this process of obtaining research funding. This chapter has attempted to provide advice and guidance on who to approach and how to approach them. It has emphasised that there are boundaries within which both funders and researchers operate, it has identified the general categories of funder and given information on specific funding bodies. It is worth while to remember that other sources of advice and guidance can be found in academic journals, newspapers and by word of mouth. An awareness of this combination will provide researchers with the necessary advice and instruction with which to pursue financial support for their research.

REFERENCES

Brown, P. & Casson, D. (1997). *A Guide to the Major Trusts*, Vol. 2, *A Further 700 trusts*. London: Directory of Social Change.

CCCR (1997). *Annual Report 1996/97, Business Plan 1997/2000*. Belfast: Centre for Child Care Research, The Queen's University of Belfast.

Fitzherbert, L., Forrester, S. & Grau, J. (1997). *A Guide to the Major Trusts*, Vol. 1: *The Top 300 Trusts*. London: Directory of Social Change.

Research Management Unit (1996). *Notes on Guidance on Work for External Bodies*. Belfast: The Queen's University of Belfast.

School of Social Sciences (1996). *A Guide to Sources of Research Funding*. Belfast: The Queen's University of Belfast.

13

PROMOTING RESEARCH THROUGH THE ESTABLISHMENT OF RESEARCH CENTRES

Dorota Iwaniec

Chapter Outline

INTRODUCTION

PROCESS AND DILEMMAS OF SETTING UP A RESEARCH CENTRE; FROM IDEA TO REALITY

STEPS TO BE TAKEN
- Organisational Arrangements
- Research Programme
- Review of Centre Activities

CENTRE FOR CHILD CARE RESEARCH
- Work Programme
- Organisational Arrangements
- Operational Management Group
- Contract Management

SUMMARY

Making Research Work: Promoting Child Care Policy and Practice
Edited by D. Iwaniec and J. Pinkerton
© 1998 John Wiley & Sons Ltd

INTRODUCTION

Many academic departments and various institutions increasingly are exploring the possibilities of setting up research centres as mechanisms to improve research capacity, productivity and stature within universities, the wider research community and the professions they represent. This is an important development for anyone interested in the promotion of child care research. These aspirations are being pursued in different ways. Usually, research capacities are generated through competitive or opportunistic research grants, or through one or two core-funded research staff. Usually this process involves appointing a part-time director, perhaps a research assistant, and getting some administrative help (Wodarski, 1990a, 1990b, 1995).

As a rule, research staff are employed on a sessional basis, or on full-time short-term contracts, depending on the size of the research project and the probabilities of securing further work. While these arrangements can produce quality research, leading to prestigious publications, they cannot provide continuity, critical mass, and a steady development of research skills as would be the case within research teams operating with job security. Persistent preoccupation with the preparation of research proposals and fund-raising diverts the attention of directors and senior staff from any real possibilities of sustained research for which there must be adequate resources in terms of time, staff and money.

Core funding and long-term contracts are increasingly advocated as appropriate ways to build skilful research teams (Williams, 1992; Bush & Hattery, 1953). Core-funded research centres as viable sources of high-quality research were recognised by the R&D strategy policies and further reinforced by both the Culyer Report (DoH, 1994a) and *A Wider Strategy for Research and Development in Personal Social Services* (DoH, 1994b)—see Chapter 1 for discussion of these documents. There are obvious advantages in building adequately funded, properly staffed, and focused research centres. Accumulation of expertise in a range of research methodologies, familiarity with the subject matter, and well-developed national and international links with researchers help to produce high-quality work in all aspects of research activities. The establishment of long-term research posts helps to create continuity and a framework within which staff can give undivided attention to research matters, improve their research skills, increase research productivity and quality, and work towards an overall improvement in knowledge.

The idea and desire of establishing research centres of some form acquired greater importance in the UK as a result of the Research

Assessment Exercises (RAE) carried out by the Higher Education Funding Council (HEFC). In order to obtain the top grade of 5, or at least 4, departments pursuing such a level of achievement are obliged to produce research of international importance, disseminate it in international or national refereed journals or books, obtain high levels of research funding, and attract a respectable number of research students undertaking higher degree programmes. All those requirements demand time and the establishment and nurturing of a research culture within departments. There are often conflicting pressures to deliver quality teaching and assistance to students on the one hand, and to produce levels and standards of research with the aim of meriting high grades on the other. These aims are particularly difficult to balance for staff involved with professional courses where teaching requirements are extensive and demanding. Some professions, and therefore professional courses, have not, as yet, fully developed a research tradition and culture. Research skills might be rare and certainly insufficient for high output and quality of research activities in any one department. Accumulation of research skills, and consequently of research capacity, can be facilitated and enhanced by research centres which, in turn, can filter those skills to teaching staff and students.

Research centres promote research culture in various ways. Wodarski (1995) refers to the following functions: firstly, they serve as a catalyst for developing knowledge that is essential for well-informed and effective practice; secondly, they provide a good context for the training of doctoral students and may facilitate means for their financial support; thirdly, for those departments located in universities where there are levels of high research productivity and traditions, research centres justify activities associated with the development of new knowledge; fourthly, they facilitate interdepartmental collaboration in research; and, fifthly, they provide experiences in publishing research and in writing research proposals that can lead to promotion and tenure. Research centres can create a stimulating environment in which other members of the academic staff and practitioners in the area can pursue their research ideas and shape them into workable and well-designed proposals (Ikenberry & Friedman, 1972).

As the writing of research proposals requires time, experience and specific skills, the staff of a centre can assist others to prepare imaginative and technically sound proposals capable of meeting the requirements of the sponsoring bodies, or, in the case of practitioners, to evaluate their work. Since most proposals have to be submitted relatively quickly once tenders are invited, a collaborative approach which can draw on the skills of centre staff may speed up the process of preparing a quality research proposal in order to secure the probability of funding, execution of the research, and subsequent publications (Porter *et al.*, 1982; Shetty, 1986). There is no doubt that training and experience are necessary in the formulation of research proposals: the latter must address the right questions and ensure that techniques are used that give the best chance of success (see Chapter 10 for full discussion).

However, core-funded research centres are not always free of problems, as they may be given little autonomy for the design, methodology, and development and analysis of projects; also, the research programme may be dictated by the funders and may provide neither freedom for research activities nor secure contracts of long enough duration for those engaged in research. Furthermore, those researchers wishing to pursue curiosity-driven topics may not be given an opportunity to do so. Williams (1992), when reviewing 13 research units funded by the Department of Health (DoH), found that the structures of those units often failed to provide cohesive frameworks for future work and that there was an urgent need for careful strategic planning. In addition, existing contracts did not give the units sufficient security to attract, train and retain the best researchers. Williams and his Review Group also identified some tension between 'policy customers' in the Department and the units, and, as far as administration was concerned, between the units and their host universities. The review was conducted against the background of the then new NHS R&D strategy in order to implement necessary changes for more satisfactory work. Williams's review in 1992 was followed by a series of expert reviews commissioned by the DoH, and in January 1995 it was announced that the outcomes of all visits were positive and that the Department's funding would continue. A number of arrangements were put in place such as:

- the future of the units would be secured by agreeing a long-term programme for each;
- the first priority of research would be determined by the Department;
- the directors of the units would be at liberty to tender competitively for additional commissions, devoting up to 10% of their time to curiosity-driven projects; and
- core staff would be on five-year contracts with prospects of renewal.

This chapter will draw on the author's experience in the development of the core-funded Centre for Child Care Research at the Department of Social Work, The Queen's University of Belfast. It will discuss the step-by-step approach leading to the creation of the Centre from initial idea to final realisation. Organisation, management structure, remit, research activities, contracting negotiating terms of partnership obligations, respective responsibilities and quality control will all be discussed.

PROCESS AND DILEMMAS OF SETTING UP A RESEARCH CENTRE; FROM IDEA TO REALITY

The creation of any core-funded research centre requires well-informed strategic planning, collation of intelligence and realistic consideration as to what such a proposed centre can offer and what will be its focus. Additionally, and most importantly, it is essential the requesting institution has a reasonable research record, a good reputation, and the expertise to build up and develop such a centre and to make it work. To do the ground work requires time, energy, resourcefulness, and perseverance, as such aspirations have many stumbling-blocks along the way. Timing may be of the essence here, as well as an ability to capture opportunities which may arise nationally and regionally as a result of major organisational changes, research strategies, new legislation, or social and political pressures and concerns regarding the working of policies and practice in particular areas. In the case of the Centre for Child Care Research, it was initiated in response to the major organisational changes in Health and Social Services Boards, the forthcoming implementation of the Children (NI) Order 1995 (DHSS, 1995), and the proposed R&D strategy in Health and Personal Social Services in the Province. Since the Department of Social Work at The Queen's University has had an established record and capacity in child care research and teaching, it was felt that it was reasonable and appropriate to pursue the idea of establishing a centre which would build on existing strengths.

STEPS TO BE TAKEN

There are many phases and steps to go through, and many difficulties to overcome along the journey from the start to the finishing point. The author's experience, as an initiator, negotiator, organiser and currently director of the Centre for Child Care Research would suggest the following six steps as one possible viable route.

Step 1: Securing Support and Approval at University Level

The idea first needs to be tested out at the department in question, and then with senior university management to secure approval and support in principle before embarking on further work. Since all universities want to improve their research standing, and departments their research rating, and try to do so within diminishing resources, support is likely for such an idea, providing it is rational, achievable, and well argued. The prospects of getting overheads from the funding levy is also attractive to the managers of resources at the universities.

For the academic department pursuing this idea it is very attractive and worth while. It provides not only a number of skilled and experienced researchers, and therefore increasing departmental high-quality research productivity, but also facilitates joint research projects with teaching staff, advice on research design, help with statistical analysis, and assistance in writing research proposals. Additionally, such research staff can teach research methods and the dissemination of research findings, at graduate and post-graduate levels and on qualifying and post-qualifying professional courses, and provide an excellent resource for research students and their academic supervisors.

Step 2: 'Testing the Waters'

A research centre proposal has a much better chance of success, and undoubtedly gets greater credibility, if it is based on a well-surveyed feasibility study conducted by an independent researcher. To this end the Department of Social Work initiated such a study and appointed a temporary researcher in order to test out whether or not such a centre should be established, and, if so, what form it should take. The feasibility study also aimed to determine needs as perceived by the social work agencies in relation to child care research dissemination and research training requirements.

The researcher consulted widely, obtaining data from the statutory and voluntary child care sector, including managers, practitioners and trainers in the region, DHSS senior officials, senior academic staff at The Queen's University, existing research units in Northern Ireland, and leading social work and child care research units in other parts of the United Kingdom. The resulting report, entitled *Establishing a Research Unit within QUB Social Work Department: A Feasibility Study* (O'Halloran, 1994), was very encouraging, clearly indicating the need for a high-quality accessible research capacity to assist the process of making informed and cost-effective practice, policy and management decisions at a time of fundamental changes, both organisational (purchaser/provider split) and legal (the Children (NI) Order 1995).

The feasibility study, on the basis of its findings, recommended that:

- establishing a child care research centre was, in principle, feasible;
- in practice, such a proposition was only feasible with core funding from the Department of Health and Social Services;
- the most satisfactory strategy for establishing and maintaining a child care research centre would involve tying it directly to practice agencies;
- the functions of such a centre should be focused and explicit;
- the collaborative nature of the child care research centre be demonstrated by the creation of formal structures linking the Department of Social Work and agencies; and
- a detailed specification for such a research unit be drawn up.

Step 3: Feasibility Study Dissemination Seminar

Once the feasibility study has been completed and the report widely distributed to all concerned, then the dissemination of its findings and the possible way forward should be discussed with key people invited to a special seminar. It should not be anticipated that an immediate decision will be made, but an opportunity will be given to clarify issues, explore problems and difficulties, and sense the mood of the possible funders. It is wise to have senior academic managers at the seminar to reassure agencies, managers, and the Department's officials of the university's commitment and support for such a development. It is advisable to present, at the end of the seminar, an outline of the proposed Centre, which should cover:

- aims;
- organisational arrangements;
- anticipated research programmes;
- required staffing, equipment, and accommodation;
- system of accountability and quality control; and
- funding.

The seminar audience should be given a reasonably clear description, at this stage, about the Centre's organisation, remit, and financial and other needs in order to become operational, and what it would offer to the agencies and professions involved. Thereafter, discussions

should reveal interest and commitment and any amendments necessary to the proposals. The debate should encourage participants to
express views and seek advice on the best way to take the proposals
forward. In the case of the Centre for Child Care Research (and this
appears to be common experience), while general enthusiasm and approval for such a development was expressed, the representatives of
Social Services were more reserved and hesitant about issues related to
funding. They felt that financial resources should be provided by the
DHSS and that they (the Social Services) should be approached directly
to discuss this issue. It was also suggested that the DHSS (Research
Branch and Social Work Inspectorate), in conjunction with The Queen's
University, should call a formal meeting, inviting Directors of Social
Services, DHSS child care officials and researchers, and Social Work
Inspectorate to start negotiations based on a formally written proposal
document submitted by The Queen's University of Belfast. It was sug-
gested that a proposal should be sent to the Directors of Social Services,
The Boards' executives, and Assistant Directors of Child Care, and that
the proposal should also be distributed within the appropriate sections
of the DHSS and The Queen's University.

Step 4: Preparing a Formal Proposal Document

The proposal document is a major working tool to make the idea of a
research centre a reality, and particular attention should be given to it.
Firstly, it should provide a base for prospective funders and other
interested parties to make a judgement regarding the validity of the
proposal, and whether required research needs are likely to be met.
Secondly, it should show clear evidence of motivation and contain a
thoroughly researched and developed business plan by the fund seek-
ers. Thirdly, it should form a sound base for negotiation and later
contracting. Such a proposal must deal with and answer three basic
questions: the what, the how, and the why of the proposed Centre.

The *what* question deals with the following:
• What are the aims and objectives of the proposed Centre?
• What is such a Centre going to offer?
• What functions is it going to take on board?
• What resources, both material and human, are needed to make it
  operational?
• What are the Centre's remit and focus?
• What is the anticipated research agenda?
• What are the lines of accountability?

The *how* question covers:
- How is the Centre going to be structured and organised?
- How is it going to be managed?
- How is it going to be monitored in terms of quality control?
- How is it going to relate and establish links with professional agencies and larger research communities?
- How is it going to disseminate its research findings?
- How is it going to provide help and assistance for practitioners, managers, service users, and students?
- How will it maintain links with the academic staff in the Department and the University at large?

The *why* question covers:
Explanations of reasons and purposes for such development. The arguments should be based on a relevant literature review, feasibility study outcomes, and any other information which are appropriate to strengthen the arguments (such as R&D strategy).

The Proposal Document put forward the following propositions:

- The Centre would be based on a partnership between the DHSS, the four Health and Social Services Boards, and The Queen's University of Belfast, representing a shared strategic commitment by the Department, the Boards, and the University in order to assist the process of making informed and cost-effective practice, policy and management decisions at a time of fundamental organisational and child care legislation changes, through the fostering and development of a high-quality, accessible research capacity.
- The proposed Research Centre would adopt the principles, and would be run according to the rules and policies, of the Regional (R&D) strategy.
- The Centre's aim would be to play a key role in influencing the development of child care policy and practice in Northern Ireland through the undertaking and dissemination of research relating to a full range of child care needs and services.
- The Centre would have three major objectives:
    (i)   to identify and conduct original research into child care needs and services through using and developing a mix of research methods and varied forms of dissemination;
    (ii) to provide access to a wide range of child care research through collating, analysing and evaluating regional, UK and international statistics and research findings in a fashion that usefully complements the existing activity of the DHSS in this area;

(iii)   to offer training and consultation on undertaking and applying child care research.

The Centre would be progressed through the development and implementation of a research agenda and a dissemination strategy com-
bining the perspectives of the DHSS, the Boards and Trusts and
Queen's University. Particular attention would be given to:

- researching practice and policy issues arising from the Children
  (NI) Order and from adoption, matrimonial and other child welfare
  related legislation;
- identifying, describing and evaluating examples of effective practice in the child care field;
- examining the impact of the organisational context on the delivery
  of child care services and, in particular, issues associated with different agencies and disciplines.

Step 5: Negotiations

Formal negotiations should take place in order to discuss in detail the
Centre Proposal Document, and to reach mutual agreement on various
aspects of the proposed Centre. In the first place, a final decision should
be made as to whether or not to establish a Research Centre; secondly,
the funding arrangements should be decided upon and put in place,
with consideration given as to how costs are to be distributed;
thirdly, decisions should be arrived at about the organisational structures, the lines of accountability, the accommodation, appointment of
staff and the length of their contracts, and all other resources required;
and, fourthly, research priorities should be clearly specified. As has
been pointed out, a major problem lay in the reluctance of the representatives of Social Services to commit themselves to financial contributions. If senior agency managers are kept fully informed those may be
encouraged and persuaded to play active roles in the establishment of
a Research Centre in all its aspects including making monetary contributions to the general funding. Being a party to negotiation gives them
full awareness of what is on offer, and enables them to judge how such
an enterprise would meet their research needs and what they can
contribute. If such agreement may be reached in principle, the next
phase of negotiations should concern detail of each agencies contribution including the amount each agency should pay, since every Board
is associated with areas of differing sizes and populations. A formula
based on population size and area should be used.

Most informal discussions with individuals or parties concerned usually occur before any of the formal meetings so that the ground can be prepared and progress speeded up. Awareness of reservations about acceptance of any part or parts of the proposal at an early stage is an advantage so that contingency plans may be made to accommodate the specific needs of each party and address any concerns. The chairing of meetings is of considerable importance, requiring skills of negotiation, familiarity with the subject matter, sensitivity and awareness of the research requirements of each agency, and a high degree of professionalism. Choosing the right person to preside over those meetings is essential to arrive at positive and speedy conclusions.

Once the Proposal Document was accepted (after being fully negotiated during three lengthy meetings) the tidying-up work was carried out by the University Bursar's office and the DHSS Research Management Branch on overheads and on the precise financial contribution from each of the H&PSS Boards and the DHSS. Sums allocated from each Board were based on the size of its population, but the DHSS was to be a major funder. It is worth mentioning that a strong presence of senior academic staff from the University, together with the skilful professionalism of the Chairperson, played an important part in ensuring success by reassuring the Social Services Directors as well as (most importantly) their Chief Executives, of the validity of and necessity for Research Centre development. The decision was taken that the Centre would be funded on the basis of five-year rolling contracts for core staff, with the possibility of renewal pending a three- to five-yearly assessment review.

Organisational Arrangements

The partnership approach would be maintained within the proposed organisational arrangements. The work of the Centre would be overseen by the Strategy and Policy Group (SPG), comprising the DHSS, the four Boards, and the Queen's University representative. The SPG functions would be to:

- agree a prioritised core research programme;
- monitor the total work programme of the Centre;
- review progress of long-term projects;
- examine the adequacy of staffing and resources;
- set forward-planning objectives;
- monitor quality arrangements and expenditure.

The Group would meet four times a year to review the Centre's work, to give direction on priorities, and would be responsible for com-

missioning a formal review of the Centre's work at three-yearly in
tervals.

Centre Staff and Lines of Accountability

Responsibility for direct management of the Centre would rest with the
University. The programme of work undertaken by the Centre would
be organised and supervised by a Director. The Director would hold
ultimate responsibility for the efficient conduct of Centre business, and
be accountable to the Strategy and Policy Group for the drawing up of
a programme of research work and for the execution of the approved
programme as well as for establishing, in consultation with the Strategy and Policy Group, advisory groups for each of the major core
projects. In addition, the Director would be accountable to the University, through the Provost of the College of Legal, Social and Educational
Sciences, for financial matters and for maintaining proper academic
standards.

A report on work in progress would be presented at each meeting of
the Strategy and Policy Group by the Director. In addition, the Director
would submit a formal Annual Report of work completed and in
progress and of the major issues associated with running of the Centre
(including finance, accommodation and staffing). The Annual Report
would set out a forward-planning statement, including details of projected expenditure.

To provide sufficient human resources to carry out the proposed
research programme, at least five research staff members would be
needed, consisting of a senior research fellow, two research officers,
one research associate and one statistician. Additionally, a full-time
secretary would be required to assist the research team. The senior
research fellow would be accountable to the Director of the Centre and
be responsible for the day-to-day work of the Centre's staff, who in turn
would be accountable to the senior research fellow.

Resources

The Centre should be funded by the DHSS, the four Boards, and The
Queen's University, and there should be approximate parity in the
contribution made by each party towards the costs of establishing and
running the Centre. All three parties should contribute, both to direct
funding and to meeting indirect costs.

Accommodation

Accommodation for a minimum of six full-time staff should be provided by the University on the campus, if possible, in close proximity to

the Department of Social Work in order to facilitate easy collaboration between research and academic staff and management of the Centre.

Publication of Research Findings

Staff of the Centre should be at liberty to disseminate research findings at local, national, and international levels. Freedom to publish should be agreed by all relevant parties, and such agreement should not be withheld unreasonably. This should be formally stated in the Centre's contract.

Research Programme

A systemic and thematic approach should be taken in the construction of the Centre's research programme. The Centre's staff should carry out a basic 'core programme' of research to be determined by the Strategy and Policy Group. The 'core programme' should be drawn up to allow for a number of empirical projects, of different duration, to run concurrently in a way that would ensure that the Centre is engaged in a continuous rolling programme of work.

Alongside the 'core programme' the Centre should develop an 'additional programme', and for this the University would be free to employ such staff and make any other arrangements it sees fit. The responsibility for the funding of projects under this programme should lie with the University, and these should come under the direction of the Operational Management Group. Work undertaken as part of the 'additional programme' would be included in the Director's Reports to the Strategy and Policy Group.

Review of Centre Activities

Continuous reviews should be ensured by the Director's Reports presented at each meeting of the Strategy and Policy Group. In addition, the Annual Report will provide a means for regularly reviewing the work of the Centre.

Step 6: Writing a Formal Contract

The final step involving all parties concerned is the drawing up of a formal contract between purchasers and providers, in which the rules and obligations are clearly set out. Such contracts are based on the principles outlined in the Central Unit on Procurement Guidances (HM Treasury, 1993, 1994, 1995) Although use of this document is not mandatory, it is considered as a good guide to professional practice and is linked to the European Community (EC) procurement directives as implemented in UK legislation, the ruling of the European Court of Justice, and other relevant European Community laws (HM Treasury, *CUP Guidance*, Nos 39, 42, 47 and 51). The Public Services Contracts Regulations (1993) provide specific guidelines for 'contracting authorities' who are seeking 'public services contracts'. The principal requirement of the Regulations is that, in seeking offers in relation to such a contract, a contracting authority must use one of three procedures: the 'open procedure', whereby any person who is interested may submit a tender; the 'restricted procedure', whereby only those persons selected by the contracting authority may submit tenders; and the 'negotiated procedures', whereby the contracting authority negotiates the terms of the public services contract with one or more persons selected by it. (The negotiated procedure may only be used in certain limited circumstances.) The negotiated procedure was used in respect of the Centre for Child Care Research. The negotiations and the formal written contract were based on the Proposal Document (Department of Social Work, 1995). Whatever the formal contracts are, they should allow a certain level of flexibility, especially in developmental work, where certain details cannot be envisaged in advance.

The Culyer Report (DoH, 1994a) also emphasised the need for flexibility when drawing up contracts relating to research facilities in order to avoid excessive bureaucracy, and too much detail leading to a paralysis of activity. Effective negotiations should aim to arrive at a mutual understanding of all that is expected from each party and how those expectations may be achieved. Attention should be directed to research activities and to the dissemination of that research; to the time needed for research, its conclusion, and its dissemination; and to the methodology of how to assess results. Such contracts should provide the means of monitoring and reviewing activities set against the desired criteria of success and expectations. No matter how complex are the issues negotiated, a contract is simply an agreement between two parties under which one party promises to do something for the other in return for a consideration, usually a payment. This places obligations on both parties to fulfil their parts of the agreement.

The contract, therefore, has to be negotiated and written in a way which ensures that both parties to it fully understand their respective obligations, and that these are fulfilled as efficiently and as effectively as possible to provide the best value for money. However, the production of a quality contract commences before the start of negotiations; the process runs from the identification of the need for such development to its final conclusion. In the case of the Centre for Child Care

Research, it began from the feasibility study and progressed to the formal and detailed Centre Proposal Document, setting a base for a negotiated contract which applies to the present day. The conditions of a formal contract call for the following aspects to be addressed:

- the legal framework within which the service will be provided;
- the payment process;
- responsibility for monitoring performance;
- responsibility for managing the contract; and
- procedures for resolution of problems, dealing with default, and termination.

CENTRE FOR CHILD CARE RESEARCH

After almost two years of preparation, the Centre for Child Care Research was established. Many lessons have been learned about how to create such an enterprise, from the birth of the idea to its final realisation. The next phase was dependent on the internal organisation and execution of the agreed Centre Proposal and contract obligations. Following the appointment of the part-time Centre Director and the full-time Senior Research Fellow as team manager, accommodation and the necessary equipment were acquired, and preparations were made to appoint research and administrative staff. Two research officers, a statistician, a research associate, and the secretary of the Centre were appointed. The first task was to organise the work of the Centre and to allocate responsibilities in line with the particular interests and skills of research staff, ensuring that overall objectives were observed and that core research projects were given priority.

Work Programme

The Centre's overall work programme falls broadly into three categories:

- conducting original research, encompassing both Core and Additional programmes relating to child care issues specifically addressing issues emerging from the Children (NI) Order 1995, using and developing a mix of innovative qualitative and quantitative research methods;
- enabling access to research to be achieved by various forms of research dissemination such as: the production of quarterly bulle-

tins; the continuous development of WWW pages; the publishing of child care research and child care statistical reviews; the production of research reports; the publication of research findings in national and international journals, chapters and books; the running of research dissemination seminars at interim and final stages of research; and helping practitioners, students and academic colleagues with literature searches for validated research projects;

- research training that involves teaching research methods on social work qualifying courses; providing research training courses for practitioners; supervising research students; providing consultancy in research design, data collection methods and data analysis; and helping with research proposal writing skills.

The Centre's work programme is being developed within a specified timetable (see Figure 14) with a view to ensuring overall coherence, academic standards, relevance to agency policy, management and practice. Particular attention is being given to addressing issues arising primarily from the implementation of the Children (NI) Order 1995. This involves undertaking work that laid the foundation for examining over time the implications of the new law through exploring the detail of the primary legislation with the associated Guidance and Regulations in order to establish projects focusing on key areas in which implementation was expected to lead to major developments. In addition, some work has been done to locate Northern Ireland child care concerns within UK, all Ireland, and international contexts.

Organisational Arrangements

In planning and developing the Centre's organisational structures and research programmes, particular attention was paid to the Centre's partnership arrangements and close links between it and the Department of Social Work. It has often been reported that research centres and the 'mother departments' tend to become alienated and, after a while, do not collaborate. In order to avoid this probability, links need to be forged and strengthened. At the Department of Social Work this has been achieved partly because the Centre Director is also the Head of Department, and the Senior Research Fellow, prior to his appointment, was a lecturer at the Department of Social Work. Mindful of the need for 'give and take', working arrangements were evolved on exchange-theory principles, and this was achieved by:

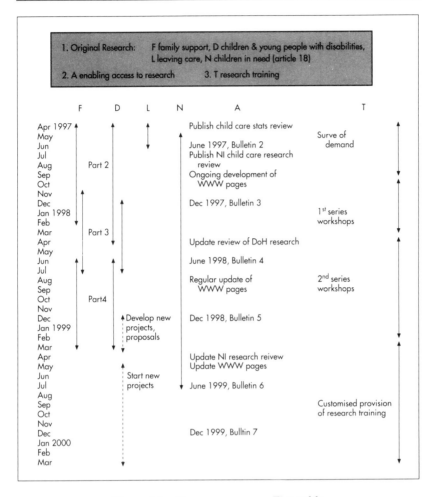

Figure 14: Core programme: Timetable

- allocating the indirect cost of £20,000 p.a. of academic staff time to the work of the Centre;
- participating in joint research projects;
- providing consultancy and advice by academic staff to researchers on child care matters;
- research staff taking over responsibility for research methods teaching on professional qualifying course;
- giving help to academic staff with statistical analysis, literature search, projects design, and the writing of proposals; and
- holding monthly joint staff meetings.

Organisational and management structures aim to achieve account-ability to the funding partners; clear lines of management within the University; a tightly-knit group of productive research staff; and an openness to collaboration beyond the funding partners to a range of voluntary organisations, pressure groups, other research units and various interested parties.

Figure 15 shows the configuration of the key bodies in the organisa-tional structures comprising the Research and Development Office, The Queen's University, DHSS, the Health and Social Services Boards, and the other parties occasionally involved in the Centre's work).

Operational Management Group

The Operational Management Group (OMG) was established with the primary function of giving effect to decisions taken by the Strategy and Policy Group (SPG) through managing the Centre's internal opera-tional matters. The OMG provides a key mechanism for quality control. Membership consists of all the Centre staff plus other members of the University or agencies' staff who are collaborating or are working jointly on specific projects. The OMG meets regularly (initially weekly,

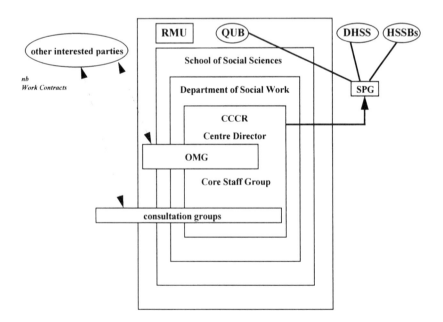

Figure 15:   CCCR organisational arrangements

currently monthly) with a standing agenda, and its business is minuted. The minutes form the basis of a regular report presented at the Department of Social Work staff meetings and provide records for the Director's reports to the SPG.

The OMG has adopted a formal project management approach to the identification and co-ordination of all key tasks associated with core and additional core programmes. Responsibility for project tasks is assigned to appropriate staff members, taking into account any other work commitments, and a week-by-week timetable is drawn up, detailing tasks and staffing for a period of six weeks (Figure 16). Progress is measured according to the agreed timetable, so that when unexpected developments or problems arise, remedial action can be implemented. In addition, a half-day per month is allocated to review core project progress in a wider and more comprehensive way.

Each project has lead-researchers who have responsibility for planning, overall management and execution of the project. The project management approach helps effective planning and management of the work of the Centre, with the implications of any piece of work being judged in terms of its impact on the rest of the Centre's activities. This is particularly important in managing the additional programme of research, or curiosity-driven projects, and ensuring that they do not detract from core programme work. An additional review of the quality of the Centre's work is provided by the external consultant. This involves an annual visit to the Centre as well as periodic advice and comments, spoken or written.

Contract Management

To ensure a high standard of research activities by the Centre, a contract management approach has been adopted. The obvious advantages from organising and monitoring any work according to the contract are detailed below.

Provision of Effective Control

Effective control ensures that all parties fulfil their obligations by agreeing the mechanism for change as well as all aspects of cost. Such systems must be identified at the earliest possible stage and incorporated into the contract document so that all parties are familiar with them. A good example is when, for whatever reasons, funders might want to change or refocus agreed research programmes, and those anticipated changes are not reflected in the costing. It is therefore

Area of work	Main task	25 November	2 December		16 December	6 January	13 January
CORE PROGRAMME Core Programme Projects *Family Support*	Stage 1 Report Second draft		Complete				
	U&SP support group meetings	JP/KH (U)					
	Stage 2 planning						
Disabilities	Stage 1 Report First draft Comments		Complete				
	Support Group Meeting						
	Stage 2 Planning						
Accessing Research	1 General 2 Dissemination: Leaving Care Putting Children on Political Agenda 3 Bulletin 4 WWW pages	JP/KH		MW MW			
Training (MSW)	Marking	PMcC/JP/MM/VS/KH					

Figure 16: Sample of a six-week timetable and task distribution

essential that the contract control system provides mechanisms for the co-ordination of knowledge, information and experience, and for their dissemination to all members involved in the contract agreement. The CCCR managers adopted this practice not only by keeping accurate records, co-ordinating activities and communicating issues needing attention to the Strategy and Policy Group, but also by using that information for planning ahead and anticipating operational developments, which then are discussed and endorsed by the SPG.

Measuring Performance to Required Standards

To ensure value for money, delivery of all CCCR research data on quality performance (measured against required standards) must be considered. Full use is made of any comments by the SPG, which are minuted and incorporated into the Centre's practice, communicated as appropriate to the support groups of the major research projects and to the external consultant. Feedback from draft project reports, annual reports, and business plans are scrutinised for quality and effectiveness. The requirements for monitoring progress and the management of information must be specified in the contract in order to avoid confusion and misunderstanding. Quality control also includes continuous assessment of whether external and internal resources are being used efficiently and effectively and keeping in touch with, and seeking objective comments from, contract partners and other interested parties.

Compliance with Contract Conditions

The contract conditions set out a framework of obligations, and managing them correctly helps to ensure that they are met. But if, for any reason, they are not met, the conditions provide for remedies to be applied properly and promptly. The CCCR Operational Management Group provides mechanisms to examine progress, evaluate quality, identify pitfalls, check timetables and suggest improvements and developments. The OMG also provides the Director with information on which a judgement of contract compliance can be made, and, if necessary, action taken to overcome difficulties.

Production of Clearly Documented Records

By adopting disciplined and continuous documentation of work records, quality control and good practice are ensured, while protection is provided in cases of dispute. Documentation enables an inde-

pendent review and assessment of the Centre's work and its professionalism to be made. It should include minutes of meetings and
records of reviews, annual reports, bulletins, financial statements, activities of staff within and outside the Centre, publication records,
training and consultancy in research methods, and documentation of
electronic dissemination of WWW pages, dissemination methods and
audiences.

Disciplined Management and Control of Change

As most requirements are subject to change due to evolving needs,
policies or strategies, the contract manager (in this case the Centre
Director) has to address those new needs with the purchasers of the
Centre's services. Changes to requirements normally affect cost and
require a revision of payment with the funding partners. It might also
involve redirection and consequently renegotiation of parts of the activities, because, for example, of new policies or strategies introduced
by the funding institutions. These changes need to be anticipated and
their effects controlled by the Centre managers who require up-to-date
information based on effective intelligence collection in order to act
upon them swiftly.

SUMMARY

The process involving key components of initiating and building the
Centre for Child Care Research has been presented as one of a few
probabilities and means of securing core funding. The partnership
approach to addressing research needs has created better opportunities
for child care agencies and academic departments, such as those of
social work, to put joint research firmly on the agenda. Growing recognition by Personal Social Services that research is essential to inform
policy and practice has, in some regions, stimulated a debate on how
that could be achieved within scarce resources.

In order to deal with unmet research needs, the agencies have to
create facilities to fill those gaps. Universities are well-positioned to
provide research services to the agencies as they have the required
research skills and up-to-date knowledge of available research
findings. However, research work requires funding, so the research
purchaser's commitment to plan it as an integral part of service delivery is necessary. Some money should be made available for research
purposes, and used in such a way that would provide the necessary

information on how to improve operational aspects of service provisions, according to set priorities. To have well-informed policies and practice, research and services should progress together; therefore, reliable continuity is advisable, where researchers, managers and practitioners work in partnership, setting up the research agendas, addressing priorities, formulating research questions, disseminating findings and devising strategies based on newly acquired knowledge. Research Centres can provide such fora, and available evidence indicates value for money from establishing such facilities.

Initiatives have to be instigated and need to be taken forward for discussions and negotiations with possible funders. The process might be lengthy and not free from obstacles and problems, but perseverance is worth while. As an example of how to make an idea a reality, the establishment of the Centre for Child Care Research offers object lessons. If departments such as Social Work with a commitment to child care are to improve research productivity and academic standing within the universities and the wider research communities, an exploration of all possibilities is essential, not least by those associated with research councils, the PSS and other child care agencies. To enhance a culture of scholarship and research-led teaching at graduate and postgraduate levels, and on qualifying and post-qualifying courses, research centres can play an important role by facilitating research opportunities for teaching staff as well as opening up access to research findings for students and the practitioners in child care agencies.

REFERENCES

Bush, G. P. & Hattery, L. H. (eds) (1953). *Team Work in Research*. Washington, DC: American University Press.

DoH (1994a). *Supporting Research and Development in the NHS*. NHS Research and Development Task Force. London: HMSO. [The Culyer Report].

DoH (1994b). *A Wider Strategy for Research and Development Relating to Personal Social Services*. An Independent Review Group Report. London: HMSO.

Department of Social Work (1995). *The Child Care Research Proposal Document*. Belfast: The Queen's University of Belfast.

DHSS (1995). Children (NI) Order 1995.

HM Treasury (1993). *Central Unit on Procurement* (CUP) *Guidance*, No. 39: *Basic Purchasing and Supply*.

HM Treasury (1993). *Central Unit on Procurement* (CUP) *Guidance*, No. 42: *Contracting for the Provision of Services*.

HM Treasury (1994). *Central Unit on Procurement* (CUP) *Guidance*, No. 47: *Contract Management*.

HM Treasury (1995). *Central Unit on Procurement* (CUP) *Guidance*, No. 51: *Introduction to the EC Procurement Rules*.

Ikenberry, S. O. & Friedman, R. C. (1972). *Beyond Academic Departments*. London: Jossey-Bass.

O'Halloran, K. (1994). *Establishing a Research Unit within QUB Social Work Department: A Feasibility Study*. Belfast: The Queen's University of Belfast.

Porter, A. L. , Chubin, D. E. , Rossini, F. A. , Broeckmann, M. E. & Connolly, T. (1982). The role of the dissertation in scientific courses. *American Scientist*, **70**, 475–481.

The Public Services Contracts Regulations (1993). *Public Procurement No. 3228*. London: HMSO.

Shetty, Y. K. (1986, Spring). Quality productivity, and profit performance: learning from research and practice. *National Productivity Review*, 166–173.

Williams, S (1992). *Review of the Role of DoH-Funded Research Units*. London: HMSO.

Wodarski, J. S. (1990a). *The University Research Enterprise*. Springfield, IL: Charles C. Thomas.

Wodarski, J. S. (1990b). The University Research Enterprise. *Research Management Review*, **4**, 53–56.

Wodarski, J. S. (1995). Guidelines for Building Research Centers in Schools of Social Work. *Research on Social Work Practice*, **5**, 3, 352–371.

INDEX

Index compiled by Mary Kirkness

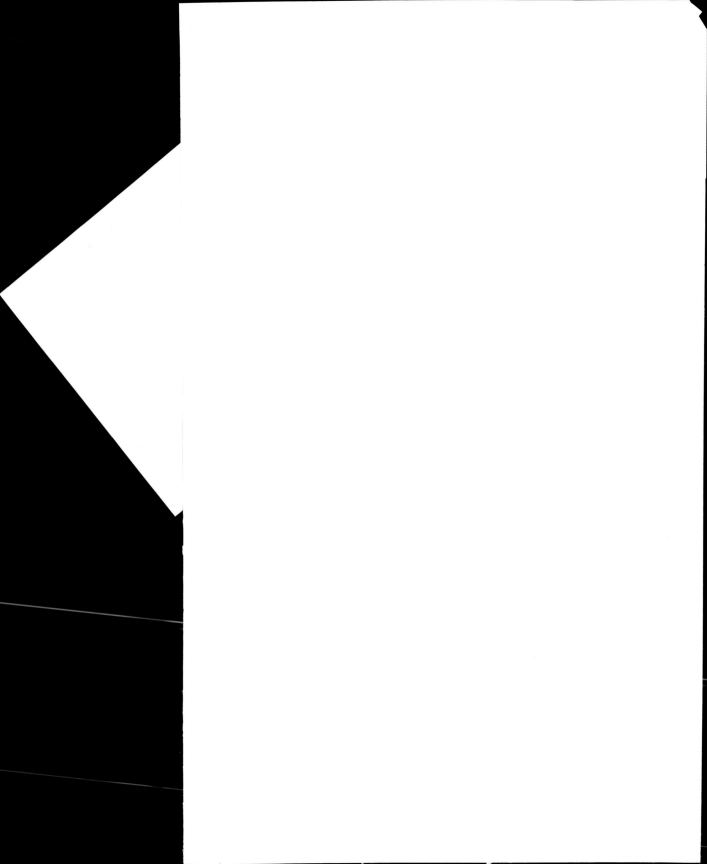

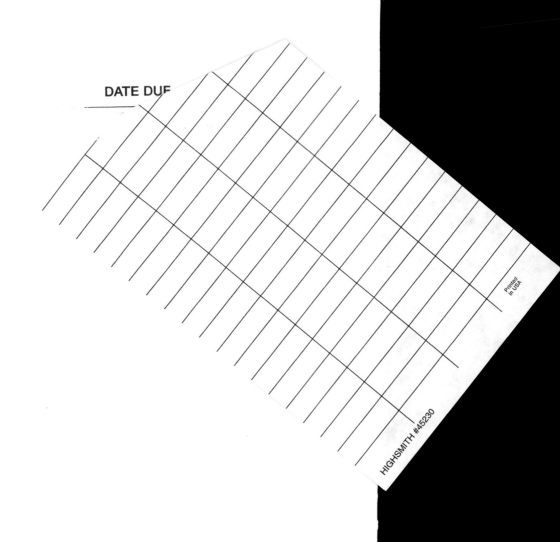

DATE DUE

HIGHSMITH #45230

Printed in USA